SUFFERINGS IN AFRICA

CAPT. JAMES RILEY.

*Engraved for his Narrative of Sufferings
and Travels in Africa.*

SUFFERINGS IN AFRICA: CAPTAIN RILEY'S NARRATIVE

AN AUTHENTIC NARRATIVE
OF THE LOSS OF THE

AMERICAN BRIG COMMERCE

Wrecked on the Western Coast of Africa, in the Month of
August, 1815.

WITH

AN ACCOUNT OF .THE SUFFERINGS

OF HER

SURVIVING OFFICERS AND CREW,

WHO WERE ENSLAVED BY THE WANDERING ARABS ON THE GREAT

AFRICAN DESART, OR ZAHAHRAH:

AND

OBSERVATIONS HISTORICAL, GEOGRAPHICAL, &c.

MADE DURING THE TRAVELS OF THE AUTHOR WHILE A SLAVE TO

THE ARABS, AND IN THE EMPIRE OF MOROCCO

BY JAMES RILEY,
LATE MASTER AND SUPERCARGO.

EDITED AND WITH AN INTRODUCTION
BY GORDON H. EVANS

THE LYONS PRESS

Introduction © 1965, 2006 by Gordon H. Evans
First Lyons Press Edition © 2000
Originally published by Clarkson N. Potter in 1965, New York

The Lyons Press is an imprint of Rowman & Littlefield.

Distributed by NATIONAL BOOK NETWORK

ISBN 13: 978-1-59921-211-0
ISBN 10: 1-59921-211-1

Library of Congress has previously cataloged an earlier edition.

INTRODUCTION

In the year 1815, a young American sea-captain out of
Hartford, Connecticut, was shipwrecked off the western
coast of North Africa. With this event began as extraordinary an odyssey as was ever recorded. The captain and
his several crewmen were captured as slaves by the Arabs
and forced to wander (with their masters) in the hostile
Sahara Desert. Sold to a new master upon the expectation
of a good ransom, they were nearly freed once only to start
their wanderings again. Almost overcome by suffering and
misery, they nevertheless survived and eventually were rescued by an Englishman in Mogadore. The ordeal was so
severe that his weight fell from 240 pounds down to a
mere 90.

In this book is Captain James Riley's own account of the
sufferings and trials he endured with his crew. It was first
published in 1817, and soon became famous. Now we would
call it a huge best seller—and many different editions
were made. We know that additional publications came
out in 1818, 1820, 1828, 1850, and 1859.

Captain Riley's narrative is one of the best travel-
adventure books that has ever been written. To be considered of such a rank, a writer must fulfill at least one or
two conditions. Either he must tell us of a part of the
world which has not been seen before by his people,
or he must have a certain depth which makes his work
much more than merely a good story. Captain Cook's *Voyages* fits the first class. Very few Europeans had visited the
South Seas before Cook, and in some of the areas he described none had ever set foot. Doughty's great *Travels in
Arabia Deserta* fulfills the second requirement. Doughty
has a meaning quite beyond simple description. Riley does
not fully meet either of these strict conditions. Nevertheless,

v

his story is so well told, so dramatic, so true to life, that it qualifies him for near greatness. Here indeed is a lost classic of its kind.

This narrative was widely read in the nineteenth century not only because its author tells of his incredible experiences in a strange land, but also because of the manner in which he relates these experiences: Riley uses a plain and refreshingly matter-of-fact style to express his accounts of barbarism and his descriptions of foreign places.

Much of the credit for this style must go to Anthony Bleeker of New York who edited the book for Riley. Plain men prefer the complex sentence, the long word, and the imagined elegance of "fine" writing. The more educated prefer just the opposite. The Anglo-Saxon word, the brief declarative sentence, the plain style of writing are normally the model of the literary man. Riley's is eminently the plain style, and reflects the hand of an unplain man.

As he tells us in his opening pages, Captain James Riley was born in Connecticut in 1777. He was probably of Irish Protestant stock. After a modest education and uneventful early life, he volunteered for the war of 1812. His service was distinguished, and he ended the war with the rank of captain. At the end of hostilities with England, he made the transfer from military to merchant service, and became the master of the American brig, *Commerce,* only to become stranded on the western coast of Africa in August, 1815, with his ship wrecked.

After many adventures he was ransomed from slavery by William Willshire, the British Consul General at Mogadore, Morocco. Several members of his crew were also rescued at the same time, or later by Mr. Willshire. Indeed this English Samaritan must for a long time have done little but bargain for lost Americans scattered about the Sahara. Riley's gratitude to Willshire lasted a lifetime, and is one of the most touching aspects of his book.

After rescue, Riley returned to the United States and lived in Washington during several sessions of Congress. He knew the principal officers of the government at the time, and it was James Monroe, then Secretary of State, who suggested he write his book. It was an immediate and vast success; between the first edition (1817) and the last (1859) almost a million were sold.

Riley became one of the best known men in the United States at the time. His description of foreign places and barbarism caught the public's imagination. He also became a domestic traveler, and in 1818 journeyed 4,000 miles through the American West, which would now be our Midwest.

Several times he returned to visit his friend Willshire at Mogadore. His health had failed toward the last, and the doctors recommended a sea voyage. Nothing better could be done but to visit Willshire; it was on this last trip to Africa that he died and was buried at sea in March 1839. He had named a son for the Englishman.

But what of the consequences of Riley's book? They may be very large, but they cannot be absolutely proven: you see, his Narrative was one of the first books Lincoln ever read. There were few books in western Indiana in the early days of the last century, but Riley's was very well represented. Indeed it is said to be one of the most popular in the region.

Lincoln's biographies tell us that as a child, he read Aesop's *Fables*, *The Pilgrim's Progress*, Weems' *Life of Washington* and Riley's *Narrative*.

One authority believes that the two episodes which inclined Lincoln's mind against slavery were his visit to the New Orleans slave market at the age of 19, and his reading of Riley's account of slavery in Africa.

Two generations later *Uncle Tom's Cabin* would set the popular mind afire against the institution. Its emotion, its black and white morality, its almost maudlin nature, was ideally suited to appeal to the mass of literate people. But a single copy of a far different book may have had an equally great effect. Lincoln, an idealistic, but realistic man, would have been far more impressed by Riley's level-gazed account of the degradation of life under slavery. There was no romanticism here, no sentimentality—merely an objective account of evil. It is hard to think of a more effective medium on which to imbue a young man with a righteous ideal. Certainly the fact that Riley was a white man held captive by dark men would not stand in the way of the moral being universalized to Negroes enslaved by Caucasians. Needless to say in his later life Riley, as Lincoln, was warm for abolition.

However, what of the truth of Riley's narrative? Oh, you may be sure that in his day Riley was accused of exaggeration. From our vantage point it is very hard to decide whether there is validity in the charge or not. Some things do seem a bit strange, but perhaps this is only because of our distance in the place and time. We must note that Ibn Kahldun, the great Arab historiographer, warns us against accepting anything which is fantastic to the degree of being quite common experience. I think only on the rarest occasion does Riley say anything which should make us suspicious by Khaldun's principle. We should also remember that, from time immemorial, travelers who returned from distant lands have been accused of falsehoods—although they have kept rigorously to the truth. Bruce, after his great journey to the sources of the Nile, was widely disbelieved in England. Later Bruce was justified.

Finally, we are curious as to what happened to the rest of Riley's crew. Several were saved by Willshire, along with Riley. Others remained in the desert. Archibald Roberts was ransomed 19 months after his captain. Davis and Brown also got out. Robbins returned to this country and produced a book, recounting his even more extensive adventures in the Sahara. Apparently, it was designed to ride on the coattails of its popular forerunners. According to Robbins, writing in 1818, several members of the *Commerce*'s crew still were in the desert.

> Poor New England sailor boys,
> Asleep in sandy dust,
> Far from the sea, and your mothers.

New York, N.Y.   G. H. EVANS

AFFIDAVIT

SOUTHERN DISTRICT OF NEW-YORK, SS.

BE IT REMEMBERED, That on the third day of October, in the forty-first year of the Independence of the United States of America, [A. D. 1816,] JAMES RILEY, of the said District, hath deposited in this Office the title of a Book, the right whereof he claims as Author and Proprietor, in the words and figures following, to wit:

"An Authentic Narrative of the loss of the American brig Commerce, wrecked on the Western Coast of Africa, in the month of August, 1815. With an account of the sufferings of her surviving Officers and Crew, who were enslaved by the wandering Arabs on the great African Desart, or Zahahrah; and observations Historical, Geographical, &c. made during the Travels of the Author, while a slave to the Arabs, and in the Empire of Morocco. By James Riley, late Master and Supercargo; preceded by a brief sketch of the Author's life, and concluded by a description of the famous city of Tombuctoo, on the river Niger, and of another large city, far south of it, on the same river, called Wassanah, narrated to the Author at Mogadore, by Sidi Hamet, the Arabian merchant."

In conformity to the Act of the Congress of the United States, entitled "An Act for the encouragement of Learning, by securing the copies of Maps, Charts and Books to the Authors and Proprietors of such copies, during the time therein mentioned." And also to an Act, entitled "An Act supplementary to an Act, entitled an Act for the encouragement of Learning, by securing the copies of Maps, Charts and Books to the Authors and Proprietors of such copies, during the times therein mentioned, and extending the benefits thereof to the arts of designing, engraving, and etching historical and other prints."

THERON RUDD, Clerk of the
Southern District of New-York.

TO THE READER.

THE following Narrative of my misfortunes and sufferings, and my consequent travels and observations in Africa, is submitted to the perusal of a candid and an enlightened public, with much diffidence, particularly as I write without having had the advantages that may be derived from an Academic education, and being quite unskilled in the art of composing for the press. My aim has been merely to record, in plain and unvarnished language, scenes in which I was a principal actor, of real and heart-appalling distresses. The very deep and indelible impression made on my mind by the extraordinary circumstances attending my late shipwreck, and the miserable captivity of myself and my surviving shipmates, and believing that a knowledge of many of these incidents might prove useful and interesting to the world, as well as peculiarly instructive to my sea-faring brethren; together with the strong and repeated solicitations of many of my valuable friends, among whom was the honourable James Munroe, Secretary of State, and several distinguished members of Congress: these considerations, together with a view of being enabled by my labours to afford some relief to the surviving sufferers, and the destitute families of that part of my late crew, whose lot it was to perish in Africa, or who are still groaning out the little remains of their existence in the cruel bonds of barbarian slavery, have induced me to undertake the very arduous and difficult task of preparing and publishing a work so large and expensive.

The Narrative up to the time of my redemption, was written entirely from memory, unaided by notes or any journal; but I committed the principal facts to writing in Mogadore, when every circumstance was fresh in my memory, (which is naturally a retentive one,) and I then compared my own recollections with those of my ransomed companions: this was done with a view of showing to my friends the unparalleled sufferings I had endured, and not for the particular purpose of making them public by means of the press. It should be remembered by the reader, that the occurrences here recorded, took place out of the common course of a sailor's life; and that each particular event was of a nature calculated to impress itself so powerfully on the mind, as not easily to be effaced. Having previously, in the course of my life, visited and travelled through several foreign countries, my mind was by no means unaccustomed to pay attention to, and make observations on whatever came within the reach of my notice, and for this reason, the strange events of the desart, and the novel objects and scenes which I had an opportunity of witnessing in the country of the Moors, were not suffered to pass without awakening and exercising my curiosity as well as interest, and becoming the subject of careful and habitual reflections.

Respecting my conversations with the Arabs, I have put down what I knew at the time to be their exact meaning, as nearly as I could translate their words and signs combined. I had, previously, learned the French and Spanish languages, both by grammar and practice, and had also been accustomed to hear spoken the Russian and different dialects of the German, as well as the Portuguese, Italian, and sev-

eral other languages; so that my ear had become
familiar with their sounds and pronunciation. Perceiving an affinity between the Arabian and Spanish,
I soon began to learn the names of common things,
in Arabic, and to compare them in my mind with
those I had met with in Turkish and other Oriental
history. I had no hope of ever being redeemed, unless I could make myself understood, and I therefore
took the utmost care to treasure up every word and
sentence I heard spoken by the Arabs, to reflect on
their bearing, and to find out their true meaning, by
which means, in the course of a very few days, I was
enabled to comprehend the general tenor and drift
of their ordinary conversation, and to find out the
whole meaning of their signs and gestures. My four
companions, however, could scarcely comprehend a
single word of Arabic, even after they were redeemed.

In regard to the route, and various courses of our
travel, I would observe, that after I was purchased by
the Arabian merchants, and taken off across the desart; I was suffering under the most excrutiating
bodily pains as well as the most cruel privations; it
will not, therefore, be a matter of wonder, if on this
vast, smooth, and trackless desert, I should have mistaken one eastern course for another, or have erred
in computing the distances travelled over; for I was
frequently in such agony and so weighed down with
weariness and despair, that a day seemed to me of
endless duration. A long experience on the ocean
had before taught me to ascertain the latitude by the
apparent height of the polar star above the horizon,
so that in this particular, I could not be much mistaken; and the tending of the coast where our boat
was driven on shore, proves it must have been near
Cape Barbas. After we approached the sea-coast
again, I became more attentive to the surrounding
objects, as my hopes of being ransomed increased,

so that not only the courses, but the distances as I have given them, will agree in all their essential points.

The designs for the engravings were drawn from my own original sketches; (and they were merely rough sketches, for I have no skill in drawing;) they have, however, been executed by artists of considerable repute, and under my own inspection.

In compiling the map, particular care has been taken to consult the best authorities, but I considered, at the same time, that the information I received from my old Arabian master was sufficiently correct, and would warrant me in giving full scope to my consequent geographical impressions, in tracing the river Niger to the Atlantic Ocean. Admitting that my idea prove hereafter to be just, and that this river actually discharges its waters with those of the Congo, into the gulf of Guinea, I am of opinion, that not less than one-fourth of the whole distance in a strait line, should be added for its bends and windings, in order to calculate its real length.

While I was at Mogadore, a number of singular and interesting transactions took place such as do not often occur even in that country; and a person might reside there for many years, without having an opportunity of witnessing a repetition of them; yet their authenticity, as well as that of the other circumstances I have related, can be substantiated by many living witnesses,—men of respectability and unquestionable veracity.

My observations on the currents which have heretofore proved fatal to a vast number of vessels, and their crews, on the western coast of Africa, are made with a view to promote the further investigation of this subject, as well as to caution the unwary mariner against their too often disastrous effects.

It gives me sincere pleasure, to acknowledge the services rendered me by my respectable friend, Anthony Bleecker, Esquire of New-York, who has, at my request, revised the whole of my manuscript and suggested some very important explanations. I have been governed, in my corrections, by his advice throughout, which was of a character that can only flow from the most pure and disinterested motives;— his talents, judgment, and erudition, have contributed in a considerable degree, to smooth down the asperities of my unlearned style, and he is preeminently entitled to my warmest thanks.

To my very intimate friend, Mr. Josiah Shippey, Jun. of New-York, I am under many obligations—he has separately perused my whole manuscript, with great care and interest, and has suggested improvements, both in point of diction and grammar;—his highly classical learning, together with his pious adherence to the true principles of sound morality, and his friendly advice, have been of essential utility, and are highly appreciated.

With respect to the extraordinary circumstance mentioned in the Narrative, of the sudden subsiding of the surf when we were about committing ourselves to the open sea, in our shattered boat, I am aware that it will be the subject of much comment, and, probably, of some raillery. I was advised by a friend, to suppress this fact, lest those who are not disposed to believe in the particular interposition of Divine Providence, should make use of it as an argument against the correctness of the other parts of my Narrative. This, probably, would have been good policy in me, as a mere author, for I am pretty sure that previous to this signal mercy, I myself would have entertained a suspicion of the veracity of a writer who should have related what to me would have appeared such an improbable occurrence. Sentiments and feelings, however, of a very different kind from any that mere worldly interest can excite, forbid me to suppress or deny what so clearly appeared to me and my companions at the time, as the immediate and merciful act of the Almighty, listening to our prayers, and granting our petition at the awful moment when dismay, despair, and death, were pressing close upon us with all their accumulated horrors. My heart still glows with holy gratitude for this mercy, and I will never be ashamed nor afraid to acknowledge and make known to the world, the infinite goodness of my divine Creator and Preserver. "The waters of the sea had well-nigh covered us: the proud waves had well-nigh gone over our soul. Then cried we unto thee, O Lord, and thou didst deliver us out of our distresses. Thou didst send forth thy commandment; and the windy storm ceased, and was turned into a calm."

JAMES RILEY.

CERTIFICATES.

CAPTAIN JAMES RILEY has submitted his Narrative to my perusal, and I have read it over with great care and attention. I was his second mate on board the Commerce, and one of his unfortunate companions through, and a sharer in his dreadful sufferings and captivity, on the inhospitable shores and desarts of Africa, and I am astonished to find with what precision the whole of those incidents are related—it recalls to my memory all those dismal occurrences and distresses, and I do hereby certify, that the Narrative up to the time of our separation in Mogadore, contains nothing more than a plain statement of facts, and that myself, as well as others of the crew, owe our lives, liberties, and restoration to our country, under God, to his uncommon exertions, fortitude, intelligence, and perseverance, and I hereby request him, as my friend, to publish this my certificate.

AARON R. SAVAGE.

Done at New-York, this 1st day of {
February, A. D. 1817.

From the Hon. De Witt Clinton.

I have read part of Captain J. Riley's Narrative of his shipwreck on the coast of Africa, and of his travels into the interior of that continent, and I am of opinion that this work, on account of its illustrations of the geography of a country hitherto so little known, and its descriptions of the manners and customs of the inhabitants, will excite great attention, and ought to command public patronage: while its affecting details of the extraordinary sufferings of himself and his companions, are calculated, in an uncommon degree, to interest the feelings of the reader. And as Captain Riley is a man of good character and respectable talents, I am persuaded that the utmost confidence may be reposed in the corrections of his Narrative.

DE WITT CLINTON.

Dated in the city of New-York, ⎱
the 17th December, 1816. ⎰

CONTENTS

CHAPTER I.

A brief sketch of the Author's Life and Education up to the month of May, 1815

I WAS born in the town of Middletown, in the state of Connecticut, on the 27th of October, in the year 1777, during the war between England and America, which terminated in 1783, with the acknowlegment by the mother country of the freedom, sovereignty, and independence of the thirteen United States. My father, Asher Riley, who still lives in the same place, was bred to the farming business, and at an early age married my mother, Rebecca Sage, who is also yet living. I was their fourth child. Owing to an attack of that dangerous disorder, the liver complaint, my father was rendered incapable of attending to his usual employment for several years, during which time, his property, very small at first, was entirely expended; but after his recovery, in 1786, he was enabled, by industry and strict economy, to support his increasing family in a decent manner.

It may not be improper here, before I speak of my education, to give a general idea of what was then termed a common education in Connecticut. This state is divided into counties and towns, and the towns into societies; in each of which societies, the inhabitants, by common consent, and at their common expense, erect a school-house in which to educate their children. If the society is too large for only one school, it is again subdivided into districts, and each district erects a school-house for its own accommodation. This is generally done by a tax levied by themselves, and apportioned according to the property or capacity of each individual. It being for the general good, all cheerfully pay their apportionment. Thus prepared, they hire a teacher to instruct their children in reading and writing, and some of them are taught the fundamental rules of arithmetic. They, for the most part, hire a male teacher for four months in the year, say from October to March, and his compensation (at the time I am speaking of) was from six to ten dollars a month, with his board. In order to obtain his board, he was under the necessity of going to each of his employers' houses in rotation, making his time in each family as equal as possible and in proportion to the number of children therein. In this way all the parents became acquainted with the master or mistress. In the summer one of the best informed girls in the neighbourhood was selected to teach the youngest children. To defray the expense arising from this system, a tax was laid, and every man, whether married or unmarried, with children or without them, was obliged to pay the sum at which he was rated, and in this manner every one contributed for the good of the whole. In each society one or more meeting-houses were established, whose congregations were either Presbyterians or Congregationalists, and a minister (as he is called) regularly ordained and located for a yearly stipend or salary, and generally during life. This was an old and *steady habit*. The minister was considered as the head of the school, as well as of the meeting, and his *like* or *dislike* was equivalent to a law. All the children in each district, whether rich or poor, went to this school: all had an equal right to this kind of country education. To one of these district schools I was sent at the age of four years, where I continued, learning to spell and read, until I was eight years old, when my father's family had increased to seven or eight children, with a fair prospect of more, (it afterwards amounted to thirteen in number.)

Finding it difficult to support us all as he wished, and I having become a stout boy of my age, he placed me with a neighbouring farmer to earn my living, by assisting him in his work. From the age of eight to fourteen years I worked on the land with different farmers in our neighbourhood, who having received but a very scanty education themselves, conceited, nevertheless, that they were overstocked with learning, as is generally the case with the most ignorant, and in this, their fancied wisdom, concluded that much less than they themselves possessed would answer my purpose, as I was but a poor boy ! ! Finding therefore that they would lose my labour during school hours, (for they had always taken great care to keep me fully employed in hard drudgery every moment I was out of school, scarcely allowing me the usual hours of refreshment and sleep,) they kept me from school, merely because, as they stated, they could not get along with their work without my help. When my parents remonstrated against such conduct in those who had come under a most solemn agreement to give me a *plenty of schooling,* they were assured "that I was a very forward boy; that I could spell and read as well as any of the boys of my age; that I could repeat whole chapters in the Bible by heart, and knew all the Catechism and Creed, viz. the Presbyterian, which then was, and still is considered, all important in that section of the union called New-England: that I could sing psalms in the *separate meetings* full as well as those who had learned to sing by note, "though indeed he cannot write, (said they) because he has no turn for writing." These representations tended in some measure

to allay the anxiety of my parents, who wished me
above all things to have a good common country
education, as they at that time had no prospect of
being able to give me any thing better. They had
taught me, both by precept and practice, that to be
honest, industrious, and prudent; to govern my passions, (which were violent,) to feel for and relieve
the distresses of others when in my power; to be mild
and affable in my manners, and virtuous in all my
actions, was to be happy; and they, generally, had
instilled into my youthful mind every good principle.

I had now attained my fifteenth year; was tall,
stout, and athletic for my age; and having become
tired of hard work on the land, I concluded that the
best way to get rid of it, was to go to sea and visit
foreign countries. My parents endeavoured to dis-
suade me from this project, and wished me to learn
some mechanical trade; but finding that I could
not fix my mind upon any other business, they, with
great reluctance, consented to my choice; and I,
accordingly, shipped on board a sloop bound to the
West Indies. Having no friend to push me forward,
no dependence but on my own good conduct and
exertions, and being ambitious to gain some distinction in the profession I had chosen, I contrived to
acquire some knowledge in the art of navigation,
theoretically as well as practically, and at the age of
twenty years had passed through the grades of cabin
boy, cook, ordinary seaman, seaman, second mate,
and chief mate, on board different vessels. I was now
six feet and one inch in height, and proportionably
strong and athletic, when finding the sphere I then
moved in to be too limited for my views and wishes,
(it extending only from Connecticut River or New-
London to the West Indies, and back again,) I went
to New-York, where I was soon appointed to the
command of a good vessel, and since that time have

continued in similar employment; making voyages in all climates usually visited by American ships; traversing almost every sea, and travelling by land through many of the principal states and empires of the world. For several years I had charge of the cargoes as well as the vessels I sailed in, and had a fair share of prosperity, until the month of January, 1808, when my ship, the Two Marys of New-York, was seized by the French, as I took shelter in Belle Isle, in the Bay of Biscay, from some English men of war, being bound for Nantz; and the ship, with her valuable cargo, was confiscated, under the memorable Milan Decree of the 17th December, 1807, founded on the well known Orders in Council, of the 11th November, of the same year. I remained in France until the ship and cargo were condemned, and did not return to my native country and family, till the latter part of the year 1809, with the loss, it is true, of early all the property I had before acquired, but wiser than I went out; for I had learned to read, write, and speak both the French and Spanish languages; had travelled pretty much all over France, where I had opportunities of witnessing many important operations in the science of war, calculated to attract my attention to the principles upon which they were founded, and I, at the same time took lessons in the school of adversity, which tended to prepare and discipline my mind for the future hardships I was destined to undergo. I now strove with all my power to stem the tide of misfortune, which began to set in against me with impetuous force. I had become a husband and the father of four children, who looked up to me for support, and I strained every nerve to retrieve my lost fortune, by trading to sea; but it was of no avail; every thing proved adverse, and after an absence of two years to Spain, Portugal, the Brazils, Rio de la Plata, or River of Silver, in South America, the West In-

dies, New-Orleans, &c. I returned home at the com-
mencement of the late war (1812) pennyless. Unarmed commerce on the ocean, my element, was at
an end in an honourable way, and I could not obtain
a station I wished for in the navy, nor could I obtain
the command of a private armed vessel that suited
my views, owing to the want of funds; nor would
I accept of the command of a vessel and the consign-
ment of a cargo navigated contrary to the laws of
war under foreign licences: this I considered would
derogate from the character I always wished to support, that of a true friend to my country, (whether
in prosperity or adversity,) and a firm supporter of
its laws and institutions, which I had proved by
long experience in the ways of the world to be as
good (at least) as those of any country under
heaven. Though the offers that were made me were
great and tempting, so that my acceptance of them
could scarcely have failed of producing me a handsome fortune, and that in a very short period, yet
I remained at home during the whole war, making
use of all my faculties to gain a decent subsistence for
my family. Soon after the burning of the Capitol and
other public and private buildings at the seat of
government, by the enemy, in August 1814, when
their commanders loudly threatened to destroy every
assailable place on the seaboard, I believed the time
was near when every arm would be required for the
general defence, particularly at the exposed seaport
towns; and having enrolled myself in a volunteer
company of military exempt artillerists, composed
chiefly of masters and mates of vessels and seamen, I
had the honour of being chosen their capitain. But
our services were not needed in the field.

CHAPTER II.

*Voyage in the Commerce from Connecticut
River to New-Orleans*

AFTER the close of the war, in April 1815, being
then in my native state, I was employed as master
and supercargo of the brig Commerce of Hartford,
in Connecticut; a vessel nearly new, and well fitted,
of about two hundred and twenty tons burden, belonging to Messrs. Riley & Brown, Josiah Savage &
Co. and Luther Savage, of that city. A light cargo was
taken on board, and I shipped a crew, consisting of
the following persons, namely; George Williams,
chief mate, Aaron R. Savage, second mate, William
Porter, Archibald Robbins, Thomas Burns, and
James Clark, seamen, Horace Savage, cabin boy, and
Richard Deslisle, (a black man) cook. This man
had been a servant during the late war to Captain
Daniel Ketchum, of the 25th regiment of United
States' infantry, who distinguished himself by taking
prisoner the English Major-General Rial, at the
dreadful battle of Bridgewater in Upper Canada,
and by several other heroic achievements.

With this crew I proceeded to sea from the mouth
of Connecticut River, on the sixth day of May, 1815,
bound for New-Orleans. We continued to steer for
the Bahama Islands, as winds and weather permitted,
until the twentieth of the same month, when we
saw the southernmost part of the island of Abaco,

7

and passing the Hole in the Wall, on the twenty-first, entered on the Grand Bahama Bank to the leeward of the northernmost Berri Islands; from thence, with a fair wind and good breeze, we steered W. S. W. twelve leagues; then S. S. W. about forty leagues, crossing the Bank, in from three to four fathoms water. On the morning of the twenty-second we saw the Orange Key on our starboard beam; altered our course, and ran off the Bank, leaving them on our starboard hand distant one league. The water on this Great Bank, in most places, appears as white as milk, owing to the white sand at the bottom gleaming through it, and is so clear that an object, the size of a dollar, can be easily seen lying on the bottom in four fathom water, in a still time. Having got off the Bank, we steered W. S. W. for the Double-headed Shot Bank, and at meridian found ourselves, by good observations, in the latitude of 24. 30. being nearly that of the Orange Keys. In the afternoon it became nearly calm, but a good breeze springing up, we continued our course all night W. S. W. I remained on deck myself, on a sharp look out for the Double-headed Shot Bank, or Keys, until four o'clock A. M. when judging by our distance we must be far past them, and consequently clear of that danger, I ordered the chief mate, who had charge of the watch, to keep a good look out, on all sides, for land, white water and breakers; and after repeating the same to the people, I went below to take a nap. At about five (then fair daylight) I was awakened by a shock and thought I felt the vessel touch bottom. I sprang on deck, put the helm to starboard, had all hands called in an instant, and saw breakers ahead and to southward, close on board; apparently a sound on our right, and land to the northward, at about two leagues distance. The vessel's head was towards the S. W. and she running at the rate of ten miles the hour. I instantly seized the helm, put it hard to port, ordered all sails to be let run, and the anchors cleared away. The vessel touched lightly, three or four times; when I found she was over the reef, let go an anchor, which brought her up in two and a half fathoms, or fifteen feet of water, which was quite smooth. We now handed all the sails, and lowered down the boat. I went in her with four hands, and sounded out a passage; found plenty of water to leeward of the reef; turned and got under way, and at seven o'clock A. M. was in the open sea again, with a fresh breeze.

This being the first time, in the course of my navigating, that any vessel which I was in had struck the bottom unexpectedly, I own I was so much surprised and shocked, that my whole frame trembled, and I could scarcely believe that what had happened was really true, until by comparing the causes and effects of the currents of the Gulph Stream, I was convinced that during the light winds, the day before, when in the Santarem Channel, the vessel had been drifted by the current that runs N. N. W. (and at that time very strong) so far north of the Double-headed Shot Bank; that my course in the night, though the only proper one I could have steered, was such as kept the current on the larboard bow of the vessel, which had horsed her across it sixty miles out of her course in sixteen hours, and would have landed her on the S. W. part of the Carysford Reef in two minutes more, where she must have been totally lost. As so many vessels of all nations who navigate this stream have perished with their cargoes, and oftentimes their crews, I mention this incident to warn the navigator of the danger he is in when his vessel is acted upon by these currents, where no calculation can be depended upon, and where nothing but very frequent castings of the lead, and a good look out, can secure him from their too often fatal consequences.

Having settled this point in my own mind, I became tranquil, and we continued to run along the Florida Keys from W. S. W. to West by South, in from thirty to forty fathoms water, about four leagues distant, seeing from one to two leagues within us many rocks and little sandy islands, just above the waters' edge, with a good depth of water all around them, until noon on the 24th, when we doubled the dry Tortugas Islands in ten fathoms, and on the 26th arrived in the Mississippi River, passed Fort St. Philip at Pluquemines the same night, having shown my papers to the commanding officer of that post (as is customary.)

My previous knowledge of the river and the manner of getting up it, enabled me to pass nearly one hundred sail of vessels that were in before me, and by dint of great and continued exertions, to arrive with my vessel before the city of New-Orleans, on the first day of June. Here we discharged our cargo, and took another on board, principally on freight, in which I was assisted by Messrs. Talcott & Bowers, respectable merchants in that city. This cargo consisted of tobacco and flour. The two ordinary seamen, Francis Bliss and James Carrington, now wished for a discharge, and received it. I then shipped in their stead John Hogan and James Barrett, both seamen and natives of the state of Massachusetts.

With this crew and cargo we sailed from New-Orleans on the twenty-fourth of June; left the river on the twenty-sixth, and proceeded for Gibraltar, where we arrived on the ninth of August following, and landed our cargo. About the thirteenth the schooner ———, Capt. Price of and from New-York, in a short passage, came into the Bay, and the captain on his landing told me he was bound up to Barcelona, and that if I would go on board his vessel, which was then standing off and on in the

Bay, he would give me a late New-York Price Current, and some newspapers. I was in great want of a Price Current for my guide in making purchases, and accordingly went on board. The wind blowing strong in, and the vessel far out, I had to take four men with me, namely, James Clark, James Barrett, William Porter, and John Hogan. Having received the Price Current, &c. I left the schooner about sunset, when they immediately filled her sails and stood on. As we were busied in stepping the boat's mast to sail back, a toppling sea struck her, and nearly filled her with water; we all jumped instantly overboard, in the hope of preventing her from filling, but she filled immediately. Providentially the captain of the schooner heard me haloo, though at least a mile from us; put his vessel about, came near us, sent his boat, and saved our lives and our boat, which being cleared of water, and it being after dark, we returned safe alongside of the brig by ten o'clock at night. When the boat filled, we were more than three miles from the Rock, in the Gut, where the current would have set us into the Mediterranean, and we must have inevitably perished before morning, but we were spared, in order to suffer a severer doom, and miseries worse than death, on the barbarous shores of Africa.

We now took on board part of a cargo of brandies and wines, and some dollars, say about two thousand, and an old man named Antonio Michel, a native of New-Orleans, who had previously been wrecked on the island of Teneriffe, and was recommended to my charity by Mr. Gavino, who at that time exercised the functions of American Consul at Gibraltar.

CHAPTER III.

Voyage from Gibraltar towards the Cape
de Verd Islands, including the shipwrecl
of the brig Commerce on the coast
of Africa

WE set sail from the bay of Gibraltar on the 23d of August, 1815, intending to go by way of the Cape de Verd Islands, to complete the lading of the vessel with salt. We passed Capt Spartel on the morning of the 24th, giving it a birth of from ten to twelve leagues, and steered off to the W. S. W. I intended to make the Canary Islands, and pass between Tene-riffe and Palma, having a fair wind; but it being very thick and foggy weather, though we got two observations at noon, neither could be much depended upon. On account of the fog, we saw no land, and found, by good meridian altitudes on the twenty-eighth, that we were in the latitude of 27. 30. N. having differed our latitude by the force of current, one hundred and twenty miles; thus passing the Canaries without seeing any of them. I concluded we must have passed through the intended passage without discovering the land on either side, particularly, as it was in the night, which was very dark, and black as pitch; nor could I believe otherwise from having had a fair wind all the way, and having steered one course ever since we took our departure from Cape Spartel. Soon after we got an observation

on the 28th, it became as thick as ever, and the darkness seemed (if possible) to increase. Towards evening I got up my reckoning, and examined it all over,
to be sure that I had committed no error, and caused
the mates to do the same with theirs. Having thus
ascertained that I was correct in calculation, I altered
our course to S. W. which ought to have carried us
nearly on the course I wished to steer, that is, for
the easternmost of the Cape de Verds; but finding
the weather becoming more foggy towards night,
it being so thick that we could scarcely see the end
of the jib-boom, I rounded the vessel to, and sounded
with one hundred and twenty fathoms of line, but
found no bottom, and continued on our course, still
reflecting on what should be the cause of our not
seeing land, (as I never had passed near the Canaries
before without seeing them, even in thick weather
or in the night.) I came to a determination to haul
off to the N. W. by the wind at 10 P. M. as I should
then be by the log only thirty miles north of Cape
Bajador. I concluded on this at nine, and thought
my fears had never before so much prevailed over
my judgment and my reckoning. I ordered the light
sails to be handed, and the steering sail booms to be
rigged in snug, which was done as fast as it could be
by one watch, under the immediate direction of
Mr. Savage.

We had just got the men stationed at the braces
for hauling off, as the man at helm cried "ten
o'clock." Our try-sail boom was on the starboard
side, but ready for jibing; the helm was put to port,
dreaming of no danger near. I had been on deck all
the evening myself; the vessel was running at the
rate of nine or ten knots, with a very strong breeze,
and high sea, when the main boom was jibed over,
and I at that instant heard a roaring; the yards were
braced up—all hands were called. I imagined at first
it was a squall, and was near ordering the sails to be

lowered down; but I then discovered breakers foaming at a most dreadful rate under our lee. Hope for a moment flattered me that we could fetch off still, as there were no breakers in view ahead: the anchors were made ready; but these hopes vanished in an instant, as the vessel was carried by a current and a sea directly towards the breakers, and she struck! We let go the best bower anchor; all sails were taken in as fast as possible: surge after surge came thundering on, and drove her in spite of anchors, partly with her head on shore. She struck with such violence as to start every man from the deck. Knowing there was no possibility of saving her, and that she must very soon bilge and fill with water, I ordered all the provisions we could get at to be brought on deck, in hopes of saving some, and as much water to be drawn from the large casks as possible. We started several quarter casks of wine, and filled them with water. Every man worked as if his life depended upon his present exertions; all were obedient to every order I gave, and seemed perfectly calm;—The vessel was stout and high, as she was only in ballast trim;—The sea combed over her stern and swept her decks; but we managed to get the small boat in on deck, to sling her and keep her from staving. We cut away the bulwark on the larboard side so as to prevent the boast from staving when we should get them out; cleared away the long boat and hung her in tackles, the vessel continuing to strike very heavy, and filling fast. We however, had secured five or six barrels of water, and as many of wine,—three barrels of bread, and three or four salted provisions. I had as yet been so busily employed, that no pains had been taken to ascertain what distance we were from the land, nor had any of us yet seen it; and in the meantime all the clothing, chests, trunks, &c. were got up, and the books, charts, and sea instruments, were stowed in them, in the hope of their being useful to us in future.

The vessel being now nearly full of water, the surf making a fair breach over her, and fearing she would go to pieces, I prepared a rope, and put it in the small boat, having got a glimpse of the short, at no great distance, and taking Porter with me, we were lowered down on the larboard or lee side of the vessel, where she broke the violence of the sea, and made it comparatively smooth; we shoved off, but on clearing away from the bow of the vessel, the boat was overwhelmed with a surf, and we were plunged into the foaming surges: we were driven along by the current, aided by what seamen call the undertow, (or recoil of the sea) to the distance of three hundred yards to the westward, covered nearly all the time by the billows, which, following each other in quick succession, scarcely gave us time to catch a breath before we were again literally swallowed by them, till at length we were thrown, together with our boat, upon a sandy beach. After taking breath a little, and ridding our stomachs of the salt water that had forced its way into them, my first care was to turn the water out of the boat, and haul her up out of the reach of the surf. We found the rope that was made fast to her still remaining; this we carried up along the beach, directly to leeward of the wreck, where we fastened it to sticks about the thickness of handspikes, that had drifted on the shore from the vessel, and which we drove into the sand by the help of other pieces of wood. Before leaving the vessel, I had directed that all the chests, trunks, and everything that would float, should be hove overboard: this all hands were busied in doing. The vessel lay about one hundred fathoms from the beach, at high tide. In order to save the crew, a hawser was made fast to the rope we had on shore, one end of which we hauled to us, and made it fast to a number of sticks we had driven into the sand for the purpose. It was then tautened on board the wreck, and made fast. This being done, the long-boat (in order to save the provisions already in her) was lowered down, and two hands steadied her by ropes fastened to the rings in her stem and stern posts over the hawser, so as to slide, keeping her bow to the surf. In this manner they reached the beach, carried on the top of a heavy wave. The boat was stove by the violence of the shock against the beach; but by great exertions we saved the three barrels of bread in her before they were much damaged; and two barrels of salted provisions were also saved. We were now, four of us, on shore, and busied in picking up the clothing and other things which drifted from the vessel, and carrying them up out of the surf. It was by this time daylight, and high water; the vessel careened deep off shore, and I made signs to have the mast cut away, in the hope of easing her, that she might not go to pieces. They were accordingly cut away, and fell on her starboard side, making a better lee for a boat alongside the wreck, as they projected considerably beyond her bows. The masts and rigging being gone, the sea breaking very high over the wreck, and nothing left to hold on by, the mates and six men still on board, though secured, as well as they could be, on the bowsprit and in the larboard fore-channels, were yet in imminent danger of being washed off by every surge. The long-boat was stove, and it being impossible for the small one to live, my great object was now to save the lives of the crew by means of the hawser. I therefore made signs to them to come, one by one, on the hawser, which had been stretched taut for that purpose. John Hogan ventured first, and having pulled off his jacket, took to the hawser, and made for the shore. When he had got clear of the immediate lee of the wreck, every surf buried him, combing many feet above his head; but he still held fast to the rope with a death-like grasp, and as soon as the surf was passed, proceeded on towards the shore, until another surf, more powerful than the former, unclenched his hands, and

threw him within our reach; when we laid hold of
him and dragged him to the beach; we then rolled
him on the sand, until he discharged the salt water
from his stomach, and revived. I kept in the water
up to my chin, steadying myself by the hawser, while
the surf passed over me, to catch the others as they
approached, and thus, with the assistance of those
already on shore, was enabled to save all the rest
from a watery grave.

CHAPTER IV.

*Description of the natives.—They make war upon
the crew, and drive them off to the wreck.*

ALL hands being now landed, our first care was to
secure the provisions and water which we had so far
saved, knowing it was a barren thirsty land; and
we carried the provisions up fifty yards from the
waters' edge, where we placed them, and then formed
a kind of a tent by means of our oars and two steering
sails. I had fondly hoped we should not be discovered
by any human beings on this inhospitable shore, but
that we should be able to repair our boats, with the
materials we might get from the wreck, and by taking advantage of a smooth, (if we should be favoured
with one) put to sea, where by the help of a compass and other instruments which we had saved, we
might possibly find some friendly vessel to save our
lives, or reach some of the European settlements
down the coast, or the Cape de Verd Islands.

Being thus employed, we saw a human figure ap-

proach our stuff, such as clothing, which lay scattered along the beach for a mile westward of us. It
was a man! He began plundering our clothing. I
went towards him with all the signs of peace and
friendship I could make, but he was extremely shy,
and made signs to me to keep my distance, while he
all the time seemed intent on plunder. He was unarmed, and I continued to approach him until within ten yards.

He appeared to be about five feet seven or eight
inches high, and of a complexion between that of
an American Indian and negro. He had about him,
to cover his nakedness, a piece of coarse woollen
cloth, that reached from below his breast nearly to
his knees; his hair was long and bushy, resembling
a *pitch mop,* sticking out every way six or eight
inches from his head; his face resembled that of an
ourang-outang more than a human being; his eyes
were red and fiery; his mouth, which stretched nearly from ear to ear, was well lined with sound teeth;
and a long curling beard, which depended from his
upper lip and chin down upon his breast, gave him
altogether a most horrid appearance, and I could
not but imagine that those well set teeth were sharp-
ened for the purpose of devouring human flesh ! !
particularly as I conceived I had before seen in different parts of the world, the human face and form
in its most hideous and terrific shape. He appeared
to be very old, yet fierce and vigorous; he was soon
joined by two old women of similar appearance,
whom I took to be his wives. These looked a little
less frightful, though their two eye-teeth stuck out
like hogs' tusks, and their tanned skins hung in loose
plaits on their faces and breasts; but their hair was
long and braided. A girl of from eighteen to twenty,
who was not ugly, and five or six children, of different ages and sexes, from six to sixteen years were
also in company. These were entirely naked. They

brought with them a good English hammer, with a
rope-laniard through a hole in its handle. It had
no doubt belonged to some vessel wrecked on that
coast. They had also a kind of axe with them, and
some long knives slung on their right sides, in a
sheath suspended by their necks. They now felt
themselves strong, and commenced a bold and indiscriminate plundering of every thing they wanted.
They broke open trunks, chests, and boxes, and
emptied them of their contents, carrying the clothing on their backs upon the sand hills, where they
spread them out to dry. They emptied the beds of
their contents, wanting only the cloth, and were
much amused with the flying of the feathers before
the wind from my bed. It appeared as though they
had never before seen such things.

I had an adventure of silk laced veils and silk
handkerchiefs, the former of which the man, women,
and children tied round their heads in the form of
turbans; the latter round their legs and arms,
though only for a short time, when they took them
off again, and stowed them away among the other
clothing on the sand hills. They all seemed highly
delighted with their good fortune, and even the old
man's features began to relax a little, as he met with
no resistance. We had no fire or side arms, but we
could easily have driven these creatures off with
handspikes, had I not considered that we had no
possible means of escaping either by land or water,
and had no reason to doubt but they would call
others to their assistance, and in revenge destroy us.
I used all the arguments in my power to induce my
men to endeavour to conciliate the friendship of
these natives, but it was with the greatest difficulty.
I could restrain some of them from rushing on the
savages and putting them to death, if they could
have come up with them; but I found they could
run like the wind, whilst we could with difficulty

move in the deep sand. Such an act I conceived
would cost us our lives as soon as we should be
overpowered by numbers, and I therefore permitted them to take what pleased them best, without
making any resistance; except our bread and provisions, which, as we could not subsist without them,
I was determined to defend to the last extremity. On
our first reaching the shore I allowed my mates and
people to share among themselves one thousand
Spanish dollars, for I had hauled my trunk on shore
by a rope, with my money in it, which I was induced
to do in the hope of its being useful to them in procuring a release from this country in case we should
be separated, and in aiding them to reach their
homes. We had rolled up the casks of water and
wine which had been thrown overboard and drifted
ashore. I was now determined to mend the long-boat,
as soon and as well as possible, in order to have a
retreat in my power, (or at least the hope of one)
in case of the last necessity. The wind lulled a little
in the afternoon, at low water, when William Porter
succeeded in reaching the wreck and procured a few
nails and a marline spike; with these he got safe
back to the shore. I found the timbers of the boat
in so crazy a state, and the nails which held them
together, so eaten off by the rust, that she would not
hold together, nor support her weight in turning
her up in order to get at her bottom. I tacked her
timbers together, however as well as I could, which
was very imperfectly, as I had bad tools to work with,
and my crew, now unrestrained by my authority,
having broached a cask of wine, and taken copious
draughts of it, in order to dispel their sorrows, were
most of them in such a state, that instead of assisting
me, they tended to increase my embarrassment. We,
however, at last, got the boat turned up, and found
that one whole plank was out on each side, and very
much split. I tacked the pieces, assisted by Mr. Sav-

age, Horace, and one or two more. We chinced a little oakum into the seams and splits with our knives, as well as we could, and worked upon her until it was quite dark. I had kept sentinels walking with handspikes, to guard the tent and provisions during this time, but the Arabs had managed to rob us of one of our sails from the tent, and to carry it off, and not content with this, they tried to get the other in the same way. This I would not permit them to do. They then showed their hatchets and their arms, but finding it of no effect they retired for the night, after promising as near as I could understand them, that they would not molest us further till morning, when they would bring camels down with them. We had previously seen a great many camel tracks in the sand, and I of course believed there were some near. One of the children had furnished us with fire, which enabled us to roast a fowl that had been drowned, and driven on shore from the wreck, on which, with some salt pork, and a little bread and butter, we made a hearty meal, little thinking that this was to be the last of our provisions we should be permitted to enjoy. A watch was set of two men, who were to walk guard at a distance from the tent, to give an alarm in case of the approach of the natives and keep burning a guard fire. This we were enabled to do by cutting up some spars we found on the beach, and which must have belonged to some vessel wrecked there before us.

Night had now spread her sable mantle over the face of nature, the savages had retired, and all was still, except the restless and unwearied waves, which dashed against the deserted wreck, and tumbled among the broken rocks a little to the eastward of us, where the high perpendicular cliffs, jutting out into the sea, opposed a barrier to their violence, and threatened, at the same time, inevitable and certain destruction to every ill fated vessel and her crew that should, unfortunately, approach too near their immoveable foundations: these we had escaped only by a few rods. From the time the vessel struck to this moment, I had been so entirely engaged by the laborious exertions which our critical situation demanded, that I had no time for reflection; but it now rushed like a torrent over my mind, and banished from my eyes that sleep which my fatigued frame so much required. I knew I was on a barren and inhospitable coast; a tempestuous ocean lay before me, whose bosom was continually tossed and agitated by wild and furious winds, blowing directly on shore; no vessel or boat sufficient for our escape, as I thought it impossible for our shattered long-boat to live at sea, even if we should succeed in urging her through the tremendous surges that broke upon the shore with such violence, as to make the whole coast tremble; behind us were savage beings, bearing the human form indeed, but in its most terrific appearance, whose object I knew, from what had already passed, would be to rob us of our last resource, our provisions; and I did not doubt, but they would be sufficiently strong in the morning, not only to accomplish what they meditated, but to take our lives also, or to seize upon our persons, and doom us to slavery, till death should rid us of our miseries.

This was the first time I had ever suffered shipwreck. I had left a wife and five young children behind me, on whom I doated, and who depended on me entirely for their subsistence. My children would have no father's, and perhaps no mother's care, to direct them in the paths of virtue, to instruct their ripening years, or to watch over them, and administer the balm of comfort in time of sickness; no generous friend to relieve their distresses, and save them from indigence, degradation, and ruin. These reflections harrowed up my soul, nor could I cease to shudder at these imaginary evils, added to my real ones, until I was forced mentally to exclaim, "Thy ways, great Father of the universe, are wise and just, and what am I! an atom of dust, that dares to murmur at thy dispensations."

I next considered, that eleven of my fellow sufferers, who had entrusted themselves to my care, were still alive and with me, and all but two of them (who were on the watch) lying on the ground, and wrapped in the most profound and apparently pleasing sleep; and as I surveyed them with tears of compassion, I felt it was a sacred duty assigned me by Providence, to protect and preserve their lives to my very utmost. The night passed slowly and tediously away; when daylight at length began to dawn in the eastern horizon, and chased darkness before it, not to usher to our view the cheering prospect of approaching relief, but to unfold new scenes of suffering, wretchedness, and distress. So soon as it was fairly light, the old man came down accompanied by his wives and two young men of the same family—he was armed with a spear of iron, having a handle made with two pieces of wood spliced together, and tied with cords: the handle was about twelve feet long. This he held balanced in his right hand, above his head, making motions as if to throw it at us; he ordered us off to the wreck, pointing, at the same time, to a large drove of camels that were descending the heights to the eastward of us, his women running off at the same time whooping and yelling horribly, throwing up sand in the air, and beckoning to those who had charge of the camels to approach. I ran towards the beach, and seized a small spar that lay there, to parry off the old man's lance, as a handspike was not long enough. He in the meantime came to the tent like a fury, where the people still were, and by slightly pricking one or two of them, and pointing at the same time towards the camels, he succeeded in frightening them, which was his object, as he did not wish to call help, lest he should be obliged to divide the spoil. The crew all made the best of their way to the small boat, while I parried off his spear with my spar, and kept him at a distance. He would doubtless have hurled it at me, but for the fear of losing it.

The small boat was dragged to the water, along-side our hawser, but the people huddling into her in a confused manner, she was filled by the first sea, and bilged. I now thought we had no resource, except trying to get eastward or westward. Abandon-ing, therefore, our boats, provisions, &c. we tried to retreat eastward, but were opposed by this formi-dable spear, and could not make much progress; for the old man was very active. He would fly from us like the wind, and return with the same speed. The camels were approaching very fast, and he made signs to inform us, that the people who were with them had fire arms, and would put us instantly to death; at the same time opposing us every way with his young men, with all their weapons, insisting on our going towards the wreck, and refusing to receive our submission, while the women and chil-dren still kept up their yelling. We then laid hold of the long-boat, turned her over, and got her into the water; and as I would suffer only one at a time to get on board, and that too over her stern, we succeeded at length, and all got off safe alongside the wreck, which made a tolerable lee for the boat, though she was by this time half filled with water.

All hands got on board the wreck except myself and another, we kept bailing the boat and were able to keep her from entirely filling, having one bucket and a keg to work with. The moment we were out of the way, all the family ran together where our tent was; here they were joined by the camels and two young men, which we had not be-fore seen, apparently about the ages of twenty and twenty-six. They were armed with scimitars, and came running on foot from the eastward. The old man and women ran to meet them, hallooing to us brandishing their naked weapons and bidding us defiance. They loaded the barrels of bread on their camels, which kneeled down to receive them; the beef and all the other provisions, with the sail that the tent was made of, &c. &c. and sent them off with the children who drove them down. The old man next came to the beach; with his axe stove in all the heads of our water casks and casks of wines, emptying their contents into the sand. They then gathered up all the trunks, chests, sea instruments, books and charts, and consumed them by fire in one pile. Our provisions and water being gone, we saw no other alternative but to try to get to sea in our leaky boat, or stay and be washed off the wreck the next night, or to perish by the hands of these barbarians, who we expected would appear in great force, and bring fire arms with them, and they would besides soon be enabled to walk to the wreck, on a sand bar that was fast forming inside of the vessel, and now nearly dry at low water. The tide seemed to ebb and flow about twelve feet. We had now made all the preparations in our power for our departure, which amounted to nothing more than getting from the wreck a few bottles of wine and a few pieces of salt pork. No water could be procured, and the bread was completely spoiled by being soaked in salt water. Our oars were all lost except two that were on shore in the power of the natives. We had split a couple of plank for oars, and attempted to shove off, but a surf striking the boat, came over her bow, and nearly filling her with water, drifted her again alongside the wreck. We now made shift to get on board the wreck again, and bail out the boat; which when done, two hands, were able to keep her free, while two others held her steady by ropes, so as to prevent her from dashing to pieces against the wreck.

CHAPTER V.

*The natives seize the author by perfidy, and
then get possession of the money—the author's
critical situation on shore—he escapes to the
wreck—Antonio Michel is massacred*

THE sight of our deplorable situation seemed to
excite pity in the breasts of the savages who had
driven us from shore. They came down to the water's
edge, bowed themselves to the ground, beckoning
us, and particularly me whom they knew to be the
captain, to come on shore; making at the same time
all the signs of peace and friendship they could.
They carried all their arms up over the sand hills,
and returned without them. Finding I would not
come on shore, one of them ran and fetched a small
goat or dog skin, which by signs, they made me
understand was filled with water, and all retiring to a
considerable distance from the beach, except the old
man who had it: he came into the water with it up
to his armpits, beckoning me to come and fetch it
and drink. He was nearly naked, and had no weapons
about him. Being very thirsty, and finding we could
not get at any water, and no hope remaining of our
being able to get out through the surf to sea, I let
myself down by the hawser, and went by means of
it to the beach, where the old man met me and gave
me the skin of water, which I carried off to the wreck,
and the people hauled it up on board. This done, he

26

made me understand that he wished to go on board, and me to remain on the beach until his return.

Seeing no possible chance of escaping or of preserving our lives in any other way but by their assistance, and that that was only to be obtained by conciliating them—telling my men my mind, I went again to the shore. The young men, women, and children were now seated unarmed on the beach, near the water—the grown people nearly, and the children entirely naked. They made all the signs of peace they knew of, looking upwards, as if invoking heaven to witness their sincerity. The old man advancing, took me by the hand, and looking up to heaven, said, "*Allah K. Beer.*" I knew that Allah was the Arabic name for the Supreme Being, and supposed *K. Beer* meant "our friend or father." I let him pass to the wreck, and went and seated myself on the beach with the others, who seemed very friendly, interlacing their fingers with mine; putting my hat on one another's head and returning it to me again; stroking down my trowsers, feeling my head and hands, examining my shoes, and feeling into my pockets, &c.

When the people had hauled the old man on board, I endeavoured to make them understand that they must keep him until I was released, but they did not comprehend my meaning, owing to the noise of the surf; and after he had satisfied his curiosity by looking attentively at every thing he could see, which was nothing more than the wreck of the contents of the hold floating in her, inquiring for baftas, for fire-arms, and for money, as I afterwards learnt, and finding none he came on shore. When he was near the beach, and I about to rise to meet him, I was seized by both arms by the two stoutest of the young men, who had placed themselves on each side of me for the purpose of safe-keeping. They grasped my arms like lions, and at that instant the women

and children presented their daggers, knives and
spears to my head and breast. To strive against them
was instant death; I was therefore obliged to remain
quiet, and determined to show no concern for my
life or any signs of fear. The countenance of every
one around me now assumed the most horrid and
malignant expressions; they gnashed their teeth at
me, and struck their daggers within an inch of every
part of my head and body. The young men still held
me fast, while the old one seizing a sharp scimitar,
laid hold of my hair at the same instant, as if to cut
my throat, or my head off. I concluded my last
moments had come, and that my body was doomed
to be devoured by these beings, whom I now considered to be none other than Cannibals, that would
soon glut their hungry stomachs with my flesh. I
could only say, "Thy will be done," mentally, and
felt resigned to my fate, for I thought it could not be
prevented. But this conduct on their part, it soon
appeared, was only for the purpose of frightening
me, and as I had not changed countenance, the old
man, after drawing his scimitar lightly across the
collar of my shirt, which he cut a little, released my
head, bidding me by signs to order all the money we
had on board to be brought directly on shore.

My mates and people then on the wreck, had witnessed this scene, and had agreed, as they afterwards
informed me, that if I was massacred, which they did
not doubt from appearances would soon be the case,
to rush on shore in the boat, armed in the best manner they were able, and revenge my death by selling
their lives as dearly as possible.

When the old man had quit his hold, and I hailed
my people, their hopes began to revive, and one of
them came on the hawser to know what they should
do. I told him all the money which they had on
board must be instantly brought on shore. He was in
the water at some distance from me, and could not

hear, on account of the noise occasioned by the surf, what I added, which was for them not to part with the money until I should be fairly released. He went on board, and all hands hoping to procure my release, put their money which they still had about them, to the amount of about one thousand dollars into a bucket, and slinging it on the hawser, Porter shoved it along before him near the beach, and was about to bring it up to the place where I sat. With considerable difficulty, however I prevented him, as the surf made such a roaring, that he could not hear me, though he was only a few yards distant; but he at last understood my signs, and staid in the water until one of the young men went and received it from him. The old man had taken his seat alongside of me, and held his scimitar pointed at my breast.

The bucket of dollars was brought and poured into one end of the old man's blanket, when he bid me rise and go along with them, he and the young men urging me along by both arms, with their daggers drawn before, and the women and children behind with the spear, and their knives near my back. In this manner they made me go with them over the sand drifts to the distance of three or four hundred yards, where they seated themselves and me on the ground. The old man then proceeded to count and divide the money. He made three heaps of it, counting into each heap by tens, and so dividing it exactly, gave the two young men one-third or heap— to his two wives one-third, and kept the other to himself. Each secured his and their own part, by wrapping and tying it up in some of our clothing. During this process, they had let go of my arms, though they were all around me. I thought my fate was now decided, if I could not by some means effect my escape. I knew they could outrun me, if I should leap from them, and would undoubtedly plunge their weapons to my heart if I attempted, and failed in the attempt. However I resolved to risk it, and made a slight movement with that view at a moment when I thought all eyes were turned from me; but one of the young men perceiving my manoeuvre, made a lounge at me with his scimitar. I eluded the force of his blow, by falling backwards on the ground; it however pierced my waistcoat. He was about to repeat it, when the old man bade him desist.

The money being now distributed and tied up, they made me rise with them, and were all going together from the beach, holding me by the arms with naked daggers all around me. There appeared now no possible means of escape, when the thought suddenly occurred to me, to tempt their avarice. I then, by signs, made them understand that there was more money in the possession of the crew. This seemed to please them, and they instantly turned themselves and me about for the beach, sending the money off by one of the young men and a boy. When they approached to within one hundred yards of the beach, they made me seat myself on the sand, between two of them, who held me by the arms, bidding me order the money on shore. I knew there was none on board the wreck, or in the boat, but I imagined if I could get Antonio Michel on shore, I should be able to make my escape. I hailed accordingly and made signs to my people to have one of them come near the shore; but as they saw, by every movement of the natives, that my situation was dreadfully critical, none of them were inclined to venture, and I waited more than an hour, was often threatened with death, and made to halloo with all my might, until I became so hoarse as scarcely to make myself heard by those around me. The pity of Mr. Savage at last overcame his fears. He ventured on the hawser, and reaching the beach in safety was about to come up to me, where he would have been certainly seized on as I was, when I endeavoured to make him understand, by signs, that he must stay in the water, and keep clear of the natives, if he valued his life; but not being able to hear me, my guards, who supposed I was giving him orders to fetch the money, obliged me to get up and approach him a little, until I made him understand what I wanted: he then returned on board the wreck, and I was taken back to my former station.

Antonio came to the shore, as soon as he knew it was my wish, and made directly towards me. The natives expecting he would bring more money, flocked about him to receive it, but finding he had none, struck him with their fists and the handles of their daggers, and stirpped off all his clothing; the children at the same time pricking him with their sharp knives, and all seemed determined to torment him with a slow and cruel death. He begged for his life upon his knees, but they paid no regard to his entreaties. In hopes of saving him from the fury of these wretches, I told him to let them know by signs that there were dollars and other things buried in the sand near where our tent had stood, and to endeavour to find them by digging. A new spy-glass, a handsaw, and several other things had been buried there, and a bag containing about four hundred dollars at a short distance from them. He soon made them undersand that something was buried, and they hurried him to the spot he had pointed out, and he began to dig. I had imagined that if this man would come on shore, I should be enabled to make my escape; yet I knew not how, nor had I formed any plan for effecting it.

I was seated on the sand, facing the sea, between the old man on my left, with his spear uplifted in his left hand, pointing to my breast, and the stoutest young man on my right, with a naked scimitar in his right hand, pointing to my head—both weapons were within six inches of me, and my guards within a foot

on each side. I considered at this time, that so soon
as any thing should be found by those who were digging, they would naturally speak and inform those
who guarded me of it; (these had let go of my arms
sometime before) and as I was pretty certain that
both of them would look round as soon as the discovery of any treasure should be announced, I carefully drew up my legs under me, but without exciting suspicion in order to be ready for a start. The
place where they were digging, was partly behind
us on our right, and upon their making a noise, both
my guards turned their heads and eyes from me
towards them, when I instantly sprang out from
beneath their weapons, and flew to the beach. I was
running for my life, and soon reached the water's
edge: knowing I was pursued, and nearly overtaken,
I plunged into the sea, with all my force, head foremost, and swam under water as long as I could hold
my breath; then rising to the surface, I looked round
on my pursuers. The old man was within ten feet
of me, up to his chin in water, and was in the act of
darting his spear through my body, when a surf
rolling over me, saved my life, and dashed him and
his comrades on the beach. I was some distance
westward of the wreck; but swimming as fast as
possible towards her, whilst surf after surf broke in
towering heights over me, I was enabled by almost
superhuman exertion to reach the lee of the wreck,
when I was taken into the boat over the stern by the
mates and people.

I was so far exhausted that I could not immediately witness what passed on shore, but was informed
by those who did, that my pursuers stood motionless
on the beach, at the edge of the water, until I was
safe in the boat: that they then ran towards poor
Antonio, and plunging a spear into his body near his
left breast downwards, laid him dead at their feet.
They then picked up what things remained, and
made off altogether. I saw them dragging Antonio's

lifeless trunk across the sand hills, and felt an inexpressible pang, that bereft me for a moment of all
sensation, occasioned by a suggestion that to me
alone his massacre was imputable; but on my recovery, when I reflected there were no other means
whereby my own life could have been preserved, and
under Providence, the lives of ten men, who had
been committed to my charge, I concluded I had
not done wrong, nor have I since had occasion to
reproach myself for being the innocent cause of his
destruction, nor did any of my surviving shipmates,
though perfectly at liberty so to do, ever accuse me
on this point; from which I think I have an undoubted right to infer, that their feelings perfectly
coincided with mine on this melancholy occasion.

CHAPTER VI.

*Providential preservation through the surf to
the open ocean— sufferings in their shattered
boat nine days at sea—landing again
on the frightful coast of the
African Desart*

HOSTILITIES had now commenced, and we could
not doubt but these merciless ruffians would soon
return in force, and when able to overpower us
would massacre us all as they had already done Antonio. The wind blowing strong, and the surf breaking outside and on the wreck twenty or thirty feet
high, the hope of getting to sea in our crazy long-boat
was indeed but faint. She had been thumping along-

side the wreck, and on a sand bank all day, and
writhed like an old basket, taking in as much water
as two men constantly employed with buckets could
throw out. The deck and outside of the wreck were
fast going to pieces, and the other parts could not
hold together long. The tide, (by being low) together with the sand bar that had been formed by the
washing of the sea from the bow of the wreck to the
beach, had very much lessened the danger of com-
municating with the shore during this day; but it
was now returning to sweep every thing from the
wreck, aided by the wind, which blew a gale on
shore every night. To remain on the wreck, or go
on shore was almost certain death; the boat could no
longer be kept afloat alongside, and being without
provisions or water, if we should put to sea, we must
soon perish. We had neither oars nor a rudder to
the boat; no compass nor a quadrant to direct her
course; but as it was our only chance, I resolved to
try and get to sea; expecting, nevertheless, we
should be swallowed up by the first surf, and
launched into eternity all together.

I, in the first place, sent Porter on shore to get the
two broken oars that were still lying there, while I
made my way through the water into the hold of the
wreck, to try once more if any fresh water could be
found. I dove in at the hatchway, which was covered with water, and found, after coming up under
the deck on the larboard side, as I expected, just
room enough to breathe, and to work among the
floating casks, planks, and wreck of the hold. After
much labour I found a water cask, partly full, and
turning it over, discovered that its bung was tight.
This gave me new courage, and after upheading it,
I came up and communicated the circumstance to
my shipmates, and we then made search for some
smaller vessel to fill from the cask. After much trouble, a small keg was found in the after hold; it might
probably hold four gallons—the head of the water-

cask was stove in, and with the help of Mr. Savage and Clark I got the keg full of water, and a good drink for all hands besides, which was very much needed. The others were in the meantime employed in rigging out spars which we had lashed together over the stern of the wreck with a rope made fast to their outer ends, in order to give the boat headway, and clear her from the wreck, when we should finally shove off. Porter had returned with the oars, and also brought the bag of money that had been buried, containing about four hundred dollars: this he did of his own accord.

We had got the small boat's sails, consisting of a jib and mainsail, into the boat, with a spar that would do for a mast, and the brig's fore-topmast stay-sail; the keg of water, a few pieces of salt pork, a live pig, weighing about twenty pounds, which had escaped to the shore when the vessel struck, and which had swam back to us again when we were driven from the shore; about four pounds of figs, that had been soaking in salt water ever since the brig was wrecked, and had been fished out of her cabin; this was all our stock of provisions.

Every thing being now ready, I endeavoured to encourage the crew as well as I could; representing to them that it was better to be swallowed up all together, than to suffer ourselves to be massacred by the ferocious savages; adding, that the Almighty was able to save, even when the last ray of hope was vanishing; that we should never despair, but exert ourselves to the last extremity, and still hope for his merciful protection.

As we surveyed the dangers that surrounded us, wave following wave, breaking with a dreadful crash just outside of us, at every instant, our hearts indeed failed us, and there appeared no possibility of getting safely beyond the breakers, without a particular interference of Providence in our favour. The particular interference of Providence in any case I had al-

ways before doubted. Every one trembled with
dreadful apprehensions, and each imagined that the
moment we ventured past the vessel's stern, would
be his last. I then said, "let us pull off our hats, my
shipmates and companions in distress." This was
done in instant; when lifting my eyes and my soul
towards heaven, I exlaimed, "great Creator and preserver of the universe, who now seest our distresses;
we pray thee to spare our lives, and permit us to pass
through this overwhelming surf to the open sea; but
if we are doomed to perish, thy will be done; we
commit our souls to the mercy of thee our God, who
gave them: and Oh! universal Father, protect and
preserve our widows and children."

The wind, as if by divine command, at this very
moment ceased to blow. We hauled the boat out; the
dreadful surges that were nearly bursting upon us,
suddenly subsided, making a path for our boat about
twenty yards wide, through which we rowed her
out as smoothly as if she had been on a river in a
calm, whilst on each side of us, and not more than
ten yards distant, the surf continued to break twenty
feet high, and with unabated fury. We had to row
nearly a mile in this manner; all were fully convinced that we were saved by the immediate interposition of divine Providence in this particular instance, and all joined in returning thanks to the
Supreme Being for this mercy. As soon as we reached
the open sea, and had gained some distance from the
wreck, we observed the surf rolling behind us with
the same force as it had on each side the boat. We
next fitted the mast, and set the small boat's mainsail. The wind now veered four points to the eastward, so that we were enabled to fetch past the
point of the Cape, though the boat had neither keel
nor rudder, it was sunset when we got out, and night
coming on, the wind as usual increased to a gale
before morning, and we kept the boat to the wind by
the help of an oar, expecting every moment to be

swallowed up by the waves. We were eleven in number on board; two constantly bailing were scarcely able to keep her free, changing hands every half hour. The night was very dark and foggy, and we could not be sure of fetching clear of the land, having nothing to guide us but the wind. In the morning we sailed back again for the land, and had approached it almost within reach of the breakers without seeing it, when we put about again. It had been my intention after we had got to sea, to run down the coast in the hope of finding some vessel, or to discover the mouth of some river, in order to obtain a supply of water. But now the dangers and difficulties we should have to encounter in doing this, were taken into consideration. If we tried to navigate along the coast, it was necessary to know our course, or we should be in imminent danger of being dashed to pieces on it every dark day, and every night. The thick foggy weather would prevent our seeing the land in the day time; whilst the wind, blowing almost directly on the land, would force us towards it, and endanger the safety of both the boat and our lives at every turn or point. We had no compass to guide us either by day or night; no instrument by which to find our latitude; no rudder to steer our boat with; nor were we in possession of materials wherewith it was possible to make one; she had no keel to steady her, nor was there a steering place in her stern, where an oar could be fixed by any other means than by lashing to the stern ring, which afforded a very unsteady hold. On the other hand, we considered that if we escaped the danger of being driven on shore or foundering at sea, and should succeed in reaching the cultivated country south of the desart, we should have to encounter the ferocious inhabitants who would not fail, in the hope of plunder, to massacre us, or doom us to slavery. On the other hand, we reflected that we had escaped from savages who had already killed one of our shipmates, had gained the open sea through divine mercy, and could stand off to the westward without fear of being driven on shore. In this direction we might meet with some friendly vessel to save us, which was our only hope in that way; and the worst that could happen to us was to sink altogether in the sea, or gradually perish through want of sustenance.

Having considered, and represented to my companions the dangers that beset us on every side, I asked their opinions one by one, and found they were unanimously in favour of committing themselves to the open sea in preference to keeping along the coast. The dangers appeared to be fewer, and all agreed that it was better to perish on the ocean, if it was God's will, than by the hands of the natives. There being a strong breeze, we stood off by the wind had at length arrived, and expecting that every approaching surge would bury him forever in a watery grave.

The boat racked like an old basket, letting in water at every seam and split; her timbers working out or breaking off; the nails I had put in while last on shore were kept from entirely drawing out, merely by the pressure of the water acting on the outside of the boat. Sharp flashes of lightning caused by heat and vapour shot across the gloom, rendering the scene doubly horrid. In this situation some of the men thought it was no longer of use to try to keep the boat afloat, as they said she must soon fill in spite of all their exertions. Having prayed to the Almighty and implored pardon for our transgressions, each one seemed perfectly resigned to his fate: this was a trying moment, however, and my example and advice could scarcely induce them to continue bailing; whilst some of them, by thrusting their heads into the water, endeavoured to ascertain what the pains of death were, by feeling the effects the water would produce on their organs. Thus passed this night; all my exertions were necessary to encourage the men to assist me in bailing the boat, by reminding them of our miraculous escape from the savages, and through the surf to the open sea, and enforcing on their minds the consideration that we were still in the hands of the same disposing power, escaping from the shore by a miracle, to be abandoned here and swallowed up by the ocean; and that for my own part I still entertained hopes of our preservation; at any rate that it was a duty we owed to God and ourselves to strive to the latest breath to prevent our own destruction. Day came on amidst these accumulated horrors; it was the first of September; thirst pressed upon us, which we could only allay by wetting our mouths twice a day with a few drops of wine and water, and as many times with our urine.

The wind continued to blow hard all this day, and the succeeding night with great violence, and the boat to work and leak in the same manner as before. Worn down with fatigues and long continued hunger and thirst, scorched by the burning rays of the sun, and no vessel appearing to save us, our water fast diminishing, as well as our strength, every hope of succour by meeting with a vessel entirely failed me, so that in the afternoon of the 2nd of September, I represented to my companions, that as we were still alive, after enduring so many trials, it was my advice to put about, and make towards the coast again; that if we continued at sea, we must inevitably perish, and that we could but perish in returning towards the land; that we might still exist four or five days longer, by means of the water and provisions that remained, and that it might be the will of Providence to send us on the coast where our vessel had been wrecked, and where means were perhaps prepared to bring about our deliverance and restoration to our country and our families. All seemed convinced that it was so, and we immediately put about with a kind of cheerfulness I had not observed in any countenance since our first disaster.

From this time all submitted to their fate with tolerable patience, and kept the boat free, though we had continual bad weather, without murmuring. We wetted our lips with wine and water twice every day, and ate the bones and some of the raw flesh of our pig, with its skin; but at length we became so faint as to be unable to take our turns in bailing, whilst the boat laboured so much as to work off nearly all the nails that kept the planks to her timbers above water.

By the 6th of September, at night, we had not made the land, and could not hope to make the boat hold together in any manner above another day. I expected we should have found the land that day, but was disappointed, and some of the people began again to despair. Impelled by thirst, they forgot what they owed to their shipmates, and in the night got at, and drank off one of the two bottles of wine we had remaining. When I mentioned the loss of the wine on the morning of the 7th, all denied having taken or drank it, adding that it was an unpardonable crime, and that those who did it ought to be thrown overboard instantly. From the heat observable in their conversation, I guessed the offenders, but the wine was gone, and no remedy remained but patience, and stricter vigilance for the future.

In a short time we discovered land at a great distance ahead, and to leeward. This gave all hands new spirits; hope again revived for a moment; the land appeared perfectly smooth in the distant horizon; not the smallest rising or hill was to be seen, and I concluded we must be near a desart coast, where our sufferings would find no relief, but in death. We continued to approach the land, driving along to the southward by a swift current, roaring

on. These locusts were dead, and crumbled to dust on the slightest touch.

We now found a good place in the sand, about one hundred feet from the sea, under a high cliff, to sleep on; here we greased our mouths by eating a small piece of salt pork, and wet them as usual with a sip of urine. All hands, except myself, had a little fresh water left; my comrades knew I had not one drop, and two of them offered to let me taste of theirs, with which I just moistened my tongue, and after sending up our prayers to heaven for mercy and relief in our forlorn and desolate condition we laid ourselves down to sleep.

I had, on setting out from home, received Horace Savage under my particular charge, from his widowed mother; his father, when living, having been my intimate friend, I promised her to take care of him, as if he was my own son, and this promise I had endeavoured to fulfill. He was now in deep distress, and I determined within myself that I would adopt him as my son, for his mother was poor; that I would watch over his ripening years, in case we both lived, and if fortune should favour me in future, that he should share it in common with my children. I now took him in my arms, and we all slept soundly till morning, though the change was so great in the night, from extreme heat to a damp cold air, that we awoke in the morning (September 9th) with benumbed and trembling limbs. Sleep, however, had refreshed us, and though our feet were torn, and our frames nearly exhausted, yet we chased away despair, and set forward on our journey.

We soon discovered at no great distance ahead, a sand beach that appeared large, and from which the shore upward seemed more sloping, as if opening a way to the surface above it; we also thought we should be able, in case we could reach the beach, to get water that would be drinkable, by digging in the sand, down to a level with the water in the sea, and letting it filter into the hole; this I had done on the little keys of the Bahama bank, with success, and expected it would be the same here;—so we made our way slowly along, as we had done the day before, until we got within a short distance of this beach, where we met with a promontory of rocks, which rose in height even with the surface above us; jutting far into the sea, whose waves had worn in under its base to the distance of fifty or one hundred feet, and now dashed in a wild and frightful manner against the projecting points, which its washings for ages had formed underneath. To climb over this formidable obstruction, was impossible; to get around it through the water, appeared equally so, as there was not sufficient time, by the greatest exertion, to pass before the return of the surf, which would inevitably hurl the adventurer into the cavities under the cliff, among the sharp rocks, where he must immediately perish.

Thus far we had all got safe; to advance by what appeared to be the only possible way, seemed like seeking instant death; to remain in our present situation, was merely to die a lingering one, and to return, was still worse, by increasing our pains, without leading to any chance of relief. Before us was a prospect of getting water, and arriving at the summit of the land, if we could only get round the promontory alive; and fortunately, at this moment, we observed a rock about half way across this point, that had tumbled down from above, and had been washed full of holes; it was covered by every surf, and its top left bare as the wave receded. I imagined I could reach it before the wave came in; and after making known my intentions, to my companions, I followed the surf out, and laid hold of the rock, just as the returning swell overwhelmed me. I clung to it for my life, the surf passing over me, and spending its fury among the crags: the instant it retired I hurried on to the steep rocks beyond the point, where I again held on, while another surf swept over me, and then left me to clamber up as quick as I was able on the flat surface of the rock, beyond the reach of the waves. The tide was not yet entirely out, though I had judged it was; and as it continued to fall, my people following the same course and embracing the same means, all got safe to the first rock, and from thence to the place where I lay prostrate to receive and assist them in getting up. Though our limbs and bodies were very much bruised in this severe encounter, yet we felt somewhat encouraged, and made for the sand beach as fast as we were able. We soon reached it, and began digging in the sand for water, at different distances from the sea, but found it to be as salt as the ocean.

After digging several holes farther off, and meeting with dry rock instead of water, I pitched upon a spot for our last effort; and while the others were digging, I told them I would go and see if I could get up the bank, and if I succeeded that I would return in a short time with the news: the bank here rose abruptly, leaving, however, in some places sufficient slope for a man to ascend it by climbing. Through one of these slopes I made my way up, in the hope of finding some green thing that might help to allay our burning thirst, and some tree to shelter us from the scorching blaze of the sun; but what was my surprise when I came to the spot so long desired, and found it to be a barren plain, extending as far as the eye could reach each way, without a tree, shrub, or spear of grass, that might give the smallest relief to expiring nature? I had exerted myself to the utmost to get there; the dreary sight was more than I could bear; my spirits fainted within me, and I fell to the earth deprived of every sensation. When I recovered, it was some time before I could recollect where I

was: my intolerable thirst however at length convinced me, and I was enabled to administer the same
wretched and disgusting relief to which I had so
frequently before been compelled to resort.

Despair now seized on me, and I resolved to cast
myself into the sea as soon as I could reach it, and
put an end to my life and miseries together. But
when I the next moment reflected that I had left
ten of my fellow creatures on the shore, who looked
up to me for an example of courage and fortitude,
and for whom I still felt myself bound to continue
my exertions, which might yet be blessed with success; and that at the moment when I supposed the
hand of relief far from me, it might be very near;
and when I next thought of my wife and children, I
felt a kind of conviction within me, that we should
not all perish after such signal deliverances. I then
made for the sea side about a mile eastward of my
men, and finding a good place between some rocks,
I bathed myself for half an hour in the sea water,
which refreshed and revived me very much, and
then returned to my men with a heart lighter than I
expected. I was very much fatigued and threw myself down on the sand. They huddled around me,
to know what success I had met with; but to waive
the subject of my sad discovery, I told them we could
go along the beach for two miles before meeting
again with the perpendicular cliffs, and would find
great relief by bathing our bodies in the salt water;
inquiring at the same time, if they had found any
fresh in the last place they had been digging. I thus
diverted their minds, in some measure, from the object they wished to inquire after; and as I found they
had dug down six or eight feet, and had found no
water, having come to a rock which frustrated all
their attempts; with heavy hearts and tottering limbs
we staggered along the shore together.

It was about mid-day when we got to the end of

the sand beach; my people thought it would be impossible for them to climb the craggy steep; so with common consent we laid ourselves down under the shade formed by a shelving rock, to rest, and to screen ourselves from the rays of the sun, which had heated the air to such a degree, that it was with the greatest difficulty we could fetch our breath. There was the wind or air stirring at this time, except the hot steam rising from the sandy beach, which had been wet by the sea at the last tide.

Having lain down in our exhausted state, neither thirst nor our reflections had power to keep our eyes open; we sunk into a lethargic sleep, which continued about two hours, during which time a light breeze from the sea had set in, and gently fanned and refreshed our debilitated bodies. We then ascended the steep bank, crawling frequently on our hands and knees. Though I had previously prepared all their minds for a barren prospect, yet the sight of it, when they reached its level, had such an effect on their senses that they sunk to the earth involuntarily; and as they surveyed the dry and dreary waste, stretching out to an immeasurable extent before them they exclaimed, " 'tis enough; here we must breathe our last; we have no hope before us of finding either water or provisions, or human beings, or even wild beasts; nothing can live here." The little moisture yet left in us overflowed at our eyes, but as the salt tears rolled down our woe-worn and haggard cheeks, we were fain to catch them with our fingers and carry them to our mouths, that they might not be lost, and serve to moisten our tongues, that were now nearly as dry as parched leather, and so stiff, that with difficulty we could articulate a sentence so as to be understood by each other.

I began now to exhort and press them to go forward; telling them that we still might find relief, and in this effort I was assisted by Hogan, who thought with me that it was time enough to lie down and die, when we could not walk. Mr. Williams and Mr. Savage were also willing, and we moved on slowly, with scarcely a hope however of meeting with the least relief. We continued along on the edge of the cliffs, which could not be less than from five to six hundred feet in perpendicular height: the surface of the ground was baked down almost as hard as flint; it was composed of small ragged stones, gravel, and reddish earth. We observed a small dry stalk of a plant, resembling that of a parsnip, though very low; and some dry remains of locusts were also scattered on the surface as we proceeded. Near night we saw some small holes dug on the surface, and on examination found they had been made in order to get at the root of the dry weed we had just before seen: this we conceived had been done by some wild beasts; but finding no tracks of any kind near them, nor on the dirt dug up, I concluded it was done by man, and declared my hopes to my desponding companions of soon meeting with human beings.

We procured after great labour in digging with sticks we had brought from the boat and the help of stones a few small pieces of a root as large as a man's finger; it was very dry, but in taste resembled smellage or celery. We could not get enough to be of any material service to us, owing to the scarcity of the plant, and the hardness of the ground; but about sunset we discovered, on a small spot of sand, the imperfect track of a camel, and thought we saw that of a man, which we took to be a very old track.

Believing from our present feelings that we could not possibly survive a day longer without drink, and no signs of finding any appearing, the last ray of hope faded away, and the gloom of despair, which had at length settled on our hearts, now became visible in every countenance. A little after sunset we saw at a considerable distance in advance, perhaps three or four miles, another sand beach, and I urged myself forward towards it as fast as I could, in hopes of getting some rest by sleeping on the sand for the night, as the ground we were now on was as hard as rock, and covered with small sharp stones. I was encouraging the men to follow on, when Clark, being near me, begged me to look towards the beach, saying, "I think I see a light!" it was the light of a fire!

Joy. thrilled through my veins like the electric spark: hope again revived within me, and while I showed it to my sinking and despairing crew, I found it communicated to them the same feelings. I told them we must approach the natives, who I could not doubt were encamped for the night, with the greatest caution, for fear of alarming them, and falling a sacrifice to their fury in the confusion we might occasion by our sudden approach in the dark. New life and spirits were infused into all the crew, and we soon reached a broken place in the bank, through which we descended carefully over the broken rocks from three to four hundred feet to a sandy spot near its base, where we laid ourselves down for the night, after imploring the protection of Almighty God, and wetting our mouths with a few drops of water still remaining in the bottles.

The sand on which we lay was heated by the sun's rays sufficiently to have roasted eggs, and as we were on the side of a sand hill, we scraped off the top of it for a foot or two deep; when finding the heat more supportable, and the cool breeze of the night setting in, all hands being excessively fatigued, soon forgot their sufferings in the arms of sleep, excepting myself; for my mind had become so excited by alternate hopes, and fears, and reflections, that I was kept awake through the whole of this long and dismal night. I had determined, as soon as daylight appeared, to show ourselves to the natives, and submit either to death or life from their hands. I had no doubt of their being Arabs who would take and hold us as slaves, and though I did not expect myself to live but a short time in that condition, I presumed some of my fellow sufferers might, and that it was a decree of Providence which had set this alternative before us.

I no longer felt any fear of death, for that would put a period to my long sufferings: my thirst had become so insupportable, that I could with difficulty breathe, and thought I would be willing to sell my life for one gill of fresh water. My distresses had been so excessive, and my cares and anxieties for my shipmates so great, that all thoughts of my family had been driven almost entirely from my mind. I could not sleep—why was I denied what all around me were enjoying!—I shut my eyes, and prayed to be permitted to sleep, if only for one hour, but all in vain. I imagined that the savages, who were near us, would not take our lives immediately, as it was contrary to the nature of man to slay his fellow-creatures, merely from a thirst for blood.

We had now no arms to defend ourselves, nor any property to excite their jealousy, revenge, or avarice —we were as miserable as human beings could be, and I hoped we should excite pity, even in the breasts of the savage Arabs. I could hardly yet think, that we were to fall a sacrifice to these people, after the providential escapes we had already experienced: next the remembrance of my wife and children flitted across my mind, and I was forced to acknowledge, that however bad their situation might be, their real distress could in no wise equal mine, and that I had no right to repine at the dispensations of Providence, since every mortal has his circle wisely marked out by heaven; and nothing but blindness to the future, occasions us to complain of the ways of our Creator.

If it was the will of the Supreme Being that I should again see and embrace my beloved family, it would certainly take place; if not, that power who ordered all things for the general good, would not forsake them.

Thus passed away the night, which had seemed to me an endless one. I was impatient to know my fate, and chid the slowness of the sun; my great anxiety and wakefulness, rendered my thirst doubly painful, and having expended all the urine I had so carefully saved, I had recourse before morning to robbery, and actually stole a sip of the cook's water, which he had made and saved in a bottle; but the only taste it had for me, was a salt one, and it seemed (if possible) to increase by burning thirst. The day at last arrived that was to decide our fate. It was the 10th of September. I awakened my companions, and told them we must now go forward and show ourselves to the natives—that I expected they would seize upon us as slaves, but had strong hopes that some of us would escape with our lives. I also mentioned to them the name of the American Consul General at Tangier, and that if it ever was in their power, they must write to him, inform him of the fate of our vessel and her crew: to write, if possible, to any Christian merchant in Mogadore, Gibraltar, or elsewhere, or to the Consul at Algiers, Tunis, or Tripoli, if they should hear those places mentioned, and exhorted all to submit to their fate like men, and be obedient, as policy required, to their future masters. I reminded them again of the former interpositions of Providence in our favour, and said all I could to encourage and persuade them, that mildness and submission might save our lives—that resistance and stubbornness would certainly tend to make them more miserable while alive, and probably prompt the natives to murder them out of resentment.

All agreed to go forward, and on rising the little

sand hills near us, we discovered a very large drove
of camels at about half a mile to the eastward of us,
with a large company of people, in a kind of valley
formed by a ridge of sand hills on the north next the
sea, and by the high land to the south, rising from
five to six hundred feet in upright and overhanging
cliffs—through which a little farther on we saw a deep
hollow that appeared to have been formed by some
convulsive shock of the earth, which had thus made
a sort of passage, through which camels were enabled
to pass up and down, but with great difficulty. The
Arabs seemed busied in giving water to their camels;
they saw us, and in an instant one man and two
women ran towards us with great speed. As they came
forward, many others of them who saw us, also began
to advance: so taking Mr. Williams and Mr. Savage
with me, I went forward to meet them, bowed myself to the ground before them, and with signs implored their compassion.

The man was armed with a scimitar, which he
held naked in his hand; he ran up to me as if to cut
me to the earth: I bowed again in token of submission, and he began without further ceremony to strip
off my clothing, while the women were doing the
same to Mr. Williams and Mr. Savage. Thirty or
forty more were arriving—some running on foot,
with muskets or naked scimitars in their hands;
others riding on swift camels, came quickly up:—by
the time they arrived, however, we were all stripped
naked to the skin. Those Arabs near us threw up
sand into the air, as the others approached; yelling
loudly, which I now learned was a sign of hostility.
The one who stript me had also taken the cook, and
had put all the clothing he had stript from us into a
blanket, which he had taken from off his own back
for that purpose, leaving himself entirely naked.
This bundle he laid on the negro's shoulders, making me understand that myself and the black man

belonged to him, and that we must not let the others take the clothes in the bundle under pain of death.

As soon as those on the camels were near, they made them lie down, and jumping off, ran to us with their scimitars naked and ready for action; those on foot now joined these, and a great noise and scuffle ensued. Six or eight of them were about me, one hauling me one way and one another—poor Dick, the black man, partook of the hauling, and each man seemed to insist most strenuously that we belonged of right to him. The one who script us, stuck to us as his lawful property, signifying "you may have the others, these are mine." They cut at each other over my head, and on every side of me with their bright weapons, which fairly whizzed through the air within an inch of my naked body, and on every side of me, now hacking each other's arms apparently to the bone, then laying their ribs bare with gashes, while their heads, hands, and thighs, received a full share of cuts and wounds. The blood streaming from every gash, ran down their bodies, colouring and heightening the natural hideousness of their appearance. I had expected to be cut to pieces in this dreadful affray but was not injured.

Those who were not actually engaged in combat, seized the occasion, and snatched away the clothing in Dick's bundle, so that when the fight was over, he had nothing left but his master's blanket. This battle and contest lasted for nearly an hour—brother cutting brother, friend slashing friend. Happily for them, their scimitars were not very sharp, so that when they rubbed off the dried blood from their bodies afterwards with sand, their wounds were not so great or deep as I expected they would be, and they did not pay the least apparent attention to them. I had no time to see what they were doing with my shipmates; only myself and the cook were near each other.

The battle over, I saw my distressed companions divided among the Arabs, and all going towards the drove of camels, though they were at some distance from me. We too were delivered into the hands of two old women, who urged us on with sticks towards the camels. Naked and barefoot I could not go very fast, and showed the women my mouth, which was parched white as frost, and without a sign of moisture. When we got near the well, one of the women called for another, who came to us with a wooden bowl, that held, I should guess, about a gallon of water, and setting it on the ground, made myself and Dick kneel down and put our heads into it like camels. I drank I suppose half a gallon, though I had been very particular in cautioning the men against drinking too much at a time, in case they ever came to water. They then led us to the well, the water of which was nearly as black and disgusting as stale bilge water. A large bowl was now filled with it, and a little sour camel's milk poured from a goat skin into it; this tasted to me delicious, and we all drank of it till our stomachs were literally filled. But this intemperance very soon produced a violent diarrhœa; the consequences of which, however were not very troublesome, and as our situation was similar to that of a beast, being totally divested of clothing, all we cared about was to slake our unabating thirst, and replenish our stomachs by repeated draughts of this washy and unwholesome swill.

We now begged for something to eat, but these Arabs had nothing for themselves, and seemed very sorry it was not in their power to give us some food. There were at and about the well I should reckon about one hundred persons, men, women and children, and from four to five hundred camels, large and small. The sun beat very fiercely upon us, and our skins seemed actually to fry like meat before the fire. These people continued to draw water for their camels, of which the animals drank enormous quantities. It was about 10 o'clock A. M. as I judged by the sun, when one company of the Arabs having finished watering, separated their camels from among the others, took Mr. Williams, Robbins, Porter, Hogan, Barrett, and Burns, mounted them on the bare backs of the camels behind the hump, by the hair of which they were obliged to steady themselves and hold on, without knowing whither they were going, or if I should ever see them again. I took an affectionate leave of them. This their Arab masters permitted me to do without interruption, and could not help showing at this scene, that the feelings of humanity were not totally extinguished in their bosoms. They then hurried them off and ascending through the hollow or crevice towards the face of the desert, they were all soon out of sight.

There remained with the party to which I belonged, Mr. Savage, Clark, Horace, and Dick the cook. Mr. Savage was permitted to retain an old Guernsey frock, and part of a pair of trowsers about his middle, which they had not pulled off: but the rest of us were entirely stripped. Mr. Savage, Clark, and Horace were forced to assist in drawing water for the camels, until all had drunk their fill: then having filled with water a considerable number of goat skins, which had been stripped off these animals over the neck, leaving them otherwise, as whole as when on their backs, they slung them by the skin of their legs on each side of the camels, after tying up the neck to prevent the water escaping, by means of a small rope which they fastened to the fore legs of the skin to keep it up. They next put on their baskets for the women and children to ride in: these were made of camel's skin, and fixed in such a manner, with a wooden rim around them, over

which the skin was sewed, that three or four could
sit in them with perfect safety and ease, only taking
care to preserve their balance. These baskets were
fastened under the camels' bellies with a strong rope:
I was obliged to assist in putting them on, and was
in hopes of being permitted to ride in one of them,
but that was not the intention of my master. I, as
well as those who were with me had drunk a great
deal of water, while we were at the well, which had
passed off, as before observed, without doing us any
injury. We had been furnished also with a little milk
in our water two or three times, which gave some
relief to our hunger. The men had saddles just large
enough for their seat: the pads are made of flat
pieces of wood: a piece of the same rises in front,
being about the length, breadth, and thickness of a
man's hand; an iron rim, or a strong wooden one,
goes round on each side, forming a circle; covered
with a piece of skin stretched and sewed tight over
it. The saddle is then placed on the camel's back
before the hump, and fastened tight by a rope under
his belly. Thus prepared we began to mount the
sand hills and to get up through the gulley. We
were forced to walk and to drive the camels and
keep them together, whilst the sand was so soft and
yielding, that we sunk into it every step nearly to
our knees. The blazing heat of the sun's rays darting
on our naked bodies, and reflected from the sand we
waded through; the sharp pointed craggy rocks and
stones that cut our feet and legs to the bone, in addition to our excessive weakness which the dysentary
had increased, rendered our passage up through this
chasm or hollow much more severe than any thing
of the kind we had before undergone, and nearly
deprived us of life. For my own part I thought I
must have died before I could reach the summit, and
was obliged to stop in the sand, until by the applica-

tion of a stick to my sore back by our drivers, I was forced up to its level; and there they made the camels lie down and rest.

CHAPTER VIII.

The author and his crew are carried on camels into the interior of the Desart of Zahahrah— the Arabs hold a council—the crew are sold and distributed—the author's remarkable dream—the skin and flesh are literally roasted off from his body, and from the bones of his companions —their dreadful sufferings while naked and wandering about the Desart with their masters, subsisting only on a little camel's milk—two Arab traders arrive

THE Arabs had been much amused in observing our difficulty in ascending the height, and kept up a laugh while they were whipping us forward. Their women and children were on foot as well as themselves, and went up without the smallest difficulty or inconvenience, though it was extremely hard for the camels to mount; and before they got to the top they were covered with sweat and froth. Having now selected five camels for the purpose, one for each of us, they put us on behind the humps, to which we were obliged to cling by grasping its long hair with both hands. The back bone of the one I was set on was only covered with skin, and as sharp as the edge of an oar's blade; his belly, distended with water, made him perfectly smooth, leaving no projection of the hips to keep me from sliding off behind; and his back or rump being as steep as the roof of a house, and so broad across as to keep my legs extended to their utmost stretch, I was in this manner slipping down to his tail every moment. I was forced however to keep on, while the camel rendered extremely restive at the sight of his strange rider, was all the time running about among the drove, and making a most woful bellowing; and as they have neither bridle, halter, or any other thing whereby to guide or govern them, all I had to do was stick on as well as I could.

The Arabs, both men and women, were very anxious to know where we had been thrown on shore, whether to the eastward or westward; and being satisfied by me on that point, so soon as they had placed us on the camels, and given the women directions how to steer, they mounted each his camel, seated themselves on the small round saddle, and then crossing their legs on the animal's shoulders, set off to the westward at a great trot, leaving us under the care of the women, some of whom were on foot, and urged the camels forward as fast as they could run. The heavy motions of the camel, not unlike that of a small vessel in a heavy head-beat sea, were so violent, aided by the sharp back bone, as soon to excoriate certain parts of my naked body; the inside of my thighs and legs were also dreadfully chafed, so that the blood dripped from my heels, while the intense heat of the sun had scorched and blistered our bodies and the outside of our legs, so that we were covered with sores, and without any thing to administer relief. Thus bleeding and smarting under the most excruciating pain, we continued to advance in a S. E. direction on a plain flat hard surface of sand, gravel, and rock, covered with small sharp stones. It seemed as if our bones would be dislocated at every step. Hungry and thirsty, the night came on, and no indication of stopping; the cold night wind began to blow, chilling our blood, which ceased to trickle down our lacerated legs; but although it saved our blood, yet acting on our blistered skins, it increased our pains beyond description. We begged to be permitted to get off, but the women paid no attention to our distress nor intreaties, intent only on getting forward. We designedly slipped off the camels when going at a full trot, risking to break our necks by the fall, and tried to excite their compassion and get a drink of water, (which they call sherub,) but they paid no attention to our prayers, and kept the camels running faster than before.

This was the first time I had attempted to walk barefooted since I was a schoolboy: we were obliged to keep up with the camels, running over the stones, which were nearly as sharp as gun flints, and cutting our feet to the bone at every step. It was here that my fortitude and reason failed to support me; I cursed my fate aloud, and wished I had rushed into the sea before I gave myself up to these merciless beings in human forms—it was now too late. I would have put an immediate end to my existence, but had neither knife nor any weapon with which to perform the deed. I searched for a stone, intending if I could find a loose one sufficiently large, to knock out my own brains with it; but searched in vain. This paroxysm passed off in a minute or two, when reason returned, and I recollected that my life was in the hand of the power that gave it, and that "the Judge of all the earth would do right." Then running with all my remaining might, I soon came up with the camels, regardless of my feet and of pain, and felt perfectly resigned and willing to submit to the will of Providence and the fate that awaited me.

From that time forward, through all my succeeding trials and sufferings, I never once murmured in my heart, but at all times kept my spirits up, doing the utmost to obey and please those whom fortune, fate, or an overruling Providence had placed over me, and to persuade, both by precept and practice,

my unhappy comrades to do the same. I had, with
my companions, cried aloud with pain, and begged
our savage drivers for mercy, and when we had
ceased to make a noise, fearing, as it were, to lose
us in the dark, they stopped the camels, and again
placing us on them as before, drove them on at full
speed until about midnight, when we entered a small
dell or valley, excavated by the hand of nature, a
little below the surface of the desart, about from
fifteen to twenty feet deep. Here they stopped the
camels, and made them lie down, bidding us to do
the same. I judge we must have travelled forty miles
this day to the S. E.: the place was hard and rocky,
not even sand to lie on, nor any covering to shelter
us or keep off the cold damp wind that blew strong
from the sea.

They soon set about milking, and then gave us
each about a pint of pure milk, warm from the
camels, taking great care to divide it for us; it
warmed our stomachs, quenched our thirst in some
measure, and allayed in a small degree the cravings
of hunger. Mr. Savage had been separated from us,
and I learned from him afterwards that he fared
better than we did, having had a larger allowance
of milk. Clark, Horace, and Dick the cook were still
with me. We lay down on the ground as close to
each other as we could on the sharp stones, without
any lee to fend off the wind from us; our bodies all
over blistered and mangled, the stones piercing
through the sore naked flesh to the ribs and other
bones. These distresses, and our sad and desponding
reflections, rendered this one of the longest and most
dismal nights ever passed by any human beings. We
kept shifting births, striving to keep off some of the
cold during the night, while sleep, that had hitherto
relieved our distresses and fatigues, fled from us in
spite of all our efforts and solicitude to embrace it;
nor were we able to close our eyes.

The morning of the 11th came on at last, and our

industrious mistresses having milked a little from the camels, and allowed the young ones to suck, gave us about half a pint of milk among four of us, being just enough to wet our mouths, and then made us go forward on foot and drive the camels. The situation of our feet was horrible beyond description, and the very recollection of it, even at this moment makes my nerves thrill and quiver. We proceeded forward, having gained the level desart for a considerable time, when entering a small valley, we discovered three or four tents made of coarse cloth near which we were met by our masters and a number of men whom we had not before seen, all armed with either a double barrelled musket, a scimitar, or dagger. They were all of the same nation and tribe, for they shook hands at meeting, and seemed very friendly to each other, though they stopped and examined us, as if disposed to question the right of property.

It now appeared there was still some difficulty in deciding to whom each one of us belonged; for seizing hold of us, some dragged one way and some another, disputing very loudly and frequently drawing their weapons. It was however decided at last, after making us go different ways for the space of two or three hours with different men, that myself and the cook should remain, for the present, in the hands of our first master. They gave Clark to another, and Horace to a third. We had come near a couple of tents, and were certainly disgusting objects, being naked and almost skinless; this was sometime about noon, when three women came out who had not before seen us, and having satisfied their curiosity by gazing at us, they expressed their disgust and contempt by spitting at us as we went along, making their faces still more horrid by every possible contortion of their frightful features; this we afterwards found to be their constant practice wherever we went until after we got off the desart.

Towards evening a great number of the men having collected in a little valley, we were made to stop,
and as our bodies were blistered and burnt to such a
degree as to excite pity in the breasts of some of the
men, they used means to have a tent cleared out for
us to sit under. They then allowed all those of our
crew present to sit under it, and, as may well be supposed, we were glad to meet one another again, miserable as we all were. Porter and Burns, who had
been separated from me shortly after our capture,
were still absent. A council was now held by the
natives near the tent; they were about one hundred
and fifty men, some very old, some middle aged,
and some quite young. I soon found they were Mo-
hamedans, and the proper names by which they
frequently called each other were *Mohamed, Hamet,
Seid, Sidéullah, Abdallah,* &c. so that by these and
the female names *Fatima, Ezimah, Sarah,* &c. I knew
them to be Arabs or Moors.

The council were deliberating about us; and having talked the matter over a long time, seated on the
ground, with their legs crossed under them in circles
of from ten to twenty each, they afterwards arose and
came to us. One of the old men then addressed me;
he seemed to be very intelligent, and though he
spoke a language I was unacquainted with, yet he
explained himself in such a plain and distinct manner, sounding every letter full like the Spaniards,
that with the help of signs I was able to understand
his meaning. He wanted to know what country we
belonged to; I told him we were English; and as I
perceived the Spanish language was in sound more
like that which they spoke than any other I knew,
I used the phrase *Inglesis;* this seemed to please him,
and he said "*O Fransah, O Spaniah;*" meaning "or
Frenchmen or Spaniards;" I repeated we were
English. He next wanted to know which point of
the horizon we came from, and I pointed to the
North.

They had seen our boat, which they called *Zooerga,* and wanted to know if we had come all the way in that boat: I told them no, and making a kind of coast, by heaping up sand, and forming the shape of a vessel, into which I stuck sticks for masts and bowsprit, &c. I gave him to understand that we had been in a large vessel, and wrecked on the coast by a strong wind; then by tearing down the masts and covering the vessel's form with sand, I signified to him that she was totally lost. Thirty or forty of the other Arabs were sitting around us, paying the strictest attention to every one of my words and gestures, and assisting the old man to comprehend me. He wished to know where we were going, and what cargo the vessel (which I now found they called *Sfenah*) had on board. I satisfied them in the best way I could, on this point, telling them that I had on board among other things, dollars: they wanted to know how many, and gave me a bowl to imitate the measure of them; this I did by filling it with stones and emptying it three times. They were much surprised at the quantity, and seemed to be dissatisfied that they had not got a share of them. They then wanted to know which way the vessel lay from us, and if we had seen any of the natives, whom they called Moslemin.

This I took to be what we call Mussulmen, or followers of the Mahommedan doctrine, and in this I was not mistaken. I then explained to them in what manner we had been treated by the inhabitants; that they had got all our clothing, except what we had on when they found us; all our money and provisions; massacred one of our number, and drove us out to sea. They then told me that they heard of the shipwreck of a vessel a great way North, and of the money &c. but that the crew were drowned in the *el M Bahar;* this was so near the Spanish (La Mar) for the sea, that I could not misunderstand it. Thus having obtained what information they wanted on those points, they next desired to know if I knew any thing about *Marocksh;* this sounded something like *Morocco:* I answered yes; next of the *Sooltaan* (the Sultan) to which instead of saying yes, I made signs of assent, for I found they did no more themselves, except by a cluck with the tongue.

They wanted me to tell his name, *Soo Mook,* but I could not understand them until they mentioned *Moolay Solimaan;* this I remembered to be the name of the present emperor of Morocco, as pronounced in Spanish, nearly. I gave them to understand that I knew him; had seen him with my eyes, and that he was a friend to me and to my nation. They next made me point out the direction towards his dominions, and having satisfied them that I knew which way his dominions lay from us, I tried to intimate to them, that if they would carry me there, I should be able to pay them for my ransom, and that of my crew. They shook their heads—it was a great distance, and nothing for camels to eat or drink on the way. My shipmates, who were with me, could not understand one syllable of what they said, or of their signs, and did not believe that I was able to communicate at all with them. Having finished their council, and talked the matter over among themselves, they separated, and our masters, taking each his slave, made off, every one his own way. Although from the conference I derived hopes of our getting ransomed, and imparted the same to my mates and crew, yet they all seemed to think I was deluding them with false expectations; nor could I convince them of the contrary. We took another leave of each other, when we parted for the night, having travelled this day, I should guess, about fifteen miles S. E.

I had been so fully occupied since noon, that no thought of victuals or drink had occurred to my mind. We had none of us ate or drank any thing this day, except about half a gill of milk each in the morning at daylight, and about half a pint of black beach water near the middle of the day. I was delivered over to an Arab named *Bickri,* and went with him near his tent, where he made me lie down on the ground like a camel. Near midnight he brought me a bowl containing about a quart of milk and water; its taste was delicious, and as my stomach had become contracted by long hunger and thirst, I considered it quite a plentiful draught. I had been shivering with cold for a long time, as I had no covering no skreen, and not even one of my shipmates to lie near me to keep one side warm at a time. I was so far exhausted by fatigues, privations, &c. that my misery could no longer keep me awake. I sank into a deep sleep, and during this sleep I was troubled in the first place with the most frightful dreams.

I thought I was naked and a slave, and dreamed over the principle incidents which had already actually passed. I then thought I was driven by Arabs with red hot iron spears pointed at me on every side, through the most dreadful fire I had ever imagined, for near a mile, naked and barefoot; the flames up to my eyes, scorched every part of my skin off, and wasted away my flesh by roasting, burning, and drying it off to the bones; my torments were inconceivable—I now thought I looked up towards heaven, and prayed to the Almighty to receive my spirit, and end my sufferings; I was still in the midst of the flames; a bright spot like an eye with rays around it, appeared above me in the firmament, with a point below it, reaching towards the N. E.—I thought if I went that way I should go right, and turned from the south to the N. E.; the fire soon subsided and I went on, still urged by them about me, with their spears pricking me from time to time over high sand hills and rocky steeps, my flesh dropping off in pieces as I went,—then descending a deep valley, I thought I saw green trees—flowering shrubs in blossom—cows feeding on green grass, with horses, sheep, and asses near me, and as I moved on, I discovered a brook of clear running water; my thirst being excessive, I dragged my mangled limbs to the brook, threw myself down, and drank my fill of the most delicious water. When my thirst was quenched, I rolled in the brook to cool my body, which seemed still consuming with heat; then thanked my God in my heart for his mercies.

My masters in the meantime kept hurrying me on in the way pointed out by the All-seeing eye, which was still visible in the heavens above my head, through crooked, thorny, and narrow paths, over high mountains and deep valleys—past hosts of armed men on horseback and on foot, and walled cities, until we met a tall young man dressed in the European and American manner, by the side of a brook, riding on a stately horse, who upon seeing me alighted, and rushing forward, wild with joy, caught me in his arms, and pressed me to his breast, calling me by the endearing name of brother, in my own language—I thought I fainted in his arms from excess of joy, and when I revived, found myself in a neat room, with a table set in the best manner before me, covered with the choicest meats, fruits, and wines, and my deliverer pressing me to eat and drink; but finding me too much overcome to partake of this refreshment, he said, "take courage, my dear friend, God has decreed that you shall again embrace your beloved wife and children." At this instant I was called by my master—I awoke, and found it was a dream.

Being daylight, (Sept. 12th) he ordered me to drive forward the camels; this I did for about an hour, but my feet were so much swelled, being lacerated by the cutting of the stones, which seemed as if they would penetrate to my heart at every step—

I could not help stooping and crouching down nearly to the ground. In this situation, my first master Hamet observed me; he was going on the same course, S. E. riding on his camel; he came near my present master, and after talking with him a good while, he took off the blanket from his back and gave it to Bickri—then coming close to me, made signs for me to stop. He next made his camel lie down; then fixing a piece of skin over his back behind the saddle, and making its two ends fast to the girths to keep it from slipping off, he bade me mount on it, while he got on his saddle and steadied me with his hand until the camel rose. He then went on the same course as before, in company with three or four other men, well armed and mounted. The sun beat dreadfully hot upon my bare head and body, and it appeared to me that my head must soon split to pieces, as it was racking and cracking with excruciating pain. Though in this horrible distress, yet I still thought of my dream of the last night—"a drowning man will catch at a straw," says the proverb, and I can verily add, that the very faintest gleam of hope will keep alive the declining spirits of a man in the deepest distress and misery; for from the moment I began to reflect on what had passed through my mind when sleeping, I felt convinced that though this was nothing more than a dream, yet still remembering how narrowly and often I had escaped immediate apparent death, and believing it was through the peculiar interposition of divine Providence, I could not but believe that the All-seeing eye was watching over my steps, and would in due time conduct me by his unerring wisdom, into paths that would lead to my deliverance, and restoration to my family.

I was never superstitious, nor ever did I believe in dreams or visions, as they are termed, or even remembered them, so as to relate any I may have had;

but this dream made such an impression on my mind, that it was not possible for me to remove it from my memory—being now as fresh as at the moment I awoke after dreaming it, and I must add that when I afterwards saw Mr. *Willshire,* I knew him to be the same man I had seen in my sleep. He had a particular mark on his chin—wore a light coloured frock coat, had on a white hat, and rode the same horse. From that time I thought if I could once get to the empire of Morocco, I should be sure to find a friend to relieve me and my companions whose heart was already prepared for it by superior Power. My mind was thus employed until we came to a little valley where half a dozen tents were pitched; as soon as we saw them, Hamet made his camel kneel down, and me to dismount—he was met by several women and children, who seemed very glad to see him, and I soon found that they were his relations. He beckoned me to come towards his tent, for he lived there apparently with his mother, and brothers and sisters, but the woman and girls would not suffer me to approach them, driving me off with sticks, and throwing stones at me; but Hamet brought me à little sour milk and water in a bowl, which refreshed me considerably.

It was about two o'clock in the day, and I was forced to remain broiling in the sun without either tree, shrub, or any other shade to shield me from its scorching rays, until night, when Dick (the cook) came in with the camels. Hamet had kept Dick from the beginning, and made him drive the camels, but allowed him to sleep in one corner of the tent, and gave him for the few first days, as much milk as he could drink, once a day; and as he was a domestic slave, he managed to steal water, and sometimes sour milk when he was dry.

In the evening of this day I was joined by Hogan, and now found that he and myself had been pur-

chased by Hamet that day, and that Horace belonged
to an ill-looking old man, whose tent was pitched in
company. This old villain came near me, and saluted
me by the name of *Rais,* asking me the name of his
boy; (Horace) I told him it was Horace, which after
repeating a few times he learned so perfectly, that
at every instant he was yelling out *"Hoh Rais"* for
something or other. Hamet was of a much lighter
colour than the other Arabs we were with, and I
thought he was less cruel, but in this respect I found
I was mistaken, for he made myself and Hogan lie
on the ground in a place he chose, where the stones
were very thick and baked into the ground so tight
that we could not pull them out with our fingers,
and we were forced to lie on their sharp points,
though at a small distance, not more than fifty
yards, was a spot of sand. This I made him understand, (pointing at the same time to my skinless
flesh) but he signified to us that if we did not remain where he had ordered, we should get no milk
when he milked the camels. I calculate we travelled
this day about thirty miles.

Here then we staid, but not to sleep, until about
the midnight hour, when Hamet came to us with
our milk—It was pure and warm from the camels;
and about a pint for each. The wind blew as is usual
in the night, and on that part of the desart the air
was extremely cold and damp; but its moisture on
our bodies was as salt as the ocean. Having received
our share of milk, when all was still in the tent, we
stole to the sandy place, where we got a little sleep
during the remaining part of the night. Horace's
master would not permit him to come near me, nor
me to approach him, making use of a stick, as well
to enforce his commands in this particular, as to
teach us to understand him in other respects.

At daylight (Sept. 13th) we were called on to
proceed. The families struck their tents, and packed

them on camels, together with all their stuff. They made us walk and keep up with the camels, though we were so stiff and sore all over that we could scarcely refrain from crying out at every step: such was our agony:—still pursuing our route to the S. E. In the course of the morning, I saw Mr. Williams; he was mounted on a camel, as we had all been the first day, and had been riding with the drove about three hours—I hobbled along towards him; his camel stopped, and I was enabled to take him by the hand—he was still entirely naked; his skin had been burned off; his whole body was so excessively inflamed and swelled, as well as his face, that I only knew him by his voice, which was very feeble. He told me he had been obliged to sleep naked in the open air every night; that his life was fast wasting away amidst the most dreadful torments; that he could not live one day more in such misery; that his mistress had taken pity on him; and anointed his body that morning with butter or grease, but said he, "I cannot live;" should you ever get clear from this dreadful place, and be restored to your country, tell my dear wife that my last breath was spent in prayers for her happiness: he could say no more; tears and sobs choked his utterance.

His master arrived at this time, and drove on his camel and I could only say to him, "God Almighty bless you," as I look a last look at him, and forgot, for a moment, while contemplating his extreme distress, my own misery. His camel was large, and moved forward with very heavy motions; as he went from me, I could see the inside of his legs and thighs —they hung in strings of torn and chafed flesh—the blood was trickling down the sides of the camel, and off his feet—"my God!" I cried, "suffer us not to live longer in such tortures."

"I had stopped about fifteen minutes, and my master's camels had gained a great distance from me,

so that I was obliged to run that I might come up
with them. My mind was so shocked with the distresses of Mr. Williams, that I thought it would be
impious for me to complain, though the sharp stones
continued to enter my sore feet at every step. My
master saw me and stopped the drove for me to
come up; when I got near him he threatened me,
shaking his stick over my head, to let me know what
I had to expect if I dared to commit another fault.
He then rode off, ordering me and Hogan to drive
the camels on as fast as we could. About an hour
afterwards he came near us, and beckoned to me to
come to him, which I did. A tall old man, nearly as
black as a negro, one of the most ill-looking and disgusting I had yet seen, soon joined my master, with
two young men, whom I found afterwards were his
sons—they were also joined by a number more on
camels and well armed.

After some time bartering about me, I was given
to the old man, whose features showed every sign of
the deepest rooted malignity in his disposition. And
is this my master, thought I? Great God! defend me
from his cruelty! He began to go on—he was on foot;
so were his two sons; but they walked faster than
camels, and the old man kept snarling at me in the
most surly manner, to make me keep up. I tried my
very best, as I was extremely anxious to please him,
if such a thing was possible, knowing the old adage
of "the devil is good when he is pleased," was correct, when applied to human beings; but I could not
go fast enough for him; so after he had growled and
kept on a considerable time, finding I could not keep
up with him, he came behind me and thrust me forward with hard blows repeatedly applied to my exposed back, with a stout stick he had in his hand.
Smarting and staggering under my wound, I made
the greatest efforts to get on, but one of his still
more inhuman sons, (as I then thought him) gave

me a double barrelled gun to carry, with his powder horn and other accoutrements: they felt very heavy, yet after I had taken them, the old man did not again strike me but went on towards the place where he meant to pitch his tent, leaving me to follow on as well as I could.

The face of the desert now appeared as smooth as the surface of the ocean, when unruffled by winds or tempests. Camels could be seen on every direction, as soon as they came above the horizon, so that there was no difficulty in knowing which way to go, and I took care to keep sight of my new master's drove, until I reached the valley, in which he had pitched his tent. I was broiling under the sun and tugging along, with my load, which weighed me down to the earth, and should have lain down despairing, had I not seen Mr. Williams in a still worse plight than myself.

Having come near the tent about four P. M. they took the load from me, and bid me lie down in the shade of the tent. I then begged for water, but could get none. The time now came on for prayers, and after the old man and his sons had performed this ceremony very devoutly, they went away. I was in so much pain, I could scarcely contain myself, and my thirst was more painful than it had yet been. I tried to soften the hearts of the women to get me a little water, but they only laughed and spit at me; and to increase my distresses as much as they could, drove me away from the shade of the tent, so that I was forced to remain in the scorching sun for the remainder of this long day.

A little after sunset my old and young masters returned; they were joined by all the men that were near, to the number of from twenty to thirty, and went through their religious ceremonies in a very solemn manner, in which the women and little children did not join them. Soon after this was over,

Clark came in with the camels and joined me; it would have been pleasant to be together, but his situation was such that it made my heart-ache still worse than it did before; he was nearly without a skin; every part of his body exposed; his flesh excessively mangled, burnt and inflamed. "I am glad to see you once more, sir," said Clark, "for I cannot live through the approaching night, and now beg of you, if you ever get to our country again, to tell my brothers and sisters how I perished." I comforted him all I could, and assured him he would not die immediately; that the nourishment we now had, though very little, was sufficient to keep us alive for a considerable time, and that though our skins were roasted off and our flesh inflamed, we were yet alive without any signs of putrefaction on our bodies; that I had great hopes we should all be carried in a few days from this desart to where we might get some food to nourish us, and as I had learned a little of the language of these people, (or savages) I would keep trying to persuade them that if they would carry us up the Moorish dominions, I should be able to pay them a great ransom for all the crew; for an old man had told me that as soon as it should rain they would journey to the N. E. and sell us.

The night came on; cold damp winds succeeded to the heat of the day, and I begged of my old master to be permitted to go under the corner of his tent, (for it was a large one) and he seemed willing, pointing out a place for us to lie down in, but the women would not consent, and we remained outside until the men had milked the camels. They then gave us a good drink of milk, near a quart each, and after the women were asleep, one of my young masters, named *Omar*, (the same that made me carry his gun the preceding day to keep his father from beating me) took pity on our distresses, and came and made us creep under one corner of the tent, without waking the women, where some soft sand served us for a bed, and the tent kept off the cold air from us; and here we slept soundly until morning. As soon as the women awoke, and found us under the tent, they were for thrusting us out with blows, but I pretended to be asleep, and the old man looking on us, seemed somewhat concerned, fearing (as I thought) he might lose his property. He told his women to let us alone, and as he was absolute, they were forced to obey him, though with every appearance of reluctance.

After they had milked the camels, and taken a drink themselves, they gave us what remained, that is to say, near a pint between us. They did not move forward this day, and suffered us to remain under the corner of the tent in the shade all the while and the next night, and even gave us a piece of a skin to cover us with in part, and keep off the night wind. They gave us a good drink of milk when they drank themselves on the second night, and Omar had given us about a pint of water each, in the middle of the day; so that the inflammation seemed to have subsided in a great degree from our flesh and feet.

This attention, together with the two good nights' rest, revived us very much—these were the 14th and 15th days of September. I had not seen any of my unfortunate shipmates except Clark, and did not know where they were during the day we remained still. The camels were driven off early in the morning by a negro slave and two of the small boys, and did not return until in the night—they went out to the east to find shrubs for them to feed on. Clark was obliged near night to go out and pull up some dry thorn bush shrubs and roots to make a fire with. At the return of the camels, the negro slave (who was a stout fellow, named Boireck) seated himself by the fire, stretching out his legs on each side of it, and seeing us under the tent, thought to drive us out;

but as he was not permitted by our old master, he contented himself by pointing at us and making comparisons: then sneeringly addressing me by the name of Rias, or chief, would set up a loud laugh, which, with the waggery he displayed in his remarks on us, kept the whole family and several strangers who had assembled on the occasion, in a constant roar of laughter until midnight, the hour for milking the camels. He would poke our sore flesh with a sharp stick, to make sport, and show the Arabs what miserable beings we were, who could not even bear the rays of the sun (the image of God, as they term it) to shine upon us.

Being tormented in this manner, my companion Clark could scarcely contain his wrath: "it was bad enough, (he said) to be reduced to slavery by the savage Arabs; to be stripped and skinned alive and mangled, without being obliged to bear the scoffs and derison of a d———d negro slave." I told him I was very glad to find he still had so much spirits left, and could feel as if he wished to revenge an insult—it proved to me that he felt better than he did the preceding night, and as I was so much relieved myself, my hopes of being able to endure our tortures and privations increased, adding, "let the negro laugh if he can take any pleasure in it; I am willing he should do so, even at my expense: he is a poor slave himself, naked and destitute, far from his family and friends, and is only trying to gain the favour of his masters and mistresses, by making sport of us, whom he considers as much inferior to him as he is to them." Clark could not be reconciled to this mode of mockery and sport, but the negro kept it up as long as we remained with his master, every night, and always had plenty of spectators to admire his wit, and laugh at his tricks and buffoonery. This reminded me of the story of Samson, when the Philistines wished to make sport with him; he was blind, and they supposed him harmless; but he became so indignant, that he was willing to suffer death to be revenged of them; the difference was, he had strength to execute his will,—we had not.

From the 15th to the 18th, we journeyed every day to the S. E. about thirty miles a day, merely to find a few shrubs in the small scattered valleys for the camels and consequently for the inhabitants to subsist on. As we went on in that direction, the valleys became less frequent and very shallow; the few thorn bushes they produced were very dry, and no other shrubs to be found; the camels could not fill their stomachs with the leaves and shrubs, nor with all that they could crop off, though they pulled away the branches as thick as a man's finger. The milk began to fail, and consequently we had to be scanted, so that our allowance was reduced to half a pint a day, and as all the water they had taken from the well was expended, they could give us no more of that precious article. There was belonging to this tribe four mares that were the general property; they were very clean limbed, and very lean; they fed them on milk every day, and every one took his turn in giving them as much water every two days as they would drink. These mares drank up the last of our water on the 19th, nor would my master allow me to drink what little was left in the bowl, not exceeding half a pint, and it was poured out as a drink offering before the Lord, while they prayed for rain, which ineded they had reason to expect, as the season they knew was approaching, when some rain generally happens. I supposed our distance from the sea, or the well that we had left, to be three hundred miles in a direct line, and feared very much that we should not find water at any other place. The substenance we received was just sufficient to keep the breath of life in us, but our flesh was less inflamed than in the first days, for we had continued to lie under a part of the tent at night, and also in the day-time when it was pitched, which was generally the case about two o'clock in the afternoon. We had, however, become so emaciated, that we could scarcely stand, and they did not attempt to make me nor Clark do any kind of work, except gather a few dry sticks, toward evening, to light a fire. The swellings had also gone down in some measure from our feet, as there was not substance enough in us to keep up a running sore; all the moisture in them seemed to dry away, and we could support the prickings and cutting of the stones better as we became lighter and more inured to it. We had endeavoured to find some of the kind of root that was met with near the sea-coast, but none could be procured. In every valley we came to, the natives would run about and search under every thorn bush, in hopes to find some herb, for they were nearly as hungry as ourselves. In some places a small plant was found, resembling what we call shepherd's sprout; they were torn up by them and devoured in an instant. I got one or two, but they proved very bitter, and were impregnated, in a considerable degree, with salt: these plants were so rare as to be scarcely of any benefit. There were also found by the natives, in particular places, a small ground root, whose top showed itself like a single short spear of grass, about three inches above the ground; they dug it up with a stick; it was of the size of a small walnut, and in shape very much like an onion; its taste fresh, without any strong flavour; but it was very difficult to find, and afforded us very little relief, as we could not get more than half a dozen in a whole day's search, and some days none at all.

On the 19th of September, in the morning, the tribe having held a council the night before, at which I could observe my old master was looked up to as a man of superior judgment and influence, they be-

gan a route back again towards the sea, and the well
near which we were first made slaves;—this convinced me that no fresh water could be procured
nearer, and as the camels were almost dry, I much
feared that myself and my companions must perish
before we could reach it. I had been in the habit
every day since I was on the desert, of relieving my
excessive thirst by the disagreeable expedient before
mentioned; but that resource now failed me for the
want of moisture, nor had any thing passed through
my body since the day I left the well. We had journeyed for seven and a half days S. E. and I concluded
it would require the same time to return; but on the
18th we steered N. E. and on the 19th we took a
N. W. direction, and in the course of the day we
entered a very small valley, where we found a few
little dwarf thorn bushes, not more than two feet
high; on these we found some snails, most of which
were dead and dry, but I got about a handful that
were alive, and when a fire was kindled, roasted and
ate them—Clark did the same, and as we did not
receive more than a gill of milk each in twenty-four
hours, this nourishment was very serviceable.

On the morning of the 20th we started, as soon as
it was light, and drove very fast all the day. We had
no other drink than the camels' urine, which we
caught in our hands as they voided it; its taste was
bitter, but not salt, and it relieved our fainting
spirits. We were forced to keep up with the drove,
but in the course of the day found a handful of
snails each, which we at night roasted and ate. Our
feet, though not swoollen, were extremely sore; our
bodies and limbs were nearly deprived of skin and
flesh, for we continually wasted away, and the little
we had on our bones was dried hard, and stuck fast
to them. My head had now become accustomed to
the heat of the sun, and though it remained un-
covered, it did not pain me. Hunger, that had preyed

upon my companions to such a degree as to cause them to bite off the flesh from their arms, had not the same effect on me. I was forced in one instance to tie the arms of one of my men behind him, in order to prevent his gnawing his own flesh; and in another instance, two of them having caught one of the boys, a lad about four years old, out of sight of the tents, were about dashing his brains out with a stone, for the purpose of devouring his flesh, when luckily at that instant I came up and rescued the child, with some difficulty, from their voracity. They were so frantic with hunger, as to insist upon having one meal of his flesh, and then they said they would be willing to die; for they knew that not only themselves, but all the crew would be instantly massacred as soon as the murder should be discovered. I convinced them that it would be more manly to die with hunger than to become cannibals and eat their own or other human flesh, telling them, at the same time, I did not doubt but our masters would give us sufficient nourishment to keep us alive, until they could sell us. On the 20th, we proceeded with much speed towards the N. W. or sea shore; but on the 21st, we did not go forward.

This day I met with Mr. Savage, Horace, Hogan and the cook, their masters' tents were pitched near ours; they were so weak, emaciated and sore, that they could scarcely stand, and had been carried on the camels for the last few days. I was extremely glad to see them, and spoke to all but Horace, whose master drove me off with a stick one way, and Horace another, yelling most horribly at the same time and laying it on Horace's back with great fury. I soon returned to our tent, and felt very much dejected; they all thought they could not live another day—there were no snails to be found here, and we had not had one drop of milk or water to drink. Horace, Hogan, and the cook were employed in attending

their masters' camels, in company with one or two
Arabs, who kept flogging them nearly the whole of
the time.

My old master did not employ me or Clark in the
same way, because he had two negro slaves to do
that work; he was a rich man among them, and
owned from sixty to seventy camels; he was also a
kind of priest, for every evening he was joined, in
his devotions, by all the old and most of the young
men near his tent. They all first washed themselves
with sand in place of water; then wrapping themselves up with their strip of cloth and turning their
faces to the east, my old master stepped out before
them, and commenced by bowing twice, repeating
at each time *"Allah Houakibar;"* then kneeling and
bowing his head to the ground twice; then raising
himself up on his feet, and repeating, *"Hi el Allah
Sheda Mohammed Rahsool Allah,"* bowing himself
twice; and again prostrating himself on the earth
as many times, then *"Allah Houakibar"* was three
times repeated. He was always accompanied in his
motions and words by all present who could see him
distinctly, as he stood before them. He would then
make a long prayer, and they recited altogether
what I afterwards found to be a chapter in the
Koran; and then all joined in chaunting or singing
some hymn or sacred poetry for a considerable time.
This ceremony being finished, they again prostrated
themselves with their faces to the earth, and the
service concluded.

About the middle of this day two strangers arrived, riding two camels loaded with goods: they
came in front of my master's tent, and having made
the camels lie down, they dismounted, and seated
themselves on the ground opposite the tent, with
their faces turned the other way. There were in this
valley six tents, besides that of my masters.

CHAPTER IX.

*Two Arabian merchants are persuaded by the
author to purchase him and four of his suffering
companions—they kill a camel and prepare
to set out for Morocco across the Desart*

ALL the men had gone out a hunting on their
camels, carrying their arms with them; that is to
say, seeking for plunder as I concluded. My old and
young mistresses went to see the strangers; they had
no water to carry, as is customary, but took with
them a large skin, with a roll of tent cloth to make
them a shelter; the strangers rose as the women drew
near, and saluted them by the words *"Labez, Labez-
Salem; Labez-Alikom;"* peace, peace be with you,
&c. and the women returned these salutations in
similar words. They next ran to our tent, and took
a couple of sticks, with the help of which and the
skin and tent cloth, they soon made an awning for
the strangers. This done, they took the bundles
which were on the camels, and placed them in this
tent, with the saddles and all the other things the
strangers had brought. The two strangers had a
couple of skins that contained water, which the
women hung up on a frame they carried from our
tent.

During the whole time the women were thus employed, the strangers remained seated on the ground
beside their guns, for they had each a double bar-

relled musket, and so bright, that they glittered in
the sun like silver. The women having finished their
attentions, seated themselves near the strangers,
and made inquiries, as near as I could comprehend,
by saying, "where did you come from? what goods
have you got? how long have you been on your journey?" &c. Having satisfied their curiosity on these
points, they next came to me, and the old woman
(in whom as yet I had not discovered one spark of
pity) told me that Sidi Hamet had come with
blankets and blue cloth to sell; that he came from
the Sultan's dominions, and that he could buy me
and carry me there, if he chose, where I might find
my friends, and kiss my wife and children.

Before my master returned I went to the tent of
Sidi Hamet, with a wooden bowl, and begged for
some water; showing my mouth which was extremely
parched and stiff, so much so, that I could with difficulty speak. He looked at me, and asked if I was
el Rais (the captain). I nodded assent; he told his
brother, who was with him, to give me some water,
but this his benevolent brother would not conde-
scend to do; so taking the bowl myself, he poured into it near a quart of clear water, saying, "Sherub
Rais"—that is, drink, captain, or chief. I drank about
half of it, and after thanking him and imploring the
blessing of Heaven upon him for his humanity, I was
going to take the rest of it to our tent, where Clark
lay stretched out on his back, a perfect wreck of
almost naked bones; his belly and back nearly col-
lapsed, and breathing like a person in the last agonies
of death: but Sidi Hamet would not permit me to
to carry the water away, bidding me drink it myself. I pointed out to him my distressed companion;
this excited his pity, and he suffered me to give
Clark the remainder.

The water was perfectly fresh, and revived him
exceedingly; it was a cordial to his desponding soul,
being the first fresh water either of us had tasted

since we left the boat: his eyes that were sunk deep in their sockets, brightened up—"this is good water (said he) and must have come from a better country than this; if we were once there, (added he) and I could get one good drink of such water, I could die with pleasure, but now I cannot live another day." Our masters soon returned, and began, with others of the tribe, who had received the news of the arrival of strangers, to form circles and chat with them and each other; this continued till night, and I presume there were at least two hundred men present. After dark they began to separate, and by 10 o'clock at night none remained but my old master's family, and three or four of their relations, at our tent. On this occasion we were turned out into the open air, and were obliged to pass the night without any shelter or covering. It was a long and tedious night; but at the time of milking the camels, our old master coming to us, as if afraid of losing his property by our death, and anxious we should live, dealt out about a pint of milk to each; this milk tasted better than any I had yet drank; it was a sweet and season-able relief, and saved poor Clark from dissolution.

This was the first nourishment of any kind our master had given us in three days, and I concluded from this circumstance that he had hopes of selling us to the strangers. The next morning Sidi Hamet came towards the tent, and beckoned me to come there; he was at a considerable distance, and I made the best of my way to him; here he bade me sit down on the ground. I had by this time learned many words in their language, which is ancient Ara-bic, and could understand the general current of their conversation, by paying strict attention to it.

He now began to question me about my country, and the manner in which I had come here—I made him understand that I was an Englishman, and that my vessel and crew were of the same nation—I found he had heard of that country, and I stated as well as

I could the manner of my shipwreck—told him we were reduced to the lowest depth of misery; that I had a wife and five children in my own country, besides Horace, whom I called my eldest son, mingling with my story sighs and tears, and all the signs of affection and despair which these recollections and my present situation naturally called forth.

I found him to be a very intelligent and feeling man—for although he knew no language but the Arabic, he comprehended so well what I wished to communicate, that he actually shed tears at the recital of my distresses, notwithstanding that, among the Arabs, weeping is regarded as a womanish weakness. He seemed to be ashamed of his own want of fortitude, and said that men who had beards like him ought not to shed tears; and he retired, wiping his eyes.

Finding I had awakened his sympathy, I thought if I could rouse his interest by large offers of money, he might buy me and my companions and carry us up from the desart—so accordingly the first time I saw him alone, I went to him, and begged him to buy me, and carry me to the Sultan of Morocco or Marocksh, where I could find a friend to redeem me. He said no, but he would carry me to Swearah, describing it a walled town and seaport. I told him I had seen the Sultan, and that he was a friend to my nation. He then asked me many other questions about Mohammed Rassool—I bowed and pointed to the east, then towards heaven, as if I thought he had ascended there: this seemed to please him, and he asked me how much money I would give him to carry me up; upon which I counted over fifty pieces of stones, signifying I would give as many dollars for myself and each of my men. "I will not buy the others," said he, "but how much more than fifty dollars will you give me for yourself, if I buy you and carry you to your friends?" I told him one hundred dollars. "Have you any money in *Swearah,*" asked he by signs and words, "or do you mean to make me wait till you get it from your country?" I replied that my friend in Swearah would give him the money so soon as he brought me there. "You are deceiving me," said he. I made the most solemn protestations of my sincerity:—"I will buy *you* then," said he, "but remember, if you deceive me, I will cut your throat," (making a motion to that effect.) This I assented to, and begged of him to buy my son Horace also, but he would not hear a word about any of my companions, as it would be impossible, he said, to get them up off the desert, which was a great distance. "Say nothing about it to your old master," signified he to me, "nor to my brother, or any of the others." He then left me, and I went out to seek for snails to relieve my hunger. I saw Mr. Savage and Hogan, and brought them with Clark near Sidi Hamet's tent, where we sat down on the ground. He came out to see us, miserable objects as we were, and seemed very much shocked at the sight. I told my companions I had great hopes we should be bought by this man and carried up to the cultivated country—but they expressed great fears that they would be left behind. Sidi Hamet asked me many questions about my men—wished to know if any of them had died, and if they had wives and children. I tried all I could to interest him in their behalf, as well as my own, and mentioned to him my son, whom he had not yet seen. I found my companions had been very much stinted in milk as well as myself, and that they had no water,—they had found a few snails, which kept them alive; but even these now failed.

The 24th, we journeyed on towards the N. W. all day—the whole tribe, or nearly so, in company, and the strangers also kept in company with us. When my mistress pitched her tent near night, she made up

one for Sidi Hamet also. I begged of him on my
knees every time I had an opportunity, for him to
buy me and my companions, and on the 25th I had
the happiness to see him pay my old master for me:
he gave him two blankets or coarse haicks, one blue
cotton covering, and a bundle of ostrich feathers,
with which the old man seemed much pleased, as he
had now three suits of clothing. They were a long
time in making the bargain.

This day Horace came with his master to fetch
something to our tent; at his approach, I went to
meet him, and embraced him with tears. Sidi Hamet
was then fully convinced that he was my son. I had
found a few snails this morning, and divided them
between Mr. Savage and Horace before Sidi Hamet,
who signified to me in the afternoon that he intended to set out with me in two days for Swearah;
that he had tried to buy my son, but could not succeed, for his master would not sell him at any price:
then said I "let me stay in his place; I will be a
faithful slave to his master as long as I live—carry
him up to Swearah; my friend will pay you for him,
and send him home to his mother, whom I cannot
see unless I bring her son with me." "You shall have
your son, by Allah," said Sidi Hamet. The whole
tribe was gathered in council, and I supposed relative to this business. In the course of the afternoon
they debated the matter over, and seemed to turn it
every way;—they fought besides three or four battles
with fists and scimitars, in their warm and loud
discussions in settling individual disputes; but in
the evening I was told that Horace was bought, as the
tribe in council had forced his master to sell him,
though at a great price. I now redoubled my entreaties with my new master to buy Mr. Savage and
Clark, telling him that I would give him a large sum
of money if he got us up safe; but he told me he
should be obliged to carry us through bands of rob-

bers, who would kill him for our sakes, and that his company was not strong enough to resist them by force of arms—I fell down on my knees, and implored him to buy Mr. Savage and Clark at any rate, thinking if he should buy them, he might be induced to purchase the remaining part of the crew.

My mind had been so busily employed in schemes of redemption, as almost to forget my sufferings since Sidi Hamet had bought me. He had given me two or three drinks of water, and had begged milk for me of my former master. On the morning of the 26th, I renewed my entreaties for him to purchase Mr. Savage, Clark, and Hogan—the others I had not seen since the second or third day after we were in the hands of the Arabs. I did not know where they were, and consequently could not designate them to my master Hamet, though I told him all their names. Mr. Savage and Hogan looked much more healthy and likely to live than Clark, and Sidi Hamet insisted that it was impossible that Clark could live more than three days, and that if he bought him, he should lose his money. I told him no, he should not lose his money, for whether he lived or died, I would pay him the same amount.

Clark was afflicted with the scalded head, rendered a raw sore in consequence of his sufferings, and his hair which was very long, was, of course, in a very filthy condition; this attracted the attention of Sidi Hamet and his brother, the latter of whom was a very surly and cross-looking fellow. They pushed the hair open with their sticks, and demanded to know what was the occasion of that filthy appearance. Clark assured them, that it was in consequence of his exposure to the sun, and as that was the reason I had assigned for the horrible sores and blisters that covered our scorched bodies and half-roasted flesh: they said, it might possibly be so, but asked why the heads of the rest of us were not in the same state.

They next found fault with my shins, which had
been a long time very sore, and they examined every
bone to see if all was right in its place, with the
same cautious circumspection that a jockey would
use, who was about buying a horse; while we, poor
trembling wretches, strove with all possible care and
anxiety to hide every fault and infirmity in us, occasioned by our dreadful calamities and cruel sufferings.

Sidi Hamet informed me this day, that he had
bought Mr. Savage and Clark, and had bargained for
Hogan, and that he was going to kill a camel that
night for provisions on our journey. Our water had
been expended for two days, and all the families
around us were also destitute. I did not get more than
a gill of milk in twenty-four hours, and a small handful of snails—these served in a little degree to support
nature, and I waited with the greatest impatience
for the killing of the camel which had been promised, hoping to have a meal of meat once more before
I died. Clark and I had been busy all the afternoon
in gathering dry sticks to make a fire, and a little
after midnight my master came to me and showed
me where to carry the wood we had collected; it was
in a little gulley that it might not be seen by our
neighbours, whilst our former master and two present ones were leading a camel up to the same place.
This camel, on its arrival, they made lie down in the
usual manner: it was a very old one, and so poor,
that he had not been able to keep pace with the
drove during the journey, and Sidi Hamet told me
he had bought him for one blanket.

The camel being down, they put a rope round his
under jaw, with a noose in it; then hauling his head
round on the left side, made the rope fast to his
tail, close up to his body; his neck was so long, that
the under jaw reached within six inches of the tail:
they then brought a copper kettle that would con-

tain probably three gallons. Thus prepared, Sidi Hamet cut open a vein on the right side of the camel's neck, close to his breast; the blood streamed out into the kettle, and soon filled it half full; this they set over the fire and boiled, stirring it all the time with a stick until it became thick, and the consistence of a beef's liver; then taking it off the fire, they passed it to me, saying, "coole, Riley," (eat Riley.) I did not wait for a second bidding, but fell to, together with Clark: our appetites were voracious, and we soon filled our stomachs with this, to us, delicious food.

Notwithstanding the lateness of the hour, and the privacy observed in killing this meagre camel, many of our hungry neighbours had found it out, and came to assist in the dressing and eating of the animal. They insisted on having some of the blood, and would snatch out a handful in spite of all our masters could do to hinder them; they were then very officious in assisting to take off the hide, which was soon done, and the entrails were rolled out; they next proceeded to put all the small entrails into the kettle, without cleaning them of their contents, together with what remained of the liver and lights; but they had no water to boil them in. Then one of them went to the camel's paunch, which was very large, and cutting a slit in the top of it, dipped out some of the filthy water in a bowl: this they poured into the kettle, and set it a boiling, stirring it round, and now and then taking out a piece, and biting off an end to ascertain whether it was cooked enough. During this time, half a dozen hungry wretches were at work on the camel, which they would not leave under pretence of friendship for our masters, for they would not suffer strangers to work, when in their company, and it being dark, they managed to steal and convey away, before morning, more than one-half of the camel's bones and meat, with half

his skin. Our masters were as hungry as any of the
Arabs, yet though they had bought the camel, they
could scarcely get a bite of the intestines without
fighting for it; for what title or argument can prevail
against the ravenous appetite of a half-starved man?
Though our masters saw the natives in the very act of
stealing and carrying off their meat, they could not
prevent them, fearing worse consequences than losing it; it being a standing maxim among the Arabs to
feed the hungry if in their power, and give them
drink, even if the owner of the provisions be obliged
to rob himself and his own family to do it.

Notwithstanding the boiled blood we had eaten
was perfectly fresh, yet our thirst seemed to increase
in consequence of it. As soon as day light appeared, a
boy of from fourteen to sixteen years old came running up to the camel's paunch, and thrusting his
head into it up to his shoulders, began to drink of its
contents; my master observing him, and seeing that
my mouth was very dry made signs for me to go and
pull the boy away, and drink myself; this I soon did,
putting my head in like manner into the paunch;
the liquid was very thick, but though its taste was
exceedingly strong, yet it was not salt, and allayed
my thirst: Clark next took a drink of the same fluid.

This morning we were busied in cutting off the
little flesh that remained on the bones of our camel,
spreading it out to dry, and roasting the bones on the
fire for our masters, who cracking them between two
stones, then sucked out the marrow and juices. Near
noon, Horace was brought where I was; he was very
hungry and thirsty, and said he had not ate any thing
of consequence for the last three days. Our common
master said to me, "this is your son Rais," and seemed
extremely glad that he had been able to purchase
him, giving him some of the entrails and meat he
had boiled and saved for the purpose. I in my turn
gave him some of our thick camel's water, which he

found to be delicious; so true it is, that hunger and thirst give a zest to every thing. Burns was brought up soon after, and my master asked me if he was one of my men; I told him he was: "his master wants to sell him," said Sidi Hamet, "but he is old and good for nothing," added he; "but I can buy him for this blanket," showing me a very poor old one—I said, "buy him, he is my countryman, I will repay you as much for him as for the others:"—so he went out, and bought him from his master, and then gave him something to eat. Poor Burns was much rejoiced to find there was a prospect of recovering his liberty, or at least of getting where he might procure something to eat and drink. During this day, the natives flocked round in great numbers, men, women, and children, and what with begging and stealing reduced our stock of meat to less than fifteen pounds before night.

Sidi Hamet now told me that he had bought Hogan: this was in the afternoon, and he came to us. I congratulated him on our favorable prospects, and our master gave him something to eat; but his former master, Hamet, now demanded one blanket more for him than had been agreed on, as he was a stout fellow: my master would not be imposed upon, nor had he indeed a blanket left. I begged very hard for poor Hogan, but it was to no purpose, and his old master drove him off, laying on his back with a stick most unmercifully. Hamet's eyes seemed fairly to flash fire as he went from us. Hogan's hopes had been raised to a high pitch—they were now blasted, and he driven back like a criminal before his brutal owner, to his former miserable abode. He had informed me that he had never as yet, since our captivity, known what it was to sleep under the cover of a tent; that his allowance of milk had been so scant, that he did not doubt but he must have died with hunger in a day or two—he was extremely wasted and sore on every side. My heart bled for him when I saw the blows fall on his emaciated and mangled frame, but I could not assist him, and all I could do was to turn round and hide my face, so as not to witness his further tortures.

This day was employed in preparing for our departure—our masters made me a pair of sandals with two thickness of the camel's skin; they also made Horace a pair in the same manner; but Clark and Burns were fitted with single ones; they had in the morning given me a small knife, which I hung to my neck in a case: this they meant as a mark of confidence; and they also gave me charge of their stuff, the camels, and the slaves. I soon perceived, however, that although I had this kind of command, yet I was obliged to do all the work. My men were so far exhausted, that even the hope of soon obtaining their liberty, could scarcely animate them to the least exertion.

In the evening Sidi Hamet told me, *Aaron*, (Mr. Savage) would be with us by and by:—that we should start in the morning for *Swearah*, and that he hoped, through the blessing of God, I should once more embrace my family; he then told me how much he had paid for each one of us—that he had expended all his property, and that if I had not told him the truth he was a ruined man—that his brother was a bad man, and had done all he could to prevent his buying us, but that he had at last consented to it, and taken a share.

He next made me repeat, before his brother, my promises to him when we should arrive at Swearah, and my agreement to have my throat cut if my words did not prove true. Late in the evening Mr. Savage joined us—he knew before that I was going to set out, and thought he should be left behind—he was very thankful to be undeceived in this particular, and to get, at the same time something to eat, for Sidi Hamet had saved some of the camel's intestines, which he immediately gave him.

After having satisfied his hunger in some measure, he began to express his doubts as to where we were going; declaring, that he did not believe a word these wretches said:—he could not understand them, and said he did not believe I could; and suggested a hundred doubts and difficulties on the subject that his ill-boding imagination supplied him with: he did not like the price I had agreed to give for our liberty,—it was too much, and I should find no body willing to advance it for me, as I was poor.

We had started what water remained in the paunch of the camel, thick as it was, into a goat skin, straining it through our fingers to keep out the thickest of the filth. The night of the 27th, as near as we could keep count by marking the day of the month on our legs with a thorn, we passed in the open air, five of us together.

At daylight on the morning of the 28th, we were called up and made to load our camels. I had strong hopes we were going to ride, but it now appeared not to be the case. All the Arabs in the valley set out in the morning with their camels, to drive them to water—they had not been watered since the 10th, having gone without any for eighteen days. They were now at least two day's journey from the well, where we had first been seized, towards which they now steered in a N. W. direction. I mention this circumstance, to show the time these wonderful animals can live without drink, and supply their masters with milk, even when nearly destitute of vegetable substances; and with water from their paunches after death.

Soon after sunrise, our masters bade us drive the camels up the bank; at this moment Archibald Robbins came with his master to see us, and I supposed his master had brought him with a view of selling him. I had not before seen him for fourteen days, and he had only arrived soon enough to witness our departure—I now on my knees begged, as I had done before of Sidi Hamet, to purchase him; but he said he could not, and so hurried us on.

I told Robbins what my present hopes were, and that if I should succeed in getting clear, I would use my utmost endeavors to procure his and the rest of the crew's redemption. I begged him to continue as long as he could with his present master, who, for an Arab, appeared to be a very good man; and to encourage Mr. Williams and all the others to bear up with fortitude, and support life as long as it was possible, in the hope, that through my help or some other means, they might obtain their redemption in a short time; and having taken my leave of him in the most affectionate manner, (in which my companions followed the example) we set out on our journey, but with heavy hearts occasioned by the bitter regret we felt at leaving our fellow sufferers behind, although I had done all in my power to make them partakers of our better fortune.

CHAPTER X.

The author and four of his companions set out to cross the Desart—their sufferings—they come to a spring of fresh water—description of its singular situation

FROM the time I was sold to Sidi Hamet, my old master and his family shunned me as they would a pestilence; and the old villain actually stole one piece of our meat from me or rather robbed me of it just as we were setting out; for he cut it off the string

by which it was tied to the camel, in spite of my efforts to prevent him. Our masters were accompanied
for a considerable distance by several men and wom-
en, who were talking and taking leave, going on very
slowly. We were ordered to keep their camels together, which I thought I did; yet when they were
finally ready to depart, they found their big camel
had marched off a great distance, probably two miles
from us, following a drove of camels going to the N.
W. Sidi Hamet bade me fetch him back—pointing
him out: notwithstanding my weak and exhausted
state, I was obliged to run a great way to come up
with him, but my rising spirits supported me, and I
succeeded in bringing him back, where the other
camels were collected by my shipmates.

Sidi Hamet and Seid had two old camels on which
they had rode, and they had bought also a young one
that had not been broke for riding. We were joined
here by a young Arab named *Abdallah:* he had been
Mr. Savage's master and owned a camel, and a couple of goat skins to carry water in; but these, as well
as those of our masters were entirely empty. Sidi
Hamet had a kind of a pack saddle for each of his old
camels; but nothing to cover the bones of his young
ones. Having fitted them as well as he could, (for he
seemed to be humane) he placed Mr. Savage, Burns,
and Horace, on the big one, and myself and Clark on
the other old one. Seid and Abdallah took their seats
on the one which belonged to Abdallah, and Sidi
Hamet mounted the young one himself to break
him, sitting behind the hump on his bare back; and
thus arranged and equipped, we set off on a full and
long striding trot. It was about nine A. M. when we
had mounted; and this trot had continued for about
three hours, when we stopped a few minutes in a
little valley to adjust our saddles. Here Sidi Hamet
pulled out a check shirt from one of his bags and
gave it to me, declaring he had stolen it, and had
tried to get another for Horace but had not been

able: "put it on," said he, "your poor back needs a covering;" (it being then one entire sore.) I kissed his hand in gratitude, and thanked him and my Heavenly Father for this mercy. Clark, a day or two before, had got a piece of an old sail, that partly covered him—Burns had an old jacket, and Horace and Mr. Savage, a small goat skin added to their dress—so that we were all, comparatively, comfortably clad. We did not stop here long, but mounted again, and proceeded on our course to the Eastward on a full trot, which was continued till night; when coming to a little valley, we found some thorn bushes and halted for the night.

Here we kindled a fire, and our masters gave us a few mouthfuls of the camel's meat, which we roasted and ate. As we had drank no water for the last three days, except a very little of what we had taken from the camel's paunch, and which was now reduced to about four quarts, we, as well as our masters, suffered exceedingly for the want of it, and it was thereupon determined to make an equal distribution of it among the whole party; which was accordingly done with an impartial hand. This we, poor sufferers, made out to swallow, foul and ropy as it was, and it considerably relieved our parched throats; and then, finding a good shelter under a thornbush, notwithstanding our unabated pains, we got a tolerable night's sleep. We had travelled this day steady at a long trot, at the rate, I judged, of between seven and eight miles an hour: making a distance of sixty-three miles at the lowest computation. Before daylight in the morning of the 28th, we were called up and mounted on the camels as before, and we set off on the long trot, on the same course, i. e. about east as on the preceeding day.

The same smooth hard surface continued, with now and then a little break, occasioned by the naked heads of rocks just rising above the plain, and forming in some places small ledges. Near one of these, we alighted a few minutes about noon, for our masters to perform their devotions; and we allayed our thirst by drinking some of the camels' urine, which we caught in our hands: our masters did the same, and told me it was good for our stomachs. The camels took very long steps, and their motions being heavy, our legs, unsupported by stirrups or anything else, would fly backwards and forwards, chafing across their hard ribs at every step; nor was it possible for us to prevent it, so that the remaining flesh on our posteriors, and inside of our thighs and legs was so beat, and literally pounded to pieces, that scarcely any remained on our bones; which felt as if they had been thrown out of their sockets, by the continual and sudden jerks they experienced during this longest of days. It seemed to me as though the sun would never go down, and when at last it did, our masters had not yet found a place to lodge in; for they wished, if possible, to find a spot where a few shrubs were growing, in order that the camels might browse a little during the night. They stopped at last after dark in a very small valley, for they could find no better place; here they kindled a little fire, and gave us about a pound of meat between us, which we greedily devoured, and then allayed our thirst in a similar manner as before mentioned.

We had started before daylight this morning, and had made but one stop of about fifteen minutes in the course of the whole day until dark night, having travelled at least fifteen hours, and at the rate of seven miles the hour, making one hundred and five miles. Here in our barebone and mangled state, we were forced to lie on the naked ground, without the smallest shelter from the wind, which blew a violent gale all night from the north—suffering in addition to the cold, the cravings of hunger and thirst, and the most excruciating pains in our limbs and numer-

ous sores; nor could either of us close our eyes to
sleep; and I cannot imagine that the tortures of the
rack can exceed those we experienced this night. Sidi
Hamet and his two companions, who had been accustomed to ride in this manner, thought nothing of
it; nor did they even appear to be fatigued; but
when I showed him my sores in the morning, and the
situation of my shipmates, he was much distressed,
and feared we would not live. He told me we should
come to good water soon, when we might drink as
much as we wanted of it, and after that he would
not travel so fast.

We were placed on our camels soon after daylight,
(this was the 29th), having nothing to eat, and
drinking a little camel's water, which we preferred to
our own: its taste, as I before observed, though bitter was not salt; and they void it but seldom in this
dry and thirsty country. Proceeding on our journey
at a long trot, about nine o'clock in the morning, we
discovered before us what seemed like high land, as
we were seated on the camels; but on our approach,
it proved to be the opposite bank of what appeared
once to have been a river or arm of the sea, though
its bed was now dry. At about 10 o'clock, we came
to the bank nearest us; it was very steep, and four or
five hundred feet deep, and in most places perpendicular or overhanging. These banks must have been
washed at some former period, either by the sea or a
river; which river, if it was one, does not now exist.
After considerable search, our masters found a place
where our camels could descend into it, and having
first dismounted and made us do the same, we drove
them down. When we had descended the most difficult part of the bank, Seid and Abdallah went forward (with their guns) to search for a spring of fresh
water, which Sidi Hamet told me was not very far
distant. He now made me walk along with him, and
let the others drive on the camels slowly after us; for

they, as well as ourselves, were nearly exhausted. He
then asked me a great many questions respecting my
country, myself and family; and whether I had any
property at home; if I had been at *Swearah*, and if I
told him the truth concerning my having a friend
there who would pay money for me? He said also,
that both himself and his brother had parted with all
their property to purchase us, and wished me to be
candid with him, for he was "my friend." "God
(said he) will deal with you, as you deal with me."
I persisted in asserting that I had a friend at Swearah, who would advance any sum of money I needed,
and answered his other questions as well as I was
able; evading some I did not choose to answer, pretending I did not understand them. "Will you buy
Clark and Burns? (said he) they are good for nothing." They certainly did look worse, if possible, than
the rest of us. I told him they were my countrymen,
and my brothers, and that he might depend upon it
I would ransom them, if he would carry us to the
empire of Morocco and to the Sultan. "No, (said
he) the Sultan will not pay for you, but I will carry
you to Swearah to your friend; what is his name?"
"Consul," said I. It seemed to please him to hear
me name my friend so readily; and after teaching
me to count in Arabic, and by my fingers up to
twenty, (which was *ashreen*) he told me I must give
him two hundred dollars for myself, two hundred
dollars for Horace, and for the others I must pay
one hundred dollars each; showing me seven dollars he had about him, to be certain that we understood each other perfectly; and he next made me
understand that I must pay for our provisions on the
road, over and above this sum. He then made me
point out the way to Swearah, which I was enabled
to do by the sun and trade wind, making it about N.
E. "Now, (said he) if you will agree before God the
most High, to pay what I have stated, in money, and

give me a double-barrelled gun, I will take you up to Swearah; if not, I will carry you off that way," pointing to the S. E., "and sell you for as much as I can get, sooner than carry you up across this long desart, where we must risk our lives every day for your sakes; and if you cannot comply with your agreement and we get there safe, we must cut your throat and sell your comrades for what they will bring." I assured him that I had told him the truth, and called God to witness the sincerity of my intentions, not in the least doubting if I could once arrive there, I should find some one able and willing to pay the sum they demanded. "You shall go to Swearah, (said he, taking me by the hand) if God please." He then showed me the broken pieces of my watch, and a plated candlestick, which he said he had bought from some person who had come from the wreck of my vessel. The candlestick had belonged to Mr. Williams—he said he bought the articles before he saw me, and wished to know what they were worth in Swearah: I satisfied him as well as I could on this point. During this conversation we kept walking on about east, as the bed of the river ran near the northern bank, which was very high, and Sidi Hamet looked at me as if his eye would pierce my very soul, to ascertain the secrets of my heart, and discover whether I was deceiving him or not, and he became satisfied that I was sincere.

By this time, we had arrived nearly opposite the place where he calculated the spring was, and his brother and Abdallah, being not far off, he hailed them to know if they had found it; to which they answered in the negative. After searching about an hour in the bank, he discovered it, and calling to me, for I was below, bade me come up to where he was, at the foot of a perpendicular cliff—I clambered up over the fragments of great rocks that had fallen down from above, as fast as my strength would per-

mit, and having reached the spot, and seeing no signs
of water, the tears flowed fast down my cheeks, for I
concluded the spring was dried up, and that we must
now inevitably perish. Sidi Hamet looked at me, and
saw my tears of despair—"look down there, said he,
(pointing through a fissure in the rock,) I looked
and saw water, but the cleft was too narrow to admit
of a passage to it; then showing me another place,
about ten or fifteen yards distant, where I could get
down, to another small spring—"Sherub Riley, (said
he) it is sweet." I soon reached it and found it sweet
indeed; and taking a copious draught, I called my
companions, who scrambled along on their way up,
exclaiming with great eagerness, "where is the water? for God's sake! where is it? Oh, is it sweet?"
I showed it to them, and they were soon convinced of
the joyful fact. This water was as clear and as sweet
as any I had ever tasted.

Sidi Hamet now allowed us to drink our fill, while
Seid and Abdallah were driving the four camels up
the bank by a zig-zag kind of a foot way, from which
the stones and other impediments had been before
removed, apparently with great trouble and labor.
This spring, the most singular perhaps in nature,
was covered with large rocks, fifteen to twenty feet
high, only after leaving a narrow crooked passage
next the high bank behind it, by which a common
sized man might descend to get at it. It might contain, I should calculate, not more than fifty gallons
of water; cool, clear, fresh, and sweet, and I presume
it communicated with the one that was first shown
me between the rocks, which was much smaller. The
camels had been driven to within fifty yards below
the spring; our masters then took off the large bowl
which they carried for the purpose of watering the
camels: then bringing a goat skin near the spring,
made me fill it with the water, my three shipmates
passing it up to me in the bowl—I kept admonishing

my companions to drink with moderation, but at the
same time I myself continued to take in large
draughts of this delicious water, without knowing
when to stop; in consequence of which I was seized
with violent pains in my bowels, but soon found
relief.

It was here that I had an opportunity of ascertain-
ing the quantity of water which a camel could drink
at one draught. We filled a large goat skin fifteen
times, containing at least four gallons, and every
drop of this water was swallowed down by our largest
camel, amounting to the enormous quantity of sixty
gallons, or two barrels. The men kept crying out,
*"has not that camel done yet? he alone will drink the
spring dry."* It was in effect drained very low; but
still held out, as the water kept continually running
in, though slowly. This camel was a very large and
old one, about nine feet high, stout in proportion,
and had not drank any water for twenty days, as I
was informed by Sidi Hamet: but the other camels
did not drink as much in proportion.

Having finished watering them, we filled two goat
skins with the water, which had now become thick
and whitish; as the rock in which the bason was
formed for holding it, appeared to be chalky, soft,
and yielding. We descended this bank, and after preparing the camels we were mounted thereon, and
proceeded as before, but along to the eastward, in
this arm of the sea's bed. I call it an arm of the sea,
because there could be no doubt in the mind of any
one who should view it, that these high banks were
worn and washed by water; they were from six to
eight or ten miles distant from each other, and the
level bottom was encrusted with marine salt. The
bank rises four or five hundred feet, and nearly perpendicular, in most places. The broken fragments
of rock, gravel and sand, that had been undermined
by the water, and tumbled down, filled a consider-

able space near the cliffs, and did not appear to have
been washed by the water for a great number of
years. I could not account for the incrustation of salt
(as we must have been at least three hundred miles
from the sea; this bottom or bed running from east
northwardly to the west or S. W.) in any other way,
than by supposing the sea water had once overflowed
this level; that it had since either retired from that
part of the coast, or formed a bar across its mouth, or
outlet, and thus excluded itself entirely; and that
the sea air combining with the saline deposit or
sediment, continued this encrustation.

The curious and interesting springs, before mentioned, are situated on the right or north side of this
dry bay or river, about one hundred feet below the
surface of the desart, and from three hundred and
fifty to four hundred feet from the bed or bottom.
There was not the smallest sign of their ever having
overflowed their basons; thereby leaving it a mystery
how they ever should have been discovered, as there
was no rill to serve as a clue.

Our masters now hurried on to the eastward, to
find a place to emerge from this dreary abyss, still
more gloomy, if possible, than the face of the desert.
As we passed along, the salt crust crumbled under
the feet of our camels, like the thin crust of snow.
We came at length to a spot in the bank at a kind of
point, where we ascended gradually from one point
to another until within, probably, two hundred feet
of the top; here we were obliged to dismount, and
drive, coax, and encourage the camels to go up. The
ascent was very steep, though in zig-zag directions,
and the flat rock over which the camels were forced
to climb, threw them down several times, when our
masters would encourage them to get up again, by
singing and making repeated trials: helping them
over the bad places by a partial lifting, and begging

the assistance of God and his prophet most fervently, as well as of all the saints.

Having at length reached the surface of the desert, they stopped a few minutes to let the camels breathe, and also that we might come up, for Mr. Savage and Clark could not keep pace with the rest of us, on account of their severe pains in consequence of over-charging their stomachs with water. The desert here had the same smooth appearance we had before observed: no rising of the ground, nor any rock, tree, or shrub, to arrest the view within the horizon—all was a dreary, solitary waste, and we could not but admire and wonder at the goodness of Providence in providing a reservoir of pure fresh water to quench the thirst of the traveller and his camel in this dry, salt, and torrid region, and we felt an inexpressible gratitude to the author of our being, for having directed our masters to this spot, where our lives had been preserved and refreshed by the cool delicious spring, which seemed to be kept there by a continual miracle.

We had not gone more than eight miles from the bank (in a N. W. direction) before we stopped for the night: here we found no lee to screen us from the strong winds, nor bush for the camels to browse on. I reckon we had travelled five hours this morning, at the rate of seven miles an hour, before reaching the bank, and five miles after getting down it, before we came to the spring; making it forty miles to, and ten miles from the spring to where we halted for the night, so that this day's march was altogether at least fifty miles.

The dry bed or bottom before mentioned, had probably been an inlet or arm of the sea that never was explored by Europeans, or any other civilized men; yet it must have had an outlet; and that outlet must be to the southward of us, and if so, its mouth must have been at least three hundred miles distant.

Here we ate the remainder of our camel's meat:—
we had no milk; for neither of our master's camels
yielded any, and our share of meat was not more
than about an ounce each.

I judged by the height of the north star above the
horizon that we were in about the latitude of twenty
degrees North. I now experienced that to have only
one want supplied, made us feel the others as less
supportable than before: for although we had drunk
as much fresh water as we could contain, and our
thirst was in a great measure allayed, still we were
rendered extremely uneasy by the gnawings of hunger, which, together with our sufferings from the
cold and piercing winds, made this a long and restless night.

CHAPTER XI.

*Journeying on the Desart—they are hospitably
entertained by Arabs, and come to a well
of fresh water*

ON the morning of the 30th we started very early;
three of us rode, while the other two walked; taking
our turns every three hours, or thereabouts. They
let the camels walk all this day, but their long legs,
and the refreshment they had enjoyed at the spring,
enabled them to step along so fast and briskly, that
those of us who were on foot, were obliged to be on a
continual small trot in order to keep up with them:
the wind at the same time blowing very strong di-

rectly against us, and our course being nearly N. W.

About two o'clock P. M. Sidi Hamet said to me, "Riley shift Gèmel;" (I see a camel;) he was very much rejoiced at it, and so were his companions; but neither I nor my companions could perceive any thing of the kind above the horizon for two hours after this. Our masters had altered their course to about East, and at length we all saw a camel, appearing like a speck in the horizon, but we did not reach the travellers, who were with a large drove of camels, until sunset. Having come up with the men, they invited our masters to go home with them; the invitation was accepted, and we drove our camels along, following them as they went towards their tents:—it was dark and quite late before we reached them, which were four in number.

We stopped at a small distance from the tents, and were obliged to pluck up a few scattered shrubs, not thicker than straw, to make a fire with. Our masters had given us neither meat nor drink this day. I begged for some water, and they gave us each a very scanty drink. We had travelled full fourteen hours this day, and at the rate of about three miles an hour, making a distance of about forty miles. We were now in a most piteous situation, extremely chafed and worn down with our various and complicated sufferings, and we were now to lie on the hard ground without the smallest screen; not even a spot of sand on which to rest our wearied limbs—we had been promised, however, something to eat by our host, and about 11 o'clock at night Sidi Hamet called me and gave me a bowl containing some boiled meat, which I divided into five heaps, and we cast lots for them. This meat was very tender, and there was just enough of it to fill our stomachs: after eating this, we had scarcely lain down when they brought us a large bowl filled with milk and water. This was indeed sumptuous living, notwithstanding our pains and the severely cold night wind.

On the morning of the 1st of October we were roused up early to pursue our journey. Sidi Hamet now called me aside, and gave me to understand that this man had got my spy glass, and wanted to know what it was worth. I requested him to show it to me, which he did; it was a new one I had bought in Gibraltar, and it had not been injured. The Arab, though he did not know the use of it, yet as the brass on it glittered, he thought it was worth a vast sum of money. Sidi Hamet had only seven dollars in money, having invested the rest of his property in the purchasing of us, was not able to buy the glass;—his fancy was as much taken with it, however, as was that of the owner. They had also several articles of clothing in their possession, which gave me reason to infer that we could not be a great distance from the place where our vessel was wrecked; but there was no method of calculating to any degree of certainty, as they all move with such rapidity in their excursions, that they seem not to know whither, or what distances they go, nor could I find out any thing from this man concerning the wreck. Taking our leave from this truly hospitable man, we pursued our course N. W. on the level desart.

Our masters had been very uneasy all the preceding day, on account of meeting with no land marks to direct their course; they were in the same dilemma this day, directing their camels by the winds and bearing of the sun; frequently stopping and smelling the sand, whenever they came to a small sandy spot which now and then occurred, but we did not come across any loose drifting sand. We took turns in riding and walking, or rather trotting, as we had done the day before, until the afternoon, when our masters walked, (or rather ran) and permitted us to ride.

About four o'clock P. M. we saw, and soon fell in with a drove of camels, that had been to the northward for water, and were then going in a S. W. direction with skins full of water, and buckets for drawing and watering the camels; their owners very civilly invited our masters to take up their lodgings with them that night, and we went in company with them about two hours to the South, where falling in with a very extensive but shallow valley, we saw about fifty tents pitched, and going into the largest clear place, unloaded and fettered our camels to let them browse, on the leaves and twigs of the small shrubs that grew there, or on the little low moss, with which the ground was, in many places, covered. As we went along near the tents, the men and women called me *el Rais,* and soon gathered around with their children to look at us, and to wonder. Some inquired about my country, my vessel, my family, &c. Having satisfied their curiosity, they left us to gather sticks to kindle our masters' fire; this done, we found, after considerable search, a soft spot of sand to lie down upon, where we slept soundly until about midnight, when we were aroused, and each of us presented with a good drink of milk: this refreshed us, and we slept the remainder of the night, forgetting our sores and our pains. I reckon we had travelled this last day about forty miles on a course of about N. W.

On the 2d of October we set out, in company with all these families, and went North fifteen or twenty miles, when they pitched their tents, and made up a kind of shelter for our masters with two pieces of tent cloth joined together by thorns and supported by some sticks. Our masters gave us a good drink of water about noon, and at midnight milk was brought from all quarters, and each of us had as much as he could swallow, and actually swallowed more than our poor stomachs could retain.

The tribe did not move, as is customary, on the 2d of October, waiting, as Sidi Hamet said, for the purpose of feasting us. They gave us as much milk as we could drink on the night of the second. Here our masters bought a sheep, of which animals this tribe

had about fifty, and they were the first we had seen;
but they were so poor, that they could with difficulty
stand and feed upon the brown moss which covered
part of the face of the valleys hereabouts, and which
moss was not more than one inch high. This tribe,
not unlike all the others we had seen, took no nourishment, except one good drink of milk at midnight,
and a drink of sour milk and water at mid-day, when
they could get it.

On the morning of the 3d of October, our masters
took leave of this hospitable tribe of Arabs, who not
only fed *them,* but seemed desirous that *we, their
slaves,* should have sufficient nourishment also, and
gave us liberally of the best they had. Our masters had
made a trade with them, and exchanged our youngest
camel for an old one that was lame in his right fore
foot, and one that was not more than half grown.
The old one they called *Coho,* (or the lame) and the
young one *Goyette,* (or the little child.) The sheep
our masters purchased was tied about the neck with
a rope, and I was obliged to lead it until about noon,
when we came to a low valley, with some small bushes in it—in the midst there was a well of tolerable
good water—here we watered the camels, and as the
sheep could go no farther, they killed it, and put its
lean carcass on a camel, after placing its entrails
(which they would not allow me time to cleanse)
into the carcass. This well was about forty feet deep,
and dug out among the big surrounding roots.

CHAPTER XII.

*They arrive amongst immense mountains of driving
sand—their extreme sufferings—their masters find
and steal some barley, and restore it again*

HAVING watered our camels, and filled two skins
with water, and drank as much as we needed—they
mounted Horace on the young camel, and all the
others being also mounted we proceeded on towards
the N. W. at a long walk, and sometimes a trot, driving the old lame camel before us until dark night, and I
think we travelled thirty-five miles this day. The entrails of the sheep were now given us for our supper;
these we roasted on a fire we made for the purpose,
and ate them, while our masters finished two of the
quarters.

We lay this night without any screen or shelter,
and early in the morning of the 4th, we set off on our
journey, all on foot, driving our camels before us, on
the same kind of flat surface we had hitherto travelled
over: but about 10 A. M. it began to assume a new
aspect, and become sandy. The sand where we first
entered it, lay in small loose heaps, through which it
was very difficult to walk, as we sank in nearly to our
knees at each step—this sand was scorching hot. The
camels were now stopped, and all of us mounted
on them, when on their rising up, we saw before us
vast numbers of immense sand hills, stretching as far
as the eye could reach from the north to the south,
heaped up in a most terrific manner; we soon arrived

among them, and were struck with horror at the sight:
—huge mountains of loose sand piled up like drifted
snow, towered two hundred feet above our heads on
every side, and seemed to threaten destruction to our
whole party: not a green or even a dry bush or shrub
of any kind in view to relieve the eye; here was no
path to guide our footsteps, nor had we a compass to
direct our course, obstructed by these dreadful barri-
ers. The trade winds which had hitherto given us so
much relief on our journey, by refreshing our bodies
when heated by the rays of an almost perpendicular
sun, and which had served, in some measure, to direct our course—even these winds, which now blew
like a tempest, became our formidable enemy:—the
loose sand flew before its blasts, cutting our flesh like
hail stones, and very often covering us from each
other's sight, while the gusts (which followed each
other in quick succession) were rushing by.

We were here obliged to dismount, and drive the
camels up the sandy steeps after our masters, who
went on before to look out a practicable passage.
The camels, as well as ourselves, trod deep in the
sand, and with great difficulty ascended the hills; but
they went down them very easily, and frequently
on a long trot, following our masters. Sidi Hamet,
Seid, and Abdallah, seemed full of apprehensions for
their own and our safety, and were very careful of
their camels.

Thus we drove on until dark, when coming to a
space where the sand was not so much heaped up,
being like a lake surrounded by mountains, we saw
a few shrubs: here we stopped for the night, unloaded, and fettered our camels, whose appetites were as
keen apparently as ours, for they devoured the few
leaves, together with the shrubs, which were as thick
as a man's finger. We next prepared a kind of
shelter with the saddles and some sand for our masters and ourselves to keep off in some measure the
fierce and chilling blasts of wind, and the driving

sand which pierced our sores and caused us much
pain. Having kindled a fire our masters divided the
meat that remained of the sheep:—It was sweet to
our taste, though but a morsel, and we pounded,
chewed and swallowed all the bones, and afterwards
got a drink of water:—then lying down on the sand
we had a comfortable night's sleep, considering our
situation. I reckon we had made thirty-five miles
this day, having travelled about eight hours before
we got among the heavy sand hills, at the rate of
three miles an hour, and five hours among the sand
hills, at the rate of two miles an hour. We were all
afflicted with a most violent diarrhœa brought on,
no doubt, by excessive drinking and fatigue.

At daylight on the morning of the 5th, I was ordered to fetch the camels, and took Mr. Savage and
Clark with me; and the two old ones being fettered,
that is, their two fore legs being tied within twelve
inches of each other, they could not wander far; we
soon found them, and I made the one I found kneel
down, and having taken off its fetters, mounted it
with a good stick in my hand for its government, as
the Arabs of the desart use neither bridle nor halter,
but guide and drive them altogether with a stick,
and by words. Mr. Savage having found the big camel,
took off his fetters, intending to make him kneel
down in order to get on his back; but the old lame
camel which had hitherto carried no load, and which
had occasioned us much trouble, in forcing him to
keep up with the others when on our march, now set
off on a great trot to the south:—the young one followed his example, so did Abdallah's, and the big
one started also, running at their greatest speed. Seeing the panic of the other camels, I endeavoured to
stop them by riding before them with my camel,
which was the most active and fleet; but they would
not stop—dodging me every way; my camel also tried
to get rid of its load by running, jumping, lying

down, rolling over and striving to bite my legs; but I made shift to get on again before he could rise, and had got some miles from where I had started, keeping near and frequently before the other camels, which appeared to be very much frightened. Our masters had watched us, and when the camels set off, had started on a full run after them; but had been hid from my view by the numerous sand hills, over and among which we passed.—Finding I could not stop the others, and fearing I should be lost myself, I stopped the one I was on, and Sidi Hamet soon coming in sight, called to me to make my camel lie down. He mounted it, and after enquiring which way the other camels went, (which were now out of sight) and telling me to follow his tracks back to our stuff, he set after them on full speed:—Seid and Abdallah followed him on foot, running as fast as possible. I returned; and picking up a few skins that had jolted off from the little camel, I joined Mr. Savage and Clark, and we reached the place where we had slept, but much fatigued; and here we remained for two or three hours before our masters returned with the camels.

We had during this interval tasted the bark of the roots of the shrubs which grew on the sand near us— it was bitter, but not ill flavoured, and we continued to eat of it until the runaway camels were brought back; it entirely cured our diarrhœa. They had overtaken the camels with much difficulty, and the creatures were covered with sweat and sand. I expected we should receive a flogging as an atonement for our carelessness in letting the big camel go, that had been fettered, and in particular, that Mr. Savage would be punished, whom I did not doubt they had seen, when he let his camel escape. So as soon as they got nigh, I began to plead for him; but it was all to no purpose, for they whipped him with a thick stick (or goad) most unmercifully. Mr. Savage did not beg as I should have done in our situation, and in a similar case, and they believed he had done it expressly to give them trouble, and continued to call him *Fonté*, (i. e. a bad fellow,) all the remaining part of the journey. Having settled this affair, and put what stuff they had on the camels, we mounted them and proceeded,—shaping our course as before, to the N. N. W. as near as the mountains of sand would permit. It was as late as nine o'clock when we started, and at eleven, having made about three leagues, winding round the sand hills on a trot, we were obliged to dismount. The hills now stood so thick, that great care was necessary to prevent getting the camels into an inextricable situation between them, and our masters went on a head, two of them at a considerable distance, to pick the way, and one to direct us how to go:—the latter keeping all the time in sight. The sand was heated (as it had been the preceding day) by the rays of the sun, to such a degree that it burned our feet and legs, so that the smart was more severe than the pain we had before experienced, from our blisters and chafing:—it was like wading through glowing embers.

During the whole of this day, we had looked for shrubs or some green thing to relieve the eye; but not a speck of verdure was to be seen. We had no food; our water was nearly exhausted, and we saw no sign of finding an end to these horrid heaps of drifting sands, or of procuring anything to relieve our fatigues and sufferings, which were now really intolerable. We continued on our route, however, as near as circumstance would permit, N. N. W. until about nine o'clock in the evening, and stopped to rest among the high and dreary sand heaps, without a shrub for our camels to eat. I calculated we had gone this day from 9 to 11 o'clock, twelve miles, and from that time till we stopped, about two miles an hour, making in all thirty-two miles. We had nothing to eat; our masters however gave us a drink of water, and being fatigued beyond description, we soon sank down and fell asleep. I happened to awake in the night, and hearing a heavy roaring to the northward of us, concluded it must be a violent gust of wind or a hurricane, that would soon bury us in the sand forever. I therefore immediately awakened my companions, who were more terrified at the noise even than myself, for a few moments; but when we perceived that the sound came no nearer, I was convinced, (as the wind did not increase) that it must be the roaring of the sea against the coast not far off. This was the first time we had heard the sea roar since the 10th of September; and it proved to us that our masters were going towards the empire of Morocco as they had promised. My comrades were much rejoiced at being undeceived on that subject, for they had all along continued to suspect the contrary, notwithstanding I had constantly told them that the courses we steered could not fail of bringing us to the coast. On the sixth, early in the morning, we started, and I found, by inquiring of Sidi Hamet, that our conjectures were true; that we were near the sea, and that the roaring we heard (and which still continued) was that of the surf: he added, "you will get no more milk," which I thought he regretted very much. We continued on our course, laboring among the sand hills until noon, when we found, that on our right, and ahead, they became less frequent, but on our left there was a string of them, and very high ones, stretching out as far as the eye could reach. The sand hills through which we had passed rested on the same hard and flat surface I have before mentioned, without being attached to it; for in many places it was blown off, leaving naked the rocks and baked soil between the towering drifts.

About noon we left these high sands, and mounting on the camels, proceeded along southward of them, where the sand was still deep, but not high, on about an East course. Near this line of sand hills our masters discovered two camels—they bore about N. E. and we made directly for them as fast as possible. On a near approach we observed they were loaded, and our masters now took off the sheaths from their guns and primed them anew; and upon coming near the camels, they dismounted and made us do the same. We saw no human being.

The camels had large sacks on their backs, made of tent cloth, and well filled with something; there was also a large earthen pot lashed on one of them, and two or three small skin bags. Seid and Abdallah drove these camels on with ours, observing strict silence while Sidi Hamet was searching for the owner of them with his double barrelled gun, cocked and primed. Mr. Savage was on the young camel, and not being able to keep up, was a mile or more behind; when Sidi Hamet found the owner of the camels asleep on the sand near where Mr. Savage was. He went towards him, keeping his gun in readiness to fire, until he saw the other had no fire arms, and was fast asleep; when stepping carefully up, he snatched a small bag from near the sleeper's head, and went slowly away with it until past the fear of waking him. He then assisted in driving Mr. Savage's camel along, and they soon came up with us, where Seid and Abdallah had made the two loaded camels lie down between some small hillocks of sand. They untied the mouth of one of the sacks, and behold its contents were barley! This was the first bread stuff we had seen, and it gave us new hopes; they poured out about fifty pounds of it, I should guess, and put into a large leather bag of their own; then tying up the neck of the sack again, they made the camels get up with their loads. They now began to examine the contents of the small bags, and found them to consist of a number of small articles: but the one that was taken from near the Arab's head was partly filled with barley meal. They were all over-joyed at this discovery, and immediately poured out some of it into a bowl; mixed it with water, and ate it; then giving us about a quart of water between us, with a handful of this meal in it, making a most delicious gruel, they hurried us on to our camels, and set off to the S. E. on a long trot, leaving the strange camels to themselves.

We had not proceeded more than half an hour, before we saw a man running swiftly in chase of us, and hallooing to make our masters stop; they knew he must be the owner of the camels they had robbed, and paid no other attention to him than to push on the camels faster. Sidi Hamet now told me that that fellow was a "poor devil—he has not even a musket," said he "and he let me take his bag while he was asleep." The man gained on us very fast. I was afraid he would get back what had been taken from him by our masters, especially the barley—so were my shipmates; one of whom wished he had a loaded mus-ket—saying, "I would soon stop him if I had one, and thus save the barley." Our masters made their signs for this man to go back, but he continued to advance, while our Arab masters finding he would come up, kept their guns cocked in their hands, and ready to fire on him, though he had no other arms than a scim-itar; and drawing near they halted; upon which the stranger making an appeal to God and bowing him-self down and worshipping, declared that he had lost a part of his property, and that he knew they must have taken it; that he was their brother, and would rather die than commit a bad action, or suffer others to do it with impunity: "you have fire arms" (Celi-beatahs) said he, "and believe you can kill me in an instant; but the God of justice is my shield, and will protect the innocent; I do not fear you." Sidi Hamet then told him to leave his scimitar where he was, and approach without fear, and then making our camels kneel down, we all dismounted. The stranger upon this came forward and asked—"is it peace?"—"It is," was the reply of Sidi Hamet; they then saluted each other with—"peace be with you—peace be to your house—to all your friends," &c. &. and shaking one another in a most cordial manner by the hand, seated themselves in a circle on the ground. After a long debate, in which our masters justified themselves for having taken the provision without leave, because we, their slaves were in a state of starvation, which was very true, they added—"you would not have refused them a morsel, if you had been awake!" and it was thereupon finally agreed, to restore all that they had taken: so they made us clear a place on the ground that was hard, and pour out the barley from our bag. They also gave him up his bag of meal, which had been much lightened, and a very small bag, which I supposed to contain opium; this they said was all they had taken; then after they had prayed together, we all mounted our camels and proceeded on our journey. Religion and honour even among thieves, thought I!

CHAPTER XIII.

Continuation of the Journey on the Desart—several singular occurrences—they come within sight of the Ocean

THIS had detained us about an hour; Mr. Savage was put on the old camel, which still continued very lame, and Horace on the smallest. These camels could not keep pace with the others, and both Mr. Savage and Horace were severely flogged for what our masters called bad management: though the true reason I suspected was the loss of the stolen barley, which had put them in a bad humour. We kept on to the East as fast as the camels could go, until late in the evening; when hearing the voices of men halloo-ing to each other at a short distance on our left, our masters seemed much frightened; kept all still; and finding a deep hollow, we silently descended its steep bank, leaving our little camel with his legs tied, on the level above, as he was so far worn down by fatigue that he could scarcely walk. When we got to the bottom of it, we found a considerable number of small bushes, and having taken the saddles from off the camels and fettered their fore legs together, as usual, we let them go to feed. I calculate we travel-led seven hours this day, at two miles an hour, among the sand hills; then two hours on camels, until we came to the strange ones, at the rate of six miles an hour including two stops, say two hours; then from four until about ten P. M. six hours at five miles an hour—total this day, fifty-six miles.

As soon as the camels were fettered, our masters examined their guns, and having ascertained that they were well primed—ascended the sand hills in this valley, (for there was much drifted sand about it in scattering heaps, and it appeared to have once been a river, whose bed was now dry.) They bade us all follow them, and went first to the lowest part of the valley; then ascending the steep sides of the sand drifts, made us crawl after them on our hands and knees. After they had gained the top, and waiting for us to climb up, they set up the most tremendous howling I had ever before heard—one counterfeiting the tone of a tiger, the other the roar of a lion, and the third the sharp frightful yell of a famished wolf. Having kept up this concert for some time, they again proceeded mounting and descending, and searching for tracks, &c.

I was much terrified, I confess, and expected they were hunting for the people we had heard halloo when we entered the valley, to rob and murder them, and that we were to share their danger, and carry their spoil. But after they had kept us mounting and descending about two hours, they found a snug retreat surrounded on all sides by high sand drifts, where however a few small bushes were growing: they made us lie down in the deep sand, and after continuing their howlings for about half an hour, bade us go to sleep, which we much needed, as our fatigues were excessive; they had not suffered us to make the least noise since we reached the valley—nor did they themselves make any, except in imitation of wild ferocious beasts. I was now fully persuaded that they were actuated by feelings of fear and not views of plunder in these manœuvres; and taking a station with their guns in their hands around us, as if afraid they should lose their slaves, we soon forgot our troubles in the arms of sleep, and did not awake until the morning of the seventh, when we repaired to our camels and found every thing safe. There were more camels, which we saw in the open valley, browsing upon the bushes, which grew higher here than any we had hitherto seen; they were of a different species, and not clothed with long thorns.

Just as we were ready to set off on our journey an old woman and a boy came where we were; the woman appeared very friendly, made enquiries respecting our situation, and if our masters as well as our selves were not hungry; and finding that we were indeed in want of food, she sent off her boy, who soon returned with the boiled remains of what I conceived to have been a sheep or goat, consisting of the entrails and a few bones; of these our masters ate the greatest part, but gave us the remainder—that is to say, the bones, which we were very glad to get, bare as they were, for our hunger was extreme.

Having gnawed and swallowed this hard food, and drank about half a pint of water each, coloured with sour milk, which the old woman kindly gave us, we proceeded on our journey, mounting this dry river's bed or gully, which had been acted upon by water at no very remote period. We here saw the first bushes that deserved that name, since we had been on this continent. They appeared to be of the willow kind, some of them as large as a man's leg, and about fifteen feet in height. It was with much difficulty the camels could ascend this bank, but when we did reach its summit, we found ourselves on the same level desart as we had before travelled on; our view on every side was bounded only by the distant horizon, except on our left, where a long string of sand-drifts of great height intercepted it. Near these sand hills, we discovered a man mounted on a camel; he rode swiftly towards us, which our masters observing, while he was yet a great way off, dismounted from their camels to wait his approach. Myself and Mr. Savage were on foot, making the best of our way along. We saw our masters dig holes in the sand, and bury two small bags which they had stolen from the stranger the day before, at the time they helped themselves to the barley. The man on his camel soon came up, and we recognized him as the same our masters had plundered; he had followed us on, and now told them they had stolen his goods and deceived him besides.

Our masters denied the charge, and after showing him that they had nothing about them of the kind he described, told him to satisfy himself fully and to go and search their stuff on the camels; protesting at the same time that he accused them wrongfully, and calling God to witness that they had nothing of his in their possession. The man seemed satisfied with their protestations, and rode off without further examination. We were going on during this time, and *they* remained on the spot to dig up the treasure after its owner had left them. When they came up with us, Sidi Hamet said to me, "that fellow wanted his bags and things, but he has not got them yet:" he then showed me the bags and their contents. There was a small box in one of the bags, containing opium and several hollow sticks of the thickness of a man's finger, and six or eight inches long; these were filled with what I supposed to be gold dust; the other bag contained tobacco stalks, and the roots of an herb, which I afterwards understood to be a specific remedy for *evil eyes,* or witchcraft; this they esteemed as of great value, even more than the gold dust and opium: the natives smoke this root through the leg or thigh bone of a sheep or goat, they having no other pipes, and then conceit themselves invulnerable. I confess I was not pleased at the discovery of our masters' propensity to thieving, and could not help being apprehensive of the consequences that might result from such licentiousness, affecting our safety and prospects of release. We travelled fast most of this day, and must have made thirty-five miles on about an E. N. E. course. It was late when we stopped for the night: we were on a hard surface, and had neither shrub, nor indeed any other thing to fend off the cold night wind, which blew extremely fierce from the N. N. E.

October the 8th, we started very early and rode on rapidly until the afternoon, when some camels' tracks were discovered, at which our masters seemed very much rejoiced, for they were extremely hungry and thirsty. We followed these tracks until about four P. M. (they being nearly on our course) when we came in sight of a large drove of camels feeding on the scattered shrubbery in a small shallow valley, with a few sheep and goats, which were nibbling a short brown moss, not more than an inch in height, that grew round about in spots. After due salutations, which were very long and tedious, the owners of the flocks and herds invited our masters to remain with them for the night, which may well be supposed was readily accepted; we having travelled this day about forty-five miles. They showed our masters the way to their tents, who, after bidding us follow, set off for them on a full trot: we reached them in about half an hour: there were about twenty in number—pitched in a little valley near a small thicket of thorn trees. I call them trees, because they were much larger than any vegetable productions we had yet seen in this country—a few of them might be eight inches in diameter. Our masters had already killed a kid they had bought, and were employed in dressing it: which being prepared and boiled soon after dark, our masters gave us the entrails, which we immediately devoured, though not cleaned, and nearly raw, as we had not patience to wait till they were roasted sufficiently; they then offered some of the meat to the Arabs, who were sitting around them on the ground, but as they only came to gratify their curiosity in viewing us, they did not accept of any. This was the first time I had known any of them refuse so tempting an offer; and I could not but consider it as a favourable omen, and that the land was becoming more fertile and productive as we advanced on our journey, and that we must shortly escape from this horrible desart.

After we had swallowed our morsel, these people gave each of us a good drink of water, and at midnight (the hour set apart by the Arabs for taking their refreshment) they awaked me and gave me a bowl, containing probably four or five pounds of a kind of stirabout, or hasty pudding, in the centre of which, in a hole made for the purpose, there was poured a pint or more of good sweet milk:—we quickly seated ourselves in a circle around the bowl, and though it was quite hot, we swallowed it in a moment. This was the most delicious food I ever tasted; the effect it produced on my palate has never since been effaced from my memory, and my companions agreed with me, that nothing half so sweet had ever before entered their mouths; and as we all took it up with our hands, each one accused the other of eating like a hog, and of devouring more than his equal share. I endeavoured to convince them that it could not be more equally divided, as each put his hand to his mouth as fast as he could. Notwithstanding every one, by the irresistible impatience of hunger, burnt his mouth and throat, yet this dish was unspeakably grateful; for hunger, sufferings and fatigue had absolutely reduced us to skeletons: it warmed our stomachs, and checked the dysentery, which had been extremely distressing for several days past. This was the first kind of bread we had tasted since we left the wreck.

Our masters had been very much out of humour (probably owing to hunger) for several days, and beat my shipmates oftentimes most unmercifully, who, in their turn, smarting under the lash, and suffering incredibly from their sores, fatigues and privations, became as cross as wild bears, notwithstanding I did all in my power to lighten their burdens, relieve their fatigues, and intercede for and beg them off when our masters were about to beat them, and frequently walking that they might ride; yet one of them would often curse me to my face, and load me with the most opprobious epithets. My kindness seemed but to inflame his petulence, and to excite in him a strange animosity, so that in the ravings of his distempered imagination, he declared that he hated the sight of me, and that my very smiles were more cutting to him than daggers presented to his naked breast: he seemed indeed to be transformed into a perfect savage in disposition, nor did this rankling humour forsake him until I showed him in *Suze* the letter I there received from Mr. Willshire, assuring me he would shortly redeem us from slavery.

Early on the morning of the 9th, we set forward in a N. Easterly direction, and having travelled about ten hours on the camels, at the rate of four miles an hour, we came to a deep well, situated in the midst of a cluster of high bushes; here was a large company of men watering many droves of camels that were round about. These people saluted our masters in a friendly manner, when they came up. I was preparing to assist in drawing water for our camels, but Sidi Hamet, would not permit me or my companions to work; indeed we were so extremely reduced and weak, that we could not without difficulty stand steady on our feet, though (from what cause I know not) our sores were fast healing, and our skins uniting in all parts over our bodies.

While Seid and Abdallah were busied in drawing water for our camels, an Arab came up with one, and led him to our masters' watering tub or bowl, which Seid observing, bade him desist; but the strange Arab swore his camel should drink there, and he (Seid) should draw water for him. This kindled the resentment of Seid; he left his bucket, ran up to the Arab, and gave him a heavy blow on his face with his fist, which staggered him near to falling; but recovering himself, he drew his scimitar, and made a powerful thrust at Seid, who saved his life by springing suddenly from him, and the scimitar but slightly pricked his breast. Sidi Hamet had by this time seized and unsheathed his gun, and presented it to the Arab's breast within a yard's distance, ready to blow him through. When he was about to fire, his hand was seized by one of the bystanders, and others of them rushing between the combatants to prevent bloodshed, laid hold of Seid and his antagonist, and having separated them by main force, they removed the Arab to the other side of the well, where some of the company drew water for his camel, which having drank its fill, they sent the fellow off, muttering curses as he went away. Our masters, during all this time, were so exasperated at the conduct of this man, that nothing less than the strength of superior numbers would have prevented them from putting him to death, and all the company agreed that they had been grossly insulted, especially as they were strangers.

When our camels had finished drinking at this well, the water of which was very brackish, we were mounted, and proceeded further east for about one hour's ride, where we found two more wells, which appeared to have been lately dug, and the water they contained was very salt. Here was a large drove of camels (probably one hundred) to be watered, and they obliged me to assist in drawing water until they had all finished; my master encouraging me, by saying, "their owner was a very good man, and would give us food." It was about sunset when we had finished drawing water, and we followed the valley in which we were for about three miles east, when we came to the tent we had been in quest of: here was no lee to keep off the cold wind, nor did we get any thing to eat, notwithstanding our masters had praised the liberality of our host, and tried by every means to obtain some provisions from him. I soon found his goodness was like that of many others; (i. e.) he was no longer liberal than while there was a prospect of profit. I presume we travelled forty-five miles this day.

As soon as daylight appeared on the morning of the 10th, we set forward, all mounted on the camels, and kept on steadily until night over this most dreary desert, and came to a halt long after dark, without any thing to keep off the wind, which was blowing a strong gale. We travelled this day about thirteen hours, at four miles an hour; as the camels went all day on a quick walk, we must have made at least fifty-two miles E. N. E.

Oct. the 11th, we set off very early on a full trot, and went on until noon, seven hours, at six miles an hour, when the land before us appeared broken, and we descended gradually into a deep valley, whose bottom was covered with sand; and on both sides of us, at a great distance, we saw very high and steep banks like those of a river, and followed the tongue of land that separated them. Our course was nearly East. At about two P. M. our masters said they saw camels ahead, but *we* could not perceive them for long time after, when keeping on a great trot, we came up with a drove about six P. M. We could however find no owners, nor in fact any human being; for all had fled and hid themselves, probably from fear of being robbed, or that contributions might be levied on their charity for some provisions. We searched some time for the owners of these camels, but not finding them, we continued on, and having come to the abrupt end of the tongue of land on which we had been travelling, we descended into the river's bed, which was dry and soft. Pushing forward, we reached a large cluster of bushes, which appeared like an island in a lake when seen at a distance, and I suppose it was ten o'clock at night before we arrived at the spot, though we saw it in the distant horizon long before dark. As we entered among the bushes, our masters preserved a profound silence; and having found a clear spot of about twenty yards in diameter, encircled by high bushes, which kept off the wind, we stopped there for the night; having travelled that day for the space of about fourteen hours, at the rate of five miles an hour, making a distance of seventy miles. We had nothing this night wherewith to allay our hunger; our fatigues and sufferings may be more easily conceived than expressed; yet as we were sheltered from the night winds, we slept very soundly until we were roused up to continue our journey.

On the 12th of October, as soon as daylight appeared, we watered the camels at a well of brackish water near the bushes before mentioned. Our masters had been careful not to make the least noise during the night, nor to kindle a fire, fearing they should be discovered and surprised by some more powerful party; but neither foe nor friend appeared; and having filled a skin with some of this brackish water, we descended a second steep bank to the bottom or lowest part of the river's bed, which was then dry, sandy, and encrusted with salt: it appeared very white, and crumbled under the feet of our camels, making a loud crackling noise. The reasons of this bed being then without water, appeared to be the recess of the tide: its left bank rose very high in perpendicular cliffs, while its right was sloping and covered with sand, evidently blown by the winds from the sea beach, and which lay in drifts up to its very summit. This bay (for it can be nothing else) ran into the land from near a S. W. to a West direction, and was not more than eight or ten miles wide here, which I afterwards found was near its mouth, but was very broad within, and extended a great distance into the country; for since we entered its former bed we had travelled twelve hours, at the rate of five miles an hour, making sixty miles, and it then extended farther than the eye could reach to the S. W.

The steep banks on both sides, which were four or five hundred feet high, showed most evident signs of their having been washed by sea water from their base to near their summits, (but at a very remote period) and that the sea had gradually retired from

them. Our masters being in a state of starvation, their
ill humour increased exceedingly; when about nine
o'clock in the forenoon we saw two men, driving two
camels, come down the sand hills on our right. Our
masters rode off to meet them, and having made the
necessary inquiries, returned to us, who had continued going forward, accompanied by Abdallah. Sidi
Hamet informed us that there were goats in an E. S. E.
direction not far distant, and that we should soon
have some meat; so we commenced climbing over
the high hills of sand, in order that we might fall in
with them. In ascending these hills, which were extremely difficult and long, our old lame camel gave
out, having fallen down several times, which caused
much delay; so finding him nearly expiring, we abandoned him and proceeded on; though this circumstance of losing the camel, also helped to increase the
rage of our masters, who now behaved like madmen.
As we were climbing up, we perceived a hole dug in
the sand, and we were told that the entrails of a camel had been roasted there which Seid discovered by
applying his nose to the surrounding earth. Sidi
Hamet having gone on before us with his gun, we
had already ascended several miles of this steep and
sandy bank; and on arriving near the level of the surrounding country, we heard the report of a musket
fired, at no great distance from where we were, and
soon perceived Sidi Hamet, accompanied by another
Arab, driving a flock of goats before them. This Arab
was much intimidated at the sight and report of a
gun, for my master had fired off one of the barrels to
frighten him. When the goats came near us, our masters, who considered possession as a very important
preliminary, ran in among the flock, and seized four
of them which they gave into our charge, until they
should settle about the price with their owner, who
was alone and unarmed, but at this moment he was
joined by his wife:—she had not been at all fright-

ened, and commenced scolding at our masters most
immoderately and loudly:—she said, she would not
consent to part with the goats, even if her husband
did, and insisted on knowing Sidi Hamet's name:
this he told her, and she began to abuse him for being so cowardly as to rob an unarmed man; said the
whole country should ring with his name and actions, and she did not doubt but she could find some
man who would revenge this injury—her husband all
this time strove to stop her tongue, but to no purpose; nor did she cease scolding until Seid presented
his gun to her breast, and threatened her if she spoke
another word, to blow her to pieces. This compelled
her to pause a moment, while our masters (taking
advantage of her silence informed them that he had
left a good camel a little distance behind, which being only tired, could not proceed with them, and
that he would give them this camel in exchange for
these four goats. I could plainly discover however
that these people did not believe him. Sidi Hamet
nevertheless spoke the truth in part; a camel was indeed left behind, but not a good one; yet as there
was no alternative, they were necessitated to submit:
the woman however insisted on exchanging one goat
we had for another, which our masters assented to,
merely to gratify her caprice.

This business being thus settled, which had taken
up nearly an hour's time, our goats were tied fast to
each other by their necks, and given into my charge;
leaving Mr. Savage and Horace to assist in driving
them. Clark and Burns were ordered to drive the
camels, whilst our masters, a little less fretful than
before, went forward to pick out a practicable passage
for them and the goats, while my party brought up
the rear. The goats were difficult to manage, but we
continued to drive them along, and generally within
sight of the camels, though with great fatigue and
exertion. Our hunger and thirst were excessive—the

direct heat of the sun, as well as that reflected from the deep and yielding sands, was intense. Mr. Savage found here a very short green weed, which he pulled and ate, telling me it was most delicious and as sweet as honey; but I begged him not to swallow any of it until I should ask our masters what was the nature of it, for it might be poison; and I refused to touch it myself, though it looked tempting. In our distressed condition, however, he thought a green thing that tasted so well could do him no harm, and continued to eat whatever he could find of it, which (happily for him) was not much: but in a short time he was convinced of the contrary, for he soon began to vomit violently:—this alarmed me for his safety, and I examined the weed he had been so delighted with, and after a close investigation, I was convinced it was no other than what is called in America the Indian tobacco. Its effects were also similar; but how these plants came to grow on those sands I cannot conceive.

Mr. Savage continued to vomit by spells for two hours or more, which, as he had very little in his stomach, strained it so excessively as to bring forth blood. I could not wait for him, because both our masters, their camels, and our shipmates, were already out of sight. When he could proceed no further, he would stop and vomit, and then by running (though in great distress) as fast as he was able, come up with us again. I encouraged him all I could—told him what the herb was, and that its effects need not be dreaded.

Ever since we had been coming near the summit of the land, we had discerned the sea; though at a great distance ahead and on our left, but as it appeared dark and smooth in the distant horizon, I supposed it to be an extensive ridge of high woodland, and hoped we should soon reach it, as our course bent that way, and that this would prove to be the termination of the desart. Horace, however, thought it appeared too dark and smooth for land, and regarding it again attentively, I discovered it was in fact the ocean, and I could plainly distinguish its mountainous waves as they rolled along, for it was greatly agitated by fierce winds. This was the first view we had of the sea since we were made slaves: it was a highly gratifying sight to us all, and particularly so, as it was quite unexpected; and it very much revived the spirits of myself and desponding companions.

CHAPTER XIV.

They travel along the sea-coast under the high banks— fall in with and join a company of Arabs—travel in the night for fear of robbers—Mr. Savage faints— is near being massacred, and is rescued by the author

DISCERNING the tracks of our camels, which we had lost sight of for a time, as they had crossed over rocks, where they had descended through a rent or chasm, partly covered with high drifts of loose sand towards the sea-shore, we followed them down immensely steep sand hills, to a tolerably inclined plane, between the first and second banks of the sea; which from appearances, had once washed the upper bank, but had long since retired:—the inclined plane had also been a beach for ages, where the stones, that now covered its surface, had been tossed and rounded, by striking against one another.

From this beach the ocean had also retired, and now washed other perpendicular cliffs of one hundred feet or more in height, at a distance of six or eight miles to the northward of the former ones, which appeared to rise in abrupt, and in many places overhanging cliffs of rocks to the height of three hundred feet. We had made our way through these cliffs, by means of a hollow, seemingly formed on purpose for a passage, as it was the only one in view; and as I did not know which way our masters went, I had stopped to view the surrounding prospect, and now give what was then my impression. I was at a loss, which way to steer my course, but our masters, who were concealed behind a small hillock on our left, discovering my embarrassment, now called to me, where I soon joined them. It was now nearly dark, and there were three or four families of Arabs near, sitting under a shelter made of skins extended by poles; here our camels were turned up to browse, and we were ordered to collect brush, which grew on the steep side of the banks, to make a fire, and to keep off the wind during the night. Mr. Savage was entirely exhausted, and I requested him to lie down on the ground, whilst the rest of us gathered the bushes required; but when I came in with my handful, Seid was beating him with a stick to make him assist. I begged he would permit Mr. Savage to remain where he was; told him he was sick, and that I would perform his share of the labour. Sidi Hamet now returned and killed one of the goats, of which they gave us the entrails: a seasonable relief indeed, and we were allowed to drink a little of the soup they were boiled in, and a small piece of meat was divided between us; and each received a drink of water:—I had before stolen a drink for Mr. Savage, whose bloody vomit continued. In the course of the night they gave us a small quantity of the same kind of pudding we had before tasted, but as Mr. Savage was sick, they refused to give him any, saying, "he has already eaten too much of something, but they did not know what." Sidi Hamet, however, saved a little of

the pudding in a bowl for him, and as he seemed unwilling to die with hunger, I gave him part of the
pudding I had, and saved my share of meat for him
until the morning. Our hunger and thirst being
somewhat appeased we slept this night pretty soundly. We had travelled this day about thirty miles.

October the 14th, early in the morning, we took
leave of these Arabs; but while we were busied in
getting off, Abdallah seized on Mr. Savage's pudding
in the bowl as a good prize, and swallowed it in an
instant; so that nothing but my care of Mr. Savage
saved him from fainting and consequent death on
this day. Our masters had purchased two more goats
from those Arabs, which increased our number to
five; these we were forced to drive, and we kept along
the sea-shore the whole of this day. On our right the
original sea-shore (or bank) rose nearly three hundred
feet perpendicularly, and in many places in overhanging cliffs. The inclined plane on which we travelled was from three to six or eight miles wide, and
very regular; covered with pebbles and many round
stones; among which grew here and there a few dwarf
bushes of different kinds from what I had seen before
in various parts of the world. A little to our left the
plane broke off abruptly, and the ocean appeared.
The bank was from one hundred and fifty to two hundred feet high above the level of the sea, and mostly
perpendicular, against which the heavy surges dashed
with great fury, sounding like loud peals of distant
thunder. Our course and that of the shore was about
east, and near dark we fell in with four families of
Arabs who were about pitching their tents near the
sea-shore. Our masters went and introduced themselves to the one who appeared to be their chief or
the principal chaacter among them, and whose
name was *Hassar.* They soon became acquainted,
and it was ascertained that Hassar and his wife, together with four men that were with him, and their

families were going the same route that we were; upon which our masters agreed to join company.

Hassar's wife, whose name was Tamar, and appeared to be an uncommonly intelligent woman, addressed me in broken Spanish and Arabic mixed:— she said she had saved the lives of some Spaniards who had been wrecked on that coast a great many years ago; that a vessel came for them, and that she went to *Lanzarote* (one of the Canary Islands) to get some goods which the Spanish captain promised to deliver to her father, who retained three of the men until the Spaniard should have fulfilled his contract, and brought her back. She represented to me the manner in which the houses in Lanzarote were built, and described the forts and batteries with their cannon, &c, so very clearly and accurately, that I had no doubt she must have seen them, and I gave her to understand I had been there also. She said Lanzarote was a bad country, and assured us, we should not die with hunger while we remained in her company.

We travelled on the 14th about twenty miles. In the night our masters killed a goat and gave us a part of the meat as well as of the entrails: Hassar's wife also gave us a small quantity of the pudding before mentioned, which the Arabs call *Lhash;* and here we had a good night's sleep. October the 15th, early in the morning, Hassar and his company struck their tents, and all these families proceeded on with us until near night; when we came to a very deep gully, which we could not pass in any other way than by going down the bank on to the sea beach; and as it was low tide, there was a kind of pathway where camels had gone down before us. We descended, and there found a tent with an Arab family in it just below the high bank; so sending on the camels, Sidi Hamet made us stop here a few moments. The owner of the tent pretended to speak Spanish, but in fact

knew only a few detached words of that language:
he mentioned to me that he knew I had promised
Sidi Hamet that my friend in Swearah would pay
him the amount I had bargained for, stating the sum
now, said this Arab—"Have you a friend in Swearah?" I answered I had:—"do not lie, (said he) for if
you do, you will have your throat cut; but if you
have told him so merely that you might get off the
desert, so as to procure something to eat, he will pardon that pretext and deception so far as only to sell
you and your comrades to the highest bidder, the first
opportunity, provided, however that you confess the
deceit now. In a few days (added he) you will find
houses and a river of running water, and should you
persist in deceiving him, you will certainly lose your
life." I made him understand that I was incapable of
lying to Sidi Hamet; that all I told him was true;
that he was the man who had saved my life, and he
should be well rewarded for his goodness by my
friend, and by our Almighty Father. This seemed to
satisfy Sidi Hamet, who was present and understood
me better than the other did, and he told me I
should see Swearah in a few days. We now went
forward, accompanied by the Arab, who piloted us
across a small arm of the sea that entered the before-
mentioned gully. We here found a pair of kersey-
mere pantaloons that had belonged to Mr. Savage,
in the possession of one of this man's little sons;—I
pointed them out to my masters and begged them to
buy them, which after a long barter with the boy,
Seid effected, by giving him in exchange a piece of
blue cotton cloth which he had worn as a kind of
shirt: they wished me to give the pantaloons to Clark
or Horace, but I gave them to Mr. Savage, although
they insisted he was *fontè*, or a bad fellow.

Having got up the steep bank again, after wading
through the salt water, which was nearly up to our
hips, and one hundred yards broad, we encamped for

the night on high dry land; and at dark our masters, taking Horace and myself with them, went near a few tents close by the sea, where we were presented with a quantity of dried muscles, which though very salt, we found excellent: these we divided among our shipmates: I conjecture we had made twenty-five miles this day. Here our masters killed their remaining goats, boiled and ate their entrails and most of their meat, as all present were hungry, and would have some in spite of every opposition; so that our share was seized and swallowed by others.

October the 16th, we made ready and started very early, but went on slowly, keeping near the sea-shore, and mostly in the broken grounds, caused by its former washings. Our masters seemed very fearful all this day, and told me there were many robbers and bad men hereabouts, who would endeavour to seize and carry us off, and that they could throw large stones with great force and precision. We had not travelled more than fifteen miles before sunset, and night coming on, our masters, who had mounted Mr. Savage, Clark, and Burns on the camels, drove them on at a great rate, while myself and Horace were obliged to keep up with them by running on foot. All this time they had their guns in their hands unsheathed, and when Horace and myself were obliged occasionally to stop, one of them always stayed with us, and then hurried us on as fast as possible. In this manner we proceeded on until about midnight, when coming to a deep gully, Mr. Savage and Clark were dismounted, and Horace and myself placed on the camels. Descending the valley, we found it full of high sand drifts, and proceeded without making the least noise: the valley was wide, and the sand lying in it, had no doubt been driven from the sea beach by the wind. All the women and children at this time were running on foot. After reaching with much labour the other side of the valley, and the

summit beyond it, we found the whole surface of the
ground making an even inclined plane, covered with
deep drifts of loose sand. I had been riding, I think,
about two hours, when Clark, who was a considerable distance behind, called to me, and said, "Mr.
Savage has fainted away, and they are flogging him
with sticks." I instantly slipped off my camel, and
ran to relieve him as fast as my legs could carry me.
Seid was striking his apparent lifeless body, which
lay stretched on the ground, with a heavy stick: Hassar had seized him by the beard with one hand, and
with the other held a sharp scimitar, with which he
was in the act of cutting his throat. I laid hold of
Hassar, jerked him away, and clasping the body of
Mr. Savage in my arms, raised him up, and called for
water. Hassar would have run me through with his
scimitar, but Sidi Hamet arrested and prevented
him. I expected to lose my life, but had determined
to save Mr. Savage's at all hazards. Our masters and
the whole company of men, women, and children,
were around me: they were possessed with the belief
that he was perverse and obstinate, and that he would
not exert himself to proceed at a time when they
were in haste to go on, lest they should fall into the
hands of robbers; for which reason they had determined to kill him. I made Sidi Hamet, however, and
the others understand, that he had fainted through
hunger and excessive fatigue, and that he was not
perverse in this instance. This surprised them exceedingly: they had never before heard of such a
thing as fainting. Sidi Hamet ordered a camel to be
brought, and a drink of water to be given him, and
when he revived, this Arab shed tears; then putting
him and Clark on a camel, one to steady the other,
they proceeded. Sidi Hamet desired me to get on
with Horace and ride, saying, with a sneer—"the
English are good for nothing—you see even our
women and children can walk and run." I told him

I could walk, that I was not a bad fellow; and began to run about and drive up the camels; this pleased him excessively, and he bade me come and walk with him, leaving the camels to the care of others, calling me "good Riley—you shall again see your children, if God please."

We continued our journey eastward along the south side of a high string of sand hills, when hearing a dog bark before us, we turned the camels suddenly off to the north, setting them off on a full trot, but passing over the sand hills without noise: we kept this course for about an hour, until having got near the sea-bank, and north of the sand hills, we resumed our former course. Near daylight we lost our way, and fearing to go amiss, as it was very dark, they made the camels lie down in a circle, placing us within it—when they kept guard over us with their muskets in their hands, while we took a nap. I should guess we travelled fifty miles this last day and night.

October the 17th, early in the morning, we set forward again, still on the same inclined plane, between the first and second banks of the sea. The high banks on our right, whose pointed rocks, where they had been washed by the ocean, were still visible all the way, began to be overtopped with high hills rising far into the country, and presenting to our view a new aspect; so that I was convinced we had left the level desart.

CHAPTER XV.

*Black mountains appear in the east—they come to a
river of salt water, and to wells of fresh water, where
they find many horses—description of a singular plant
—come to cultivated land; to a fresh water river, and
a few stone huts*

THE black tops of high mountains appeared in the
distant horizon to the eastward about noon, and the
camel paths were very much trodden. We kept on
until near night, when meeting with a deep valley,
we wound our course through it to the southward,
and then went down south-eastwardly through another deep valley, where there was a good path. The
black bare mountains on both sides of us gave us
great hopes that we should soon come to running
water and cultivated lands; and in reality near night
we came to a stream of water, with high grass and
bushes growing on its margin. The water, however,
was very brackish, and could not be drank; but on its
opposite bank we saw a company of men at some
wells, watering about forty fine looking horses and
some camels. Our masters saluted those men, and
crossing the stream, which in this part was about two
feet deep and thirty feet wide, we watered our camels also at the same place. This river, whose water
was clear as crystal, was literally filled with beautiful
large fish, which were jumping above the surface
every moment; but the Arabs did not seem to want
them, for they could have been caught very easily.
The company with the horses and camels left the

wells, and went on to the south, riding at a full trot along the river's side; they were armed only with scimitars. Our company then went towards the sea, and Hassar's women pitched their tents for the night; here they cooked a goat, which they divided among all the party, and what fell to our share cannot be supposed to have been much. I believe we made thirty-six miles this day, as we rode nearly all the time.

October the 18th, we ascended the hill, climbing up in a zig-zag path on the steep side of the east bank of this river; and having gained the surface we found it to be a continuation of the same inclined plane on which we had before been travelling. The bank on our right, to the south, still continued to give indubitable proofs of its having been washed by the ocean; whose surges had worn in under the shelving rocks, which hung in immense masses of from two to three hundred feet high over the surface of the inclined plane below, while the plane itself adjoining the cliffs was covered with fragments that had fallen from above, and with other stones that had been washed and worn round by the ocean's waves, leaving the most positive marks of its having retired to its present bed. These observations, with those I had made before, and was enabled to make afterwards, fully satisfied my mind, that the sea had gradually retired from this continent;—I must leave it to philosophers to account for the cause. The only green thing we had seen for several days past, except what grew immediately on the bank of the river, (which were some bushes resembling dwarf alders and bulrushes) was a shrub that rose in a small bunch at the bottom, having frequently but one stalk, from three to twelve inches in thickness; the limbs spreading out in every direction, like an umbrella, into innumerable branches, making a diameter of from fifteen to twenty feet, and not more than six feet in height; its leaves very green, smooth, pointed, and about four inches long, by one and a half broad: its bark resembled that of the hard or sugar maple tree; its branches terminated abruptly, the point of each twig being nearly as thick as the end of a man's finger: this shrub, or weed, was very tender, and as we broke off the twigs, a great many drops of glutinous liquid, resembling milk, flowed from them, but its odour and taste were of the most disagreeable kind, and the camels would not feed on it. We saw a good deal that had grown up before, and had died, and become dry: on breaking it off, I found it was hollow, and almost as light as a common dry weed. Neither our masters nor the other Arabs would light a fire with it, on account of its disagreeable smell when burning; the taste of the milk issuing from this plant was the most nauseous and disgusting in nature, though very white and beautiful to behold. About noon we came to the foot of the high mountains we had seen the day before, and turned in between two of them to the southeast, leaving the sea entirely. We went up through a chasm in the bank, over rocks and through a narrow footway, formed by the treading of camels and horses; for we had seen many horse-tracks, and also the tracks of one animal of the kind called neat cattle.

As we proceeded on foot, winding upwards, we discovered on our left a few stones piled up in the form of a wall, round a pit of ten or twelve feet across, and six feet deep, dug in the earth by art. There were lying on the ground around the wall, several earthern pots that would contain from three to four gallons each; and which appeared to have been made for and used as boilers. One of our young men directly took up one of them, and was lashing it on his camel as a good prize, when Hassar and Sidi Hamet, observing the circumstance, made him untie and carry it back again to the spot where he had found it. As I already knew the propensity all had for plundering, I could not but imagine that they

now restrained themselves through fear. About sunset we came to a small spot of land that had been
cultivated, and fell in with a heap of barley straw.
Here was the first sign of cultivation we had seen on
this continent, and we hailed it as the harbinger of
happier days. We had travelled full thirty miles
this day, and our masters now gave us the putrid
remains of the goat which had hung on one of the
camels for four days; this we roasted and found it a
delicious morsel; it was tender, and needed no sea-
soning. Some of my comrades, as if their taste had
become depraved by the rage of hunger, declared
that putrid meat as far preferable to fresh; that it
wanted neither salt nor pepper to give it a relish, and
that if ever they got home again, they should prefer
such food to any other. Having finished our savoury
supper, we lay down on the straw, and enjoyed a
most charming, sound, and refreshing sleep. To us,
who for so long a time had been obliged to repose
our wearied limbs and wasted frames on the hard-
baked bosom of the desert, or the dead sides of the
barren sand drifts; this solitary heap of fresh straw
seemed softer and sweeter than a bed of down strewn
over with the most odoriferous flowers.

October the 19th, we resumed our journey very
early in the morning, and travelled on foot, all except Burns, who was so far exhausted as to be unable
to walk. Our course rounded from S. E. to E. N. E.
keeping the bottom of the valleys, most of which had
been cultivated by the plough at no very remote
period, but only in a narrow strip. The sides of the
mountains were entirely barren and naked of foliage,
and we kept on winding as the valleys permitted, until about two o'clock, P. M. when, suddenly through
a deep valley before us, a few rough stone huts broke
upon our view, and a moment afterwards we beheld
a stream of clear water purling over a pebbly bottom,
and meandering through banks covered with green
bushes and shrubs in full blossom. On the farther

side, cows, asses, and sheep, were feeding on green grass, and a number of date trees adorning and shading the margin of the rivulet. This was a sight none of us expected to behold, and I poured out my soul in rapturous effusions of thankfullness to the Supreme Being. Excess of joy had so far overpowered our faculties, that it was with difficulty we reached the water's edge; but urging forward to the brink with headlong steps, and fearlessly plunging in our mouths, like thirsty camels, we swallowed down large draughts, until satiated nature bade us stop. The rivulet was fresh, and fortunately not so cold as to occasion any injurious effects: it was quite shallow, and not more than about five yards in width; it appeared, however, very evidently that when the rain falls in the surrounding country, it flows with a much deeper and broader current. It is called by the Arabs *el Wod noon*, or the river Nun; comes from the south-east, and runs from this place to the sea in a northerly direction. We had arrived on its right bank, where some barren date trees grew, and which offered us nothing but their shade: hungry, however, as we were, our fatigue got the better of every other want, and as these were the first trees we had met with during our distressing pilgrimage, we embraced the kindly offer, and enjoyed about two hours of refreshing sleep: I was then awakened by Sidi Hamet, who directed me to come with my companions and follow him: this we instantly did, and going near one of the small houses he divided amongst us, to our inexpressible joy, about four pounds of honey in the comb. This was indeed a dainty treat; and with the hungriness of greedy bears, we devoured it, comb and all, together with a host of young bees just ready for hatching, that filled two-thirds of the cells; our hearts at the same time swelling with gratitude to God, and tears of joy trickling down our fleshless cheeks.

Hassar's men pressed around and endeavoured to snatch from us this delicious food, of which they had no share; but Sidi Hamet placing the bowl on his knees, passed the honey-comb to us piece by piece in one hand, while he held his gun in the other, ready to fire on anyone who should attempt to deprive us of our meal. The eyes of these fellows seemed to flash fire at the preference we enjoyed, and we dreaded the effects of their malicious envy; for the Arabs set no bounds to their anger and resentment, and regard no law but that of superior force. Having finished our luscious repast, we were told by our masters to go to rest, which we did, and soon fell asleep in the shade formed by a beautiful umbrella palm-tree.

About dark we were called up and ordered to gather fuel, and were afterwards presented with some pudding of the same kind we had before eaten, though mixed with oil, that I afterwards ascertained was the argan oil, which though fresh, had a very strong smell, and my stomach being cloyed with honey, I declined eating any. My companions however relished this oil very much, and preferred it afterwards to butter during our stay in Africa. We found a good shelter this night near a burying place with a small square stone building in the centre, whitewashed and covered with a dome; and I afterwards learned that this was a sanctuary or saint house: it was fenced in with thorn bushes, and was the first burying place we had seen in this country. I computed we had travelled this day (Oct. 19) about eighteen miles.

On the morning of the 20th, we did not go forward, and a number of Arabs and Moors came to see our masters and us. This place appeared to be a great thoroughfare: large droves of unloaded camels were passing up to the eastward from the way we had come, as well as from the southward, and also great numbers of loaded camels going towards the desart. Their loading consisted principally of sacks of barley, some salt and iron, together with other merchandise.

During the fore part of this day, several parties of men, in all from sixty to eighty, passed us; all mounted on handsome horses of the Arabian breed, well-bred and high-spirited: their riders were covered with cloaks or sulams, and every one had a single barrelled musket in his hand, the stocks of which were curiously wrought and inlaid with small pieces of various coloured wood and ivory, arranged and fitted in a very particular manner. The locks of these muskets were of the Moorish kind, and very unhandy, though substantial, and they seldom miss fire, although their powder is bad and coarse grained. This and a good scimitar slung on their right side constitute the whole of their weapons, they depend more upon the scimitar for close quarters in battle than upon their musket, for, say they, this will never miss fire; being similar to the practice which it is said the Russian General (Suwarrow) used to inculcate on his soldiers—"the ball will lose its way, the bayonet never—the ball is a *fool;* the bayonet a hero." A Moor is ashamed to be without his scimitar; their scabbards are made of brass, and plated on the outside with silver, but those worn by the Arabs are made of leather: these weapons both of the Moors and Arabs, are suspended from the neck by cords made of woolen yarn died red, or a strong braided leather throng. They call a scimitar or long knife *el skine.*

These natives were of a different race of men from any we had hitherto seen; they wear a haick or piece of woolen cloth wrapped about their bodies, which covering them, falls down below their knees; or else a cloak called *gzlabbia*, made in a similar manner, cut with short sleeves, and one fold of the haick generally covered the head; but those who had not their heads covered with their haick or the hood of their gzlabbia, or sulam, wore a kind of turban; the cloak or sulam, is made of coarse black cloth, very shaggy, and much in the form of the European cloak, with a hood or head-piece to it; it is, however, sewed together part of the way down in front, so that to get it on, they slip it over their heads, and it covers their arms. They are generally stout men, of five feet eight or ten inches in height, and well set; their complexion a light olive—they wear their beards as long as they will grow, and consider a man without a great bushy beard an effeminate being, and hold him in great contempt. Their saddles were well made and very high, at least eight or ten inches, fitted before and behind so as almost to make it impossible for the horse to throw his rider; their bridles are of the most powerful Arabian kind; their stirrups are made of broad sheets of iron that cover almost the whole foot—many of them are plated with silver. All the men wore slippers and spurs, and had their stirrups tied up very short.

While we remained here, a very respectable looking old man, who spoke a few words of Spanish, after learning from our masters who we were, came to me and inquired about my country and my friends in Swearah; said he knew all the consuls there, and told me their names were *Renshaw, Josef, Estevan,* and *Corte.* He said he was going to Swearah, and should be there in ten days, and would carry a letter for me if my master would let me write: but we had no paper. I informed him that my friend was named *Renshaw,* guessing him to be the English consul. This old man told my master he believed I spoke the truth, and that I had been at Swearah, which from his discourse I understood to be the same as Mogadore. He then set off eastward on his mule, which was a very large and handsome one. All the people that passed here appeared very friendly to our masters; they wished to know our story, and requested my opinion of their horses, saddles and bridles, muskets, scimitars, and accoutrements in general, &c. all of which I declared to be of the best possible kind. This morning, Sidi Hamet bought a hive of honey, and undertook to give some of it to us, but was not able to carry his kind intentions into effect, for at the moment he was handing some to me, Hassar's men rushed on him and got possession of the whole, which they devoured in a minute; there was no getting it back, and after a long and violent dispute with Hassar and his company respecting it, he procured another hive, and being assisted by the man from whom he bought it, and a number of strangers, he succeeded in distributing amongst us about three pounds of the poorest part of the comb.

CHAPTER XVI.

*The company is divided—they set off to the eastward
—their masters are attacked by a band of robbers*

AFTER we had eaten this, our masters prepared the camels, and Hassar's company divided, that is to say, two men and all the women and children took the plain great route which led east in a deep valley, driving off about one-half of the camels; Hassar and the others drove off the rest (including ours) in a N. E. direction, and we with our masters, accompanied by two other men, proceeded along the river's eastern bank to the northward for a short distance, and then ascended the high, steep, and craggy mountains eastward of us. The labour in clambering up these steep precipices is indescribable; we continued mounting them as fast as possible for about four hours, and I was fully convinced our masters took that route for fear they should be followed and surprised in the night by some who had seen us, and thus be robbed of their slaves and other property. After climbing over the highest peaks of these mountains, we saw Hassar and part of his company who had driven the camels, and had gotten up by another and more practicable path. It was now near night, and we travelled along the craggy steeps, assisting one another over the most difficult parts, while Hassar sought out the easiest places for the ascent of the camels. Coming at length to a small level spot of ground, we saw some tents, and directed our course towards them: the tents were twelve in number and placed in a semicircle. Having approached to within one hundred yards in front of the largest one, our masters seated themselves on the ground with their backs towards the tents, and a woman soon came out bringing a bowl of water, which she presented to them after the usual salutations of *Labez*, &c. &c.

Our masters drank of the water and Sidi Hamet was soon after presented with a bowl filled with dates lately plucked from the trees and not fully ripe: these he gave to us; though Seid, Abdallah, and Hassar snatched each a handful to which we were forced to submit: we found them excellent, but did not know at that time what sort of fruit they were. Here we remained during the night, and rested our emaciated bodies, which were, if possible, more fatigued than they were ever before.

October the 21st, we set off to the northward very early, and made down towards the sea through numerous steep gullies, and got into the inclined plane below the former sea-shore, about mid-day; here were the same sort of marks in this bank that we had before observed, and the same signs of its having been laved by the ocean. We went along through the same kind of thick bushes as those I have before described, near to the cliffs that at present formed a barrier to the mighty waters, where we discovered a number of tents, and soon reached them. Here our masters Sidi Hamet and Hassar, were recognized by some of the men, who were in all about twenty, with their families: these people had large sacks of barley with them, which they had procured far eastward up the country. Sidi Hamet was now sick with violent pains in his head and in all his limbs. These people (who were Arabs, as all are who live in tents in the country) took compassion on him, and cleared a tent for him, to lie under, where having made up a large fire, he kept his head towards it, turning about and almost roasting his brains, but obtained no relief from this manner of treating his disorder; he next had recourse to another singular remedy: he had a large knife put into the fire and heated red hot; then made his brother draw the back of it, hot as it was, several times across the top of his head, making it hiss (as may well be supposed) in all directions:—when it had in some measure cooled, he would again heat it as before, then making bare his legs and arms, he went through with the process of striking its back along them at the distance of three or four inches, scorching off the skin; and though it made him twitch and jump at every touch, he continued to do it for the space of an hour or more. Burns had been very ill for some time, and was so weak that he scarcely was able to stand, and could not walk—he was therefore, always placed on a camel, and as Sidi Hamet was now applying to himself a remedy for what he thought a stroke of the moon, he undertook to administer the red hot knife to the limbs of poor Burns, who from mere want of bodily strength was not able, poor fellow, to jump, but would at every touch cry out, "God have mercy upon me." As I was hungry, I begged of my masters to let me go and search for muscles on the sea-beach, (for there was a hollow at a little distance, though which we might gain it) but they refused, saying, "tomorrow, if God please, we shall be on the sea-beach: there are no muscles on this part of the coast;"—here, however, we received a good supper of *Ihash* or pudding, and rested our wearied limbs under the tent with our masters.

October the 22d, we went forward, driving our own camels only; as Hassar had taken the young one, we had but three remaining; so we rode by turns, crossing the deep hollows which had been worn down by the rains or other causes, until afternoon, when we were forced to have recourse to the sea-beach to get past one of these deep places, whose sides were so steep as to render a passage down it impracticable. When we gained the beach, we found ourselves on a narrow strip of land, which was then dry, the tide being out; this extended in length eight or ten miles, but from the water's edge to the perpendicular cliffs on our right, not more than ten yards: these cliffs appeared to be one hundred and fifty feet in height. When we came to the sea-water, I went into it, and let a surf wash over me, that I might once more feel its refreshing effects; but my master, fearing I should be carried away by the receding waves, told me not to go near them again. As we proceeded along this narrow beach, and had passed over half its length, the huge cliffs overhanging us on our right, with the ocean on our left; just as we were turning a point, we observed four men, armed each with a musket and scimitar, spring from beneath the jutting rocks, to intercept our march. Our masters were at this time on the camels, but they instantly leaped off, at the same time unsheathing their guns: to retreat would betray fear, and lead to inevitable destruction—so they determined to advance, two against four, and Sidi Hamet, though still in so weak a state as to be thought incapable of walking before he saw these men, now ran towards them with musket in his hand,

while Seid, that cruel coward, lagged behind—so true
it is that the most generous and humane men are
always the most courageous. The foe was but a few
paces from us, and stood in a line across the beach—
Sidi Hamet, holding his gun ready to fire—demanded
if it was peace? while he eyed their countenances to
see if they were deceitful—one of them answered, "it
is peace," and extended his hand to receive that of
Sidi Hamet, who gave him his right hand, suspecting
no treachery; but the fellow grasped it fast, and would
have shot him and Seid in a moment, but at that critical juncture, two of Hassar's men came in sight, running like the wind towards us, with each a double-
barrelled gun in his hand, all ready to fire; the robbers saw them as they turned the point, and the fellow who had seized Sidi Hamet's hand, instantly let
it go, turning the affair off with a loud laugh, and
saying he only did it to frighten him: this excuse was
deemed satisfactory, merely because our men did not
now feel themselves sufficiently strong to resent this
insult, and we proceeded on: but these fellows, who
were very stout and active, hovered around us, slaves
endeavoring to separate us from our masters, as it appeared, in the hope of seizing on us as their own,
which Sidi Hamet observing, ordered me with my
men to keep close to the camels' heels, while he and
his company (now strong, though none of them
armed with scimitars) kept between us and the banditti. When they found that our masters were too
vigilant for them, they took French leave of us, and
ran along the beach with incredible swiftness, chas-
ing each other, and taking up and throwing stones,
that I should suppose would weigh from six to eight
pounds, with a jerk that made them whiz through
the air like cannon balls:—they threw them against
the cliffs of rocks, which resounded with a blow, and
many of the stones were dashed to pieces as they
struck. I could see the marks they aimed at, and that

the stones went with great precision, as well as force. I had before no idea that it was possible for men to acquire by practice such enormous power of arm; for they threw these stones with such velocity, that I am convinced they would have killed a man at the distance of fifty yards at least.

Having come to the end of the beach, we ascended the bank again, leaving these formidable ruffians masters of the shore, where they, no doubt, got some plunder before they left it. After we had mounted the bank and were clear, Sidi Hamet told me that the fellows we had met were very bad men, and would have killed him and Seid, and would have taken us away where I could never hoped to see my wife and children again, if the great God had not at that time sent to our relief the two men; he then asked if I would fight to save his life? I told him I would, and that no one should kill him while I was alive, if it was in my power to prevent it; "good Riley, (said he,) you are worth fighting for, God is with you, or I must have lost my life there."

CHAPTER XVII.

Some fresh fish are procured—they pass several small walled villages, and meet with robbers on horseback

NEAR evening we met and passed a man driving an ass laden with fish, probably of from ten to twelve pounds weight each: they had much the shape and appearance of salmon, and our masters endeavoured

to procure one from the owner for me, as I gave them
to understand I was very fond of fish, and that it
would be good for Burns, but the man would not
part with one of them on any terms. At evening we
found Hassar's and his family's tents already pitched
on a little hill near the cliffs, and we joined this company. Soon after, Seid, Abdallah, and two of Hassar's
men, went out with their guns:—in about two hours,
those with us, namely, Sidi Hamet, Hassar, and two
others, hearing footsteps approaching, seized their
muskets, and springing forward from their tents, demanded, who came there? It was Seid and his company, who came towards me, and unfolding a blanket
turned out four large fish of the same kind we had
seen before. "Riley, (said Sidi Hamet,) are these
good to eat?" I answered in the affirmative—"take
them and eat them, then, (said he) but be careful not
to choke yourselves with the bones." I took three of
them, cut them into pieces, and put them into an
earthen pot, that belonged to Hassar, (this pot the
Arabs call *giderah*,) added some water, and boiled
them directly, and we ate till we were satisfied. We
drank the soup, which was extremely grateful and
invigorating, and helped to check the dysentery, with
which we were all much troubled since eating the
honey-comb. We had travelled this day, I think,
about forty miles, and slept at night within a circle
formed by our masters and their camels, out of which
we were not suffered to go, as Sidi Hamet told me
there were many robbers in this place, who would
seize on us, and carry us off in a minute, without the
possibility of my ever being restored to my family.

October 21st, at day break we set forward on our
journey, all in company, (except Hassar and the
women and children.) The fresh fish we had eaten
the night before, had made us very thirsty; and about
noon we came to a kind of cistern, or reservoir of
water on the pathway side: this reservoir was built

of stone and lime; its top was arched like a vault, rising about four feet from the ground, and the cistern
was at least eighty feet in length, eight or ten feet in
breadth in the inside, and appeared to be twenty feet
deep. It was now nearly full of water, which had been
led into it by means of gutters, formed and arranged
so as to receive and conduct the rain water when it
descends from the neighbouring hills, and is collected
in a stream in this valley. I understood this water was
the common property of all travellers along this
route, and that the cistern was built by a very rich
and pious man, solely for the purpose of refreshing
the weary traveller, and that it contained water the
whole year round, even though there should be a
continued drought for a twelve-month—but no person of our party ventured to water his camel from it,
considering it as sacred for the use of man alone. We
were still travelling on the slope between the first
and second banks of the sea, which in these parts was
much cut up, occasioned by the waters which had
from time to time poured down from the neighbouring mountains, and formed steep and very deep gullies, across which we were obliged to climb. The
path on this inclined plane was not much frequented,
and the margin of the bank on our right hand had
been newly ploughed in many places here and there
in the nooks or fertile hollows. On the high lands we
saw two small walled towns. with prickly-pear bushes
planted around them. Near these towns or walled
villages, some men were employed in ploughing with
a pair of beasts, generally a cow and an ass poked together in a very singular manner, which I shall hereafter describe, and others were watching flocks of
sheep and goats on the surrounding eminences, while
the women were seen lugging down wood on their
backs from the tops of the lofty hills, and large jars
or pitchers of water from a distant valley. They generally had a child on their backs, clinging with its

arms round the neck of the mother, and the jar or pitcher rested on their shoulders in a manner that reminded me of the story of the beautiful Rebekah, in holy writ, coming to the well with her pitcher.

About noon, we came near a considerable walled village, that stood close by the road; it had gardens close by the walls on all sides, and there was one near the gateway planted with prickly-pear. These gardens were defended by heaps of dry thorn bushes, which served as an outward defence to the town: these heaps were about six feet high, and the walls fifteen feet. Our masters stopped near the gate for some moments and no one seemed disposed to give them a drink of water, contenting themselves with gazing at them over the walls; so on they went, cursing the inhospitality of these villagers. Near night we descended into a delightful valley, whose bottom was level and well-disposed into handsome gardens, fenced in with thorn bushes and stone walls, and divided into numerous separate plots. Round about them, and at their corners, stood many fine fig-trees, which looked healthy, though they were leafless, owing to the lateness of the season: we saw also a few pomegranate-trees. These gardens or plots were planted with different kinds of vegetables, such as turnips, cabbage, onions &c. they were watered by a small stream that flowed from the hills at a short distance above, and was conducted round and through the whole of them by gutters dug for that purpose.

The owners of these gardens lived in two little walled villages, near the top of the bank on the east side, but they offered us no refreshment. We passed in the course of the day, three beds of streams or rivers, which were now dry, and one whose mouth was filled with sand, so as to stop its communication with the sea, though there was some water in it, where people from all quarters were watering their cows, sheep, goats, asses, and camels, and carrying it

off in skins and pitchers. In the afternoon, a company
of ten men on horseback, and well armed, rode towards us on the plain, making a loud jingling with
their spurs against their stirrups, and crying out,
Hah! hah! hah! hah! Our company consisted of
our two masters, and two of Hassar's men Abdallah,
and one stranger, who had joined us that day, and
being armed with five double barrelled muskets, and
some scimitars, they all sprang from their camels on
the approach of the strangers, drew their guns from
their sheaths, primed them anew, and took a station
in front of the property, in a line ready for action.

The horsemen rode up to within five yards of our
men at full speed, and then stopped their horses
short. I expected now to see a battle, though I rather
feared our men would be trampled to death by the
horses; for their arms could not have saved them
from the shock of this impetuous onset, yet they were
on the point of firing the moment the horses stopped.
The chief of the horsemen then demanded in a very
imperious tone who our masters were? where they
came from? if they knew *Sidi Ishem?* what countrymen we, their slaves were? and where they had found
us? Sidi Hamet replied to all their questions in a
sharp quick manner, and as briefly as possible, and
in his turn demanded, "who are you? where do you
come from? and, what right have you to ride up to
me in such a manner, and stop me and my slaves on
the road?" This is as near as I could understand what
they said. A loud dispute was kept up on both sides
for half an hour, when it ceased, and we were allowed
to proceed; while the others rode off to the southward among the mountains. The force on both sides
was so nearly equal, that I have little doubt this was
the only circumstance that prevented a battle.

We travelled on till long after dark, when we came
to a number of tents, and stopped for the night, and
here we were treated with some dried muscles and

barley pudding. Hassar and his family had not travelled with us the last day, but the two men who had
assisted in relieving us from our critical situation on
the beach, were in company, and we had also been
joined by one more Arab, and two camels. Ever since
we had come to the cultivated country off the desart,
we had found the people sickly; many of them were
afflicted with swelled legs, and some with what I took
to be the leprosy; and also with pains in different
parts of their bodies and limbs; though when on the
desart we did not see the smallest sign of sickness or
disorder among its inhabitants. They now considered
us as skilled in medicine, and consulted me wherever
I came; one of the women here had a swelled breast,
which was astonishingly large, and very much inflamed: she was in such pain as to cry out at every
breath. They wished me to examine it, and prescribe
a remedy, which I did by recommending a poultice
of the barley *lhash*, or pudding, to be applied, and
renewed often until the swelling should subside or
burst. The woman was very thankful, gave me a
drink of water and a handful of muscles, and requested I would examine a swelled leg of her brother; this was also inflamed, and very painful:—perceiving no skin broken, I directed a thick plaster of
coarse salt to be bound round it, so as fully to cover
the afflicted part; this they did immediately, and the
man thought he felt instantaneous relief.

From the great expedition we had used, I think we
must have travelled this day about fifty miles, as we
were almost continually on the camels, and they
going a great part of the time on a trot. In the afternoon of this day, we discovered land that was very
high, a good way eastward of us, stretching about
north as far as the eye could reach. We saw it when
on a high hill and at an immense distance; looking
over the ocean which was near us, it appeared like a
high and distant island: "there is Swearah, Riley,"

(said Sidi Hamet) pointing to the northernmost land in view: it was a great way off. I asked him how many days it would take us to get there? he answered, "ten, at our slow pace."

CHAPTER XVIII.

Their masters commit an error which they are com-
pelled to redress—Sidi Hamet and his brother Seid
fight—Horace's critical situation
—they come to villages

OCTOBER the 23d, we were awakened without making any noise, two hours before daylight, and went on our journey; I suspected there was some roguery going on, because we had never before started in the night; and we had not travelled more than two leagues, when, just at the dawn of day, we heard the sound of horses' feet coming up at full speed behind us, the clanking of the arms of their riders against each other, and spurs against their stirrups, made a great noise. Our masters stripped the covers from their guns, and gave them to me to carry. The horsemen, four in number, came up by this time, and passing us at a short distance on our right, rode round before our camels, and stopped them. Our men were five in number, with four double-barrelled guns; and bidding me to keep as close to them as possible with my men, they ran at their greatest speed to the encounter, whilst we followed on as fast as we could, fearing to be separated from them, (as

it was still quite dark) and falling into the hands of
the banditti. They approached each other with loud
cries; the voices of those on horseback sounded like
trumpets, and those of our masters were very little
lower, so that the mountains near rang again with
the sound. I expected every moment a slaughter
would commence; each one strained his throat to
speak, or rather to yell louder than his opponents. I
had approached near my master, and could distinctly hear one of the horsemen accuse him of a
breach of hospitality, and reproach him in the most
opprobrious terms, for some wrong which he alleged
had been done to him, the others were at the same
time wrangling with our other men. This war of
words having subsided a little, one of them asked my
master his name, and after considerable delay on
account of punctilio, (each insisting that the other
should tell his name first), my master told him his
name was *Sidi Hamet*—the other then said his name
was *Ali Mohammed*:—then ensued a long dispute
between them, they mutually charging each other
with perfidy, &c. During this interval, and as daylight appeared, our adversaries gained strength, for
they were joined by many armed and unarmed men,
running on foot, and according as they increased in
force, our party lowered their tone; but the clamour
was still so loud that I frequently could understand
nothing of what was said. The Arab who had joined
our company with two camels the day before, did not
set out with us this morning, but he now came running up: our masters had driven off his camels, and
this was the cause of the uproar that was now raging.
The purloined camels were then in our drove, and
while the others were quarreling about the matter,
the owner ran round and drove his camels back.
When our *honest* masters found they could not keep
what they had feloniously taken, they began to lower
their voices. By this time the sun had made its ap-

pearance, and for two hours prior I had every moment expected a bloody scuffle. I knew our masters were brave, but I had no doubt they would be overpowered by numbers, in which event we should fall to the lot of the conquerors, who were strangers to us; and it was not probable that these men would be as humane to us as Sidi Hamet had been; nor was I indeed certain that we ourselves should not be killed in the contest, both parties being much enraged. I felt our situation to be dreadful, indeed; but at length Sidi Hamet spoke to Ali Mohammed in a low tone of voice, and requested he would ride apart from the others with him, with which he complied, and they came near where I sat, trembling with apprehension. Sidi Hamet now told Ali that his party had not the least intention of driving off any camels but their own, and that the mistake had been occasioned entirely by the darkness of the night. He then went on protesting that he was incapable of committing an unworthy action, that he abhorred a robber and a thief, and that as he was entirely innocent of intentionally driving off the man's camels, he would not acknowledge he had done wrong designedly, but would rather lose his life in maintaining his character, and would sell it as dearly as possible. *Ali Mohammed* on this appeared to be satisfied and said to him, "I am el Rais, (the chief) and am your friend because you are a brave man:" so making Sidi Hamet's excuse to those about him, and the lost camels being recovered, they left us to pursue our journey.

We had gone up from the sea-board, and were passing between high mountains towards the southeast, when the late affray happened, but about noon we reached a plain, and took an eastern direction. Hassar's men with their camels, and Abdallah with his camel, now filed off to the left, leaving us with our masters and their own camels only, and were soon out of sight, among the bushes. The mortifying re-

sult of the morning's enterprise, had rendered Seid
uncommonly ill natured; he had claimed Horace as
his slave from the very beginning, and Mr. Savage
also belonged to him. He had always doubted my
word to his brother, and would not believe that a
miserable wretch like me could find a friend to advance money for my ransom, though both he, Hassar,
and all the company, had a high opinion of my courage, since I put my own life in jeopardy to save that
of Mr. Savage, at the time he fainted:—Seid had endeavoured to sell his slaves at every place we came to,
after leaving the desert. Hassar, as well as others, took
a particular fancy to Horace, and had offered a large
sum for him in camels and other merchandise, but
the interference of Sidi Hamet, who had sworn that
Horace should not be separated from me, aided by
my often renewed entreaties and my tears, whenever
I heard it suggested, had saved him thus far. As we
were now approaching the Moorish dominions,
powerful chiefs, with large bodies of armed men intent on plunder, were riding about and scouring the
country in every direction, and Seid had come to a
determination to take his slaves and make the most
of them. Seid was a younger brother of Sidi Hamet,
and had, until now, submitted in some degree to his
counsel, though they had many slight quarrels at different periods of the journey.—Where we stopped
the preceding night, the Arabs strove hard to get
possession of Horace. Seid had to my knowledge
made a bargain to sell him in the morning, but was
dissuaded from fulfilling it, by his brother.

We, slaves, were now five in all, travelling on foot,
but moving forward very slowly, for we were worn to
the bones by our various and complicated sufferings.
It seemed that the breath of hope alone had kept the
vital spark from being totally extinguished. Sidi Hamet was riding on his big camel before us, when Seid
ordered us to halt, but the other desired us to come

on; upon which Seid laid hold of Mr. Savage and
Horace, and stopped them. It was now that Sidi Hamet's wrath was kindled—he leaped from his camel,
and darting like lightning up to Seid, laid hold of
him and disengaged Mr. Savage and Horace from his
grasp. They clinched each other like lions, and with
fury in their looks, each strove to throw the other to
the ground. Seid was the largest and stoutest man;
they writhed and twined in every shape until both
fell, but Sidi Hamet was undermost: fire seemed to
flash from their eyes, whilst they twisted around each
other like a couple of serpents, until at length Sidi
Hamet, by superior activity or skill, disengaged himself from his brother's grasp, and both sprang up on
their feet. Instantly they snatched their muskets at
the same moment, and each retiring a few paces with
great rapidity and indignation, tore the cloth covers
from their guns, and presented them at each other's
breast with dreadful fury:—they were not more than
ten yards asunder, and both must have fallen dead,
had they fired. Horror had seized and chilled my
blood, so that I could neither get from them, nor
move, indeed, in any direction. My mind was filled
with inexpressible apprehensions—"my God, (I cried
aloud) have mercy on these unfortunate brothers, I
pray thee, for our sakes, and suffer them not to spill
each other's blood." In the midst of this ejaculation,
I was started by the report of two muskets, and imagined that both the brothers had fallen; but on turning my eyes again to this direful scene, I perceived
that Sidi Hamet had fired the contents of both his
barrels into the air, having had a moment's reflection,
whilst priming and cocking his piece. He now threw
it on the ground, then making bare his bosom, he
advanced with a firm step towards Seid, and with an
energetic voice, exclaimed, "I am now unarmed,
fire! your brother's heart is ready to receive your
balls; glut your vengeance on your benefactor." He

stopped short; Seid hesitated. Mr. Savage and Horace were near Seid, who threatened them with instant death if they moved. Sidi Hamet finding his brother's mind wavered, ran to Horace, and sent him towards me, telling his brother, he should have Clark in Horace's stead, whom he ordered to come near, but Seid would not consent to the exchange, whereupon my master added Burns; that is, two for one. Seid had made Mr. Savage sit down and had placed one of his feet on his thigh, to keep him there; while his brother ordered me to go with Horace, first to the south and then to the eastward, following the camels; still resolving that we should not be separated, and bade Mr. Savage follow us, but Seid, presenting his gun, told him if he offered to go, he would blow his brains out. As Sidi Hamet, however, bade him run, he obeyed, and when he came near me we were all ordered to stop and our masters seated themselves on the ground to settle the dispute by figuring on the sand with their fingers. Here they calculated it every way Clark and Burns were again offered for Horace, but Seid would not take them: he would keep the slave he had bought with his money: "You shall not separate him from his father, (said my master) I have sworn it." "Then I will destroy him," exclaimed Seid furiously, and springing up, he seized Horace by the breast and dashed him on the ground with all his might. The force of the blow beat the breath from his body, and he lay stretched out apparently dead. Overwhelmed with the most heart-rending emotions, I sank to the earth in an agony of despair. My master observing my anguish, said, "go, Riley," pointing to the east. With tears and sobs, I told him I could not go, for Horace, my son, was dead. After a flood of tears had relieved my swelling heart, I reflected that it was useless to bewail the fate of my adopted child, as I did not know how soon it might be my turn to suffer a similar, or perhaps a more cruel death. Seid's passion now began to subside a little, and my master then went to Horace, and taking him by the hands, raised him upon his seat: his breath returned and he revived. Sidi Hamet melted into tears at the sight: I saw the big drops roll down his cheeks, while in a tender tone, he said to Horace, "go to Riley." The spot where his head fell happened to be clear of stones, which entirely covered the ground on every side, otherwise his brains must have been dashed out. I went up to him as quick as I could, and folding him in my arms, asked him if he was much hurt; but being in great pain, and his breathing being not yet perfectly restored, he was incapable of answering me: his heart, however, was in unison with mine, in thanking the Author of our being that his life was spared, and in imploring his future protection. Our masters again seated themselves, in order to discuss this affair thoroughly, and began to speak very loud, when, fortunately for us, some strangers came in sight which reminded them that their united force was necessary for the defense of themselves and their property; so they agreed to seek a village, and take counsel as to what was best to be done.

Then turning to our left up a hill, we soon came in sight of a village, and entered it by passing between high walls. Having come to its farther extremity, an old, but a very respectable looking man, (a Moor) of a light olive colour, came out of his gate, and welcomed our masters, saluting them, (as is customary) and seeing us behind, told us to sit down in a shade formed by his wall, and rest ourselves; adding, "I will give you some food." We accordingly all seated ourselves, and while the food was preparing, our host inquired much about me and my men, and wished to know how I could make myself understood, (being a Christian.) Our owners told him all our stories, together with my promises, which they made me repeat in his presence. They wanted again to know in what my property consisted; if I had any money in my own country, or a house; how much money, how many

horses, cows, sheep, goats, asses, camels, &c.? and
lastly what number of wives and children I had. Having answered all these interrogations to their satisfaction, they made me tell what Mr. Savage, Horace,
Clark, and Burns, were worth to me? how much property I thought they had in their own country? and
our host who spoke a few words of broken Spanish, asked me if Swearah was not called *Mogdola* by
the English ? I answered in the affirmative:—this was
the first time I had heard this name mentioned on
this continent, though I had endeavoured by inquiring of all people I had spoken with to ascertain the
point; but it appeared they had never heard of the
name. One bowl of boiled barley unhulled, was
brought out to our masters, and one for us—this last
was a very large one, and the old host told us to eat,
saying, *"coole rais,"* (*eat captain.*) We had now before us for the first time, enough of this food, and
falling to with keen appetites, we filled our stomachs,
and were satisfied, leaving some in the bowl, which
they tried hard to make us finish, but we could not.
Sidi Hamet would not trust himself again with his
brother, without having some person in company to
take his part: so he hired a stout young fellow, named
Bo-Mohammed, to go along with us to another place
or village, not far distant, and we set off for it, travelling at first down towards the sea-coast, and passing
along a kind of sandy beach where the salt water
flowed in at high tides, we saw there, under the side
of a shelving rock, two boiling springs of fresh water,
which formed a considerable stream. This was the
first spring I had seen in this country, and having
taken a good drink and watered our camels, we proceeded toward the south-east among sands that had
drifted from the sea-beach; there we remained until
it was nearly dark, our masters fearing, as it were, to
go forward. About dark we resumed our course, and
soon afterwards arrived at a village, where, while
the barking of numerous dogs announced to their

owners the arrival of strangers, a grave looking man
came out, and silencing the curs, bade our masters
welcome, and invited both them and us to sit down
near his walls, until he should prepare some supper.
We had no desire, however, for food, some of us having oppressed our stomachs to such a degree with the
boiled barley, as to be racked with pain, and scarce
able to breathe, particularly Mr. Savage. Our present
host, (whose name I soon learned was *Sidi Mohammed)* after causing a mat to be spread near his wall,
seated himself and our masters theron, and desired
me to come and do the same. He now made similar
enquiries to those made by the former persons we
met, and I satisfied his curiosity as well as I could.
He then informed me he had been many times in
Swearah, and had seen the consuls, and wished me to
repeat my promise to Sidi Hamet which I did. He
had a lamp for a light, so that he could see every
motion that I made well enough to comprehend me
entirely. By this time some cakes had been baked,
which were presented to our masters, and of which
they gave us some: these cakes were made of barley
meal, ground coarse; yet it was bread, and it being
the first we had seen, we ate a little of it, though our
stomachs were not yet prepared to enjoy the treat.
After they had eaten and washed their hands and
feet, and talked over their affairs, Sidi Hamet again
called me to him, and told me he should set out in
the morning for Swearah in company with our host
Sidi Mohammed, where he hoped, with God's blessing, to arrive in three days, for he should travel on a
mule, *bugelah,* and push on night and day: that I
must write a letter to my friend, which he would
carry, and said he, "if your friend will fulfill your
engagements and pay the money for you and your
men, you shall be free; if not, you must die-for having deceived me, and your men shall be sold for what
they will bring. I have fought for you, (added he)
have suffered hunger, thirst, and fatigue, to restore

you to your family, for I believe God is with you. I have paid away all my money on your word alone: Seid and Bo-Mohammed will stay and guard you during my absence; they will give you as much *khobs* (bread) and *phash* (pudding) as you can eat; so go and sleep till morning." This night was spent on my part in a state of anxiety not easy to conceive: to whom should I write ? I knew nobody at Mogadore, and yet I must take my chance. I remembered my remarkable dream—it had literally come to pass thus far,—why should I doubt its whole accomplishment; yet I could not rest.

CHAPTER XIX.

*They author writes a letter—Sidi Hamet sets out for
Swearah—the arrival of Sheick Ali,
an extraordinary character*

EARLY the next morning we were called up and directed to go within the gates. My master said to me—"come, Riley, write a letter," giving me at the same time a scrap of paper, not so wide as my hand, and about eight inches long; he had also got a little black staining liquid and a reed to write with. I now begged hard to be taken along with him, but he would not consent, though I told him I would leave my son, whom I loved more than myself, behind me as an hostage, and three men; but all would not do, the thing was determined on. He then told me, that what I had agreed to give him was not sufficient; that

I must tell my friend, in the letter, to pay two hundred dollars for myself, two hundred for Horace, two hundred for Aaron, one hundred and sixty for Clark, and the same for Burns, adding that I had promised him a good double-barrelled gun, and I must give him that, and one to Seid also. "Seid is a bad man, (said he) but helped to save your life, and must have a gun." So I took the reed, and wrote on the slip of paper, as near as I can recollect, the following letter.

"SIR,

"The brig Commerce from Gibraltar for America, was wrecked on Cape Bajador, on the 28th August last; myself and four of my crew are here nearly naked in barbarian slavery: I conjure you by all the ties that bind man to man, by those of kindred blood, and every thing you hold most dear, and by as much as liberty is dearer than life, to advance the money required for our redemption, which is nine hundred and twenty dollars, and two double barrelled guns: I can draw for any amount, the moment I am at liberty, on Batard, Sampson, & Sharp, London—Cropper & Benson, Liverpool—Munroe & Burton, Lisbon, or on Horatio Sprague, Gibraltar. Should you not relieve me, my life must instantly pay the forfeit. I leave a wife and five helpless children to deplore my death. My companions are Aaron R. Savage, Horace Savage, James Clark, and Thomas Burns. I left six more in slavery on the desert. My present master, Sidi Hamet, will hand you this, and tell you where we are—he is a worthy man. Worn down to the bones by the most dreadful of all sufferings—naked and a slave, I implore your pity, and trust that such distress will not be suffered to plead in vain. For God's sake, send an interpreter and a guard for us, if that is possible. I speak French and Spanish.

JAMES RILEY, *late Master and Supercargo of the brig Commerce.*

While I was writing the above, they procured an additional scrap of paper, being a part of a Spanish bill of lading, on which I wrote a part of my letter, that could not be written legibly on the first scrap. Having folded them up, I directed them to the "English, French, Spanish, or American consuls, or any Christian merchants in Mogadore or Swerah." I purposely omitted mentioning that we were Americans, because I did not know that there was an American agent there, and I had no doubt of there being an English consul or agent in that place. My master was hurrying me while I was writing, and both he and my host, Seid, and the young man, and many others who stood by, were surprised to see me make the Arabic numerals; for the characters we use in arithmetic are no other than the real ancient Arabic figures, which have served them for thousands of years; they remarked to each other that I must have been a slave before, to some Arabian who had taught me the use of them, contrary to their law, because he had found me to be a smart active fellow. My master taking my letter, then mounted one mule, and Sidi Mohammed another, and rode off together very fast to the east.

We remained here seven days, during which time they kept us shut up in the yard in the day time, where the cows, sheep, and asses rested, and at night they locked us up in a dreary cellar. Seid and Bo Mohammed guarded us all the day, not because they feared we would attempt to escape, but because some of the neighbouring people might steal and run off with us, and in the night they lay on their arms outside the door, to prevent a surprise. We had as much barley-bread twice a day as we wanted, l'hash once a day and plenty of water. This food, though palatable, produced and kept up a continual dysentery; our bowels seemed to ferment like beer, and we were tortured with cholics. Our numerous sores

had now time to heal, and our bodies became mostly
skinned over before our masters returned; but the
hoemorroids distressed us extremely. All the inhabitants who lived near, and all those who heard that
Christians were in the place, (for they call all Europeans Christians) came to see us. Some were very
familiar, and all wished to know if we were
mechanics: from that circumstance I concluded that
mechanics were very much wanted, and of great importance among these people, and that there would
be no possibility of getting clear of them, if once
they should find out our usefulness in that way. I
therefore told them that we were all brought up
sailors from our childhood, and knew no other business. One tried to make me lay out and hew a pair
of posts for a door to a house that was building within the wall of the village, and gave me a line to
measure the length of them, and tried to teach me to
span it off; but I would not understand him. They
next put a kind of adze into my hand, and bade me
fit the posts in. I took the tool, and began to cut at
random, gouging out a piece here, and splitting it
there, doing more hurt than good; and, at the same
time, by my awkward and clumsy manner, taking
care to make them believe that I could do no better.
Some were satisfied that I had done my very best, but
by far the greater part of them were of opinion that
a smart application of the whip would put my mechanical powers into complete operation, and I
really expected they would apply this stimulus; for
one of them ran and fetched a stout stick, and was
about to lay it on, when Bo Mohammed, who represented Sidi Hamet, interfered and saved me from a
cudgelling. Mr. Savage, Clark, Burns, and Horace,
were each tried in their turns, who following my in-
structions, were soon relieved from all further requi-
sition. From this circumstance it is evident, that the
less useful a Christian makes himself when a slave

to the Arabs, especially in a mechanical way, the less value they will set upon him, and he will not only have a chance of getting ransomed, but it may be effected on easier terms than otherwise; for I am fully convinced, that if we had shown ourselves capable in those arts, which the Arabs highly prize, such as carpenters, smiths shoemakers, &c. &c. we should have been sold at high prices, and soon carried away beyond the possibility of redemption.

Four days after Sidi Hamet's departure, some papers were shown to me by one of the men who lived in the neighbourhood, which I found on examination, to be, first, the register of the Spanish schooner *Maria*, issued by the custom-house at Cadiz in May 1814; second—a bill of sale of the same schooner, made out at the Island of Grand Canary in 1812, of the same date with the Register. Many articles of clothing that had belonged to her crew were also shown me; and the topmast, jib-boom, and other small spars of a vessel, served to support the floor over our nightly prison. I made enquiries as far as it was possible, in order to find out something respecting this vessel, which I presumed must have been wrecked near this place; and was informed that the preceeding year a schooner anchored on this part of the coast to catch fish, and to trade; that these people found means to get alongside of her in the night in boats, and after killing the captain and three men, got possession of her; when having taken out the money and other valuables, they cut her cables, and ran her on shore: that they then made the surviving part of the crew assist in tearing the wreck to pieces, and in carrying it up to build houses with. I asked how many people were on board her, and where the remainder of the crew were; and was informed by a serious looking old man, that it consisted of seventeen souls at first; that four were slain in the conflict when she was captured; that five more had died since, and that the remaining eight were a great way off to the southeast, where they were employed in working on the land and making houses. Others said, they had gone to Swearah, and from thence to their own country; but I could easily perceive by their looks that those poor fellows had either been massacred, or were now held in slavery, where neither the voice of liberty, nor the hand of friendship, was ever likely to reach them. The people here both old and young, could speak many words of Spanish, though they did not know their meaning, but made use of them at a venture at all times—these were a set of the very coarsest and most vulgar words the Spanish language affords, and had been uttered, no doubt by poor unfortunate slaves, natives of Spain, when they were suffering the greatest misery, and when excrating these savages. One young fellow spoke several words of English, such as "good morning—good night," &c. and was master of a considerable list of curses. He one day came up to Mr. Savage, and said—"button, cut it wit a nif," and at the same time laid hold of a button on his pantaloons. Mr. Savage was very much surprised to hear a language he could understand, but these words and the oaths and curses, constituted the whole of his English education. Every person here had either a long knife or a scimitar always slung by his side. Among the rest several negroes came to look at us, some of whom were slaves and some free, and they were all Mohammedans—these were allowed to sit on a mat beside our masters, and make remarks on us as we were placed among the fresh manure at a short distance. Seid desired to know what we called black men; I told him *negroes;* at which name the negroes seemed very indignant, and much enraged.

On the sixth day of my master's absence, a man arrived and took up his lodging with our guards—he was about six feet in height, and proportionably

stout; his colour was something between that of a
negro and an Arab; when he came in he was saluted
by Seid and the others in company by the name of
Sheick Ali, (or Ali the chief.) This man possessed
talents of that superior cast which never fail to
command the greatest respect, and at the same time
to inspire dread, awe, and reverance. He appeared to
be only a guest or visitor. In his deportment he was
grave and dignified: he raised his voice on occasions
terribly, and spoke in tones almost of thunder; yet
when he wished to please by condescension and
courtesy, it thrilled on the ear like sounds of softest
music; his manner and air were very commanding,
and his whole aspect and demeanour bore the stamp
of the most daring courage and unflinching firmness.
He was the most eloquent man I had ever heard
speak; persuasion dwelt upon his tongue; while he
spoke, all the company observed the most profound
silence, and with open mouths seemed to inhale his
honied sentences. He pronounced with the most
perfect emphasis; the elegant cadence so much admired in eastern oratory seemed to have acquired
new beauties from his manner of delivery: his artic-
ulation was so clear and distinct, and his countenance
and actions so intelligent and expressive, that I could
understand him perfectly, though he spoke in the
Arabic language. He would settle all controverted
points among the disputants when applied to, in
an instant, and yet with the utmost gracefulness and
dignity. This extraordinary chief was often conversing in a low tone of voice with Seid respecting me
and my men—he said he believed me to be a very
artful fellow, and capable of any action either good
or bad; and said he did not doubt but my friends
would raise any sum of money that might be demanded for my ransom. He regretted very much that
he had not seen Sidi Hamet before he set out for
Swearah, and concluded to remain with us until his

return. He questioned me very particularly as to
my country, my friends, family, property, &c.—he
also wished to know all the story of my shipwreck,
and was very curious to find out what quantity of
money and what other property fell into the hands
of those who first met with us after the vessel was
wrecked, and what crime was committed to induce
these Moslemin to kill Antonio. He next examined
our bodies all over, and on one of Clark's arms his
attention was arrested by a cross, and several other
marks of Christian insignia that had been pricked
in with Indian ink, in the manner of the Spanish
and other sailors; the stain remained entire, though
the skin had many times been changed, and now
seemed tight over the bone. This being a conclusive
proof in the Sheick's mind of *Christianity*, he pronounced him "a Spaniard," and said he should not
be redeemed, but must go to the mountains and work
with him. Every thing that this man said, seemed
to carry with it a weight that bore down all opposition.

We had, during Sidi Hamet's absence, (after the
fifth day) been in constant expectation of receiving
news from him, or that he himself would return, and
our keepers inquired of every stranger who came
from the eastward, if they had seen him, but obtained no news until the seventh day, when one of
the most fierce and ill-looking men I had ever beheld,
approached the wall, and hailed Seid by name, ordering him in an imperious tone to open the gate directly. Seid demanded to know who he was—he replied, *Ullah Omar;* that he came from Swearah, and
had met Sidi Hamet near that place, who requested
him to call and tell Seid where he was, and that God
had prospered his journey so far. The gate was now
opened and the stranger entered: he was of a dark
complexion, nearly six feet in height, and extremely
muscular; had a long musket in his hand, a pair of

horse pistols hanging in his belt, and a scimitar and two long knives slung by his sides, with the haick or blanket for a dress, and a large white turban on his head; he had a pair of long iron spurs, which were fastened to his slippers of yellow Morocco leather; he rode a beautiful horse, which seemed fleet and vigorous, and he appeared to be about forty years of age. This was the first man I had seen harnessed in this way. Sheick Ali knew him, and shook him most cordially by the hand, and after exchanging salutations all round, hearing I was the captain, he addressed me, and told me he had seen my friend, Sidi Hamet; that he met him within one day's ride of Swearah; that he would no doubt be here on the morrow, for that God had prospered his journey on account of me, and added, that he hoped my friend in Swearah or Mogdola would be as true to me as Sidi Hamet was: he then spoke to all my men, who, though they did not understand him, were rejoiced to hear through me, that there was a prospect of my master's returning soon. This man had two powder horns slung from his neck, and a pouch in which he carried a wooden pipe and some tobacco, besides a plentiful supply of leaden balls and slugs. My shipmates wanted some tobacco very much, and I asked him for a little, upon which he gave me a handful of very good tobacco, and seemed exceedingly pleased to have it in his power to administer comfort to such miserable beings. I imagined from his whole deportment that he resembled one of those highspirited, heroic, and generous robbers, that are so admirably described in ancient history. Seid furnished him with some food, which I now learned they called *cous-koo-soo*, with some slices of pumpion or squash spread over it in the bowl, and well peppered. This dish, which is made of small balls of flour, boiled with a fowl and vegetables, looked (for I had not the pleasure of tasting it) like a very nice dish.

After they had washed, drank water, eaten, washed again, and prayed together, Ullah Omar took his leave. During the whole of the time we remained here, our keepers washed themselves all over with water twice a day, before mid-day and evening prayers, and always washed their hands before and after eating.

The state of my mind, in the meantime, can be more easily conceived than described: during this day and the next, which was the eighth, I longed to know my fate; and yet I must own, I trembled at the thoughts of what it might be, and at the conditions I had myself proposed at my last purchase, and had so often since confirmed. If my master should find no one who should be willing to pay the money for my redemption, my fate was sealed. I had already agreed to have my throat cut! this could not be prevented; yet when I made this agreement I was naked and on a vast and dreary desart, literally without a skin; my remaining flesh was roasted on my body; not a drop of fresh water to quench my burning thirst, nor even an herb or any other thing to satisfy the cravings of hunger: my life was fast wasting away, and there was not even a hope remaining, or a possibility of existing long in my then forlorn condition: both myself and my companions would have sold our lives for a drink of fresh water or a morsel of bread. In that most dismal and desperate situation, I imagined that if I could once get to the cultivated country beyond the desart, I should find some food to support nature, and fresh water to allay our thirst. My remarkable dream had also given me courage to hope for redemption; but if I was not redeemed myself, I felt it my duty to exert myself to the utmost to preserve the lives of my shipmates; they might some of them, I fancied, possibly survive, even though I should not, and be at length restored to their country and friends, in consequence of my exertions, and convey to my distressed family the sad things of my wretched fate. Circumstances were now changed; I had passed the dangers of the desert, and arrived in the cultivated country; we had now plenty of good water, and some food and shelter; and though my flesh was nearly all wasted away, yet a new skin had succeeded and nearly covered my bones. My desire to live kept pace with the increase of my comforts; I longed for the return of my master, and yet I anticipated it with the most fearful and dreadful apprehensions. I could not sleep; alternate hope and fear kept me in a state of continual agitation. I calculated on the moment of his arrival as decisive of my fate. It would either restore me to liberty, or doom me to instant death; I trembled at every noise occasioned by the opening of the gate on any new arrival.

CHAPTER XX.

*A Moor arrives from Mogadore, bringing a letter—
the letter—they set out for that city*

THE eighth day of my master's absence passed tediously away; when after dark we heard a trampling outside the walls: Seid went forth to learn its cause, and soon returned with Sidi Mohammed, followed by a well looking Moor: they came directly to that part of the yard where we were sitting on the ground, trembling with apprehension and with cold. When they came near me, the Moor called out and said in English, "How de-do, Capetan." This raised

me and all my men from the ground; I felt as if my
heart was forcing its way up into my throat, and it
entirely obstructed my breath. I eagerly seized his
hand, and begged to know who he was, and what was
my doom, and if Sidi Hamet had come back; he then
asked me in Spanish if I spoke that language, and
being answered in the affirmative, he informed me
in Spanish, that he came from Mogadore; that my
letter had been received by one of the best of men,
an Englishman, who was his friend, and who had
shed tears on reading my letter: that he had paid
the money to my master immediately, and had sent
him (the Moor) off, without giving him scarcely a
moment's time to take leave of his wife, and that he
had been on his mule ever since he left Swearah,
travelling on as fast as possible, night and day. The
anxiety of my companions by this time had risen to
such a pitch that they broke in upon his story, on
which I communicated to them the thrice welcome
and happy intelligence, that we had a friend who
would redeem us from slavery. Our souls were overwhelmed with joy, and yet we trembled with apprehension lest it might not be true: alas! perhaps it was
only a delusive dream, or some cruel trick to turn
our miseries into mockery. At this moment however
the Moor handed me a letter: I broke it open; but
my emotions were such, that it was impossible for
me to read its contents, and I handed it to Mr. Savage: for my frame trembled to such a degree, that
I could not stand, and I sank to the earth, but, thank
God, not senseless; while by means of the light of a
fire, he read as follows:—

Mogadore, October 25, 1815.
MY DEAR AND AFFLICTED SIR,
    I have this moment received your two notes
by *Sidi Hamet*, the contents of which, I hope, you
will be perfectly assured have called forth my most

sincere pity for your sufferings and those of your companions in captivity.

By a Gibraltar paper I discover, under the arrivals from the 5th to the 11th August, the name of your vessel, and that she was American, from which I conclude both you and your crew must be subjects of the United States: had it not been for the paper adverted to, some delay would have occured, as you do not state in your notes to what nation you belong.

I congratulate you most sincerely on the good fortune you and your fellow sufferers have met, by being in the hands of a man who seems to be guided by some degree of commiseration.

I can in some measure participate in the severe and dangerous sufferings and hardships you must have undergone; but, my dear Sir, console yourself, for, thanks be to God, I hope they will soon have a happy issue; for which purpose I devoutly pray the great Disposer of all things will give you and your unfortunate companions health and strength once more to visit your native land.

This letter will be delivered you by *Rais bel Cossim,* in whom you may place the fullest faith; he speaks Spanish, and has directions to pay attention to your orders, and render you every care your severe misfortunes may require:—be pleased to write me an immediate answer, stating every particular relating to yourself, your crew, and vessel, as I have given orders to the Moor to forward it to me without delay.

I have agreed to pay the sum of nine hundred and twenty hard dollars to Sidi Hamet on your safe arrival in this town with your fellow sufferers; he remains here as a kind of hostage for your safe appearance.

I have been induced to trust implicitly to your word, and the respectable references you have given, in confidence that those gentlemen, or yourself, will readily reimburse me the whole of the expenses that may be incurred in obtaining your redemption.

I have the most sincere pleasure to acquaint you, you will be at liberty to commence your journey for this town on the receipt of this letter, and make what stages you please on the road, as I do not advise you, in the eagerness all of you must feel, to run into danger by over-exertion and fatigue: I would, therefore, recommend the greatest precaution on this point. I have sent under charge of Rais bel Cossim, shoes and cloaks, which I have no doubt you will find very useful in preserving you from rain or cold on the road.

I have also forwarded you some provisions and spirits, that you may enjoy a foretaste of returning liberty.

I beg to recommend the greatest secrecy of your circumstances until your arrival here, for should the Moors suppose you able to pay more, they would throw difficulties in the way, and thereby much retard your redemption.

I shall send off an express to-morrow to the United States' Consul General at Tangier, and a letter to Mr. Horatio Sprague of Gibraltar, informing them of your loss, and of the favourable hopes I entertain of your immediate release.

I have appointed with *Rais bel Cossim,* on your arrival at a short distance from Mogadore, to wait at the garden of a friend of mine, and send me notice of the same, when I shall immediately set out to meet you.

I trust there is no occasion for me to say how truly I commiserate and enter into all your misfortunes: when God grants me the pleasure to embrace you, it will be to me a day of true rejoicing.—I beg you will assure every one with you of my truest regard; and with sentiments embittered by the thoughts of the miseries you have undergone, but with the most sanguine hope of a happy end to all your sufferings, I subscribe myself, with the greatest esteem, my dear Sir, your friend,   WILLIAM WILLSHIRE.

P. S. I willingly agree to advance the money, considering a month or more must elapse before I could receive an answer from Mr. Sprague. I therefore concluded you would prefer being at liberty in this town, to experiencing a prolongation of your sufferings during that period. I shall be happy in rendering you every comfort that my house and this country can afford.   W.W.

My feelings, during the reading of this letter, may perhaps be conceived, but I cannot attempt to describe them; to form an idea of my emotions at that time, it is necessary for the reader to transport himself in imagination to the country where I then was, a wretched slave, and to fancy himself as having passed through all the dangers and distresses that I had experienced: reduced to the lowest pitch of human wretchedness, degradation, and despair, a skinless skeleton, expecting death at every instant: then let him fancy himself receiving such a letter from a perfect stranger, whose name he had never before heard, and from a place where there was not an individual creature that had ever before heard of his existence, and in one of the most barbarous regions of the habitable globe: let him receive at the same time clothes to cover and defend his naked, emaciated and trembling frame, shoes for his mangled feet, and such provisions as he had been accustomed to in his happier days—let him find a soothing and sympathising friend in a barbarian, and one who spoke perfectly well the language of a Christian nation; and with all this, let him behold a prospect of a speedy liberation and restoration to his beloved family:—here let him pause, and his heart must, like mine, expand near to bursting with gratitude to his all-wise and beneficent Creator, who had upheld his tottering frame and preserved in his bosom the vital spark, while he conducted him, with unerring wisdom and goodness, through the greatest perils and sufferings, by a continued miracle, and now prepared the heart of a stranger to accomplish what had been before determined.

The letter being finished, we could only raise our eyes and hearts to heaven in adoration and silent thankfulness, while tears of joy trickled down our haggard cheeks. Amidst these joyful and heart thrilling sensations, my attention was aroused by the thundering voice of *Sheick Ali*, who stormed away most furiously on being informed that Sidi Hamet had given me and my companions for such a paltry sum: —he said, Sidi Hamet must be a fool and a madman to put himself in the power of a villanous Christian, who would undoubtedly murder him and take back his money so soon as we should arrive in Swearah. The Moor, who had hitherto remained silent, now spoke out in a very spirited manner, and told the Sheick in a very firm, but eloquent and persuasive tone, that he had bought me and my companions with his own money, which he had paid to Sidi Hamet before he left Swearah; and that he (Sidi Hamet) remained there voluntarily as a hostage for his (*Rais bel Cossim's*) safety, as well as security for the delivery of the slaves.

"We are of the same religion, (added Rais) and owe these Christian dogs nothing; we have an undoubted right to make merchandise of them, and oblige them to carry our burdens like camels. That fellow (said he, pointing to me) calls himself the captain of a vessel,—he has deceived his master and you; for he was nothing more than cook on board, and the captain has long been dead." This the Sheick would not believe; if it was so, how could I write a note to induce a stranger to pay so much

money for me and my men? "It was only a short one,
(added he) and its writer must be a man of much
consequence, as well as knowledge. I fear you
(though a Moslemin) have leagued with a Christian
against Sidi Hamet, first to rob him of his slaves, and
then to take his life." "No—by Allah! I am incapable
of such an act of treachery," (retorted Rais) and told
the Sheick I was indeed the cook, but being a stout
fellow, had been able to endure fatigues better than
the others: "but (added he) give them paper, pen,
and ink, and they will soon convince you they can all
write, and much better than Riley." This contro-
versy continued a long time, and I found that Rais
bel Cossim was a man of great courage, as well as
knowledge and eloquence; and he certainly displayed great address and management in checking
the avaricious calculations of the Sheick, by insisting
upon my not being a captain, and thus depreciating
my value as a slave. Seid seemed to have sunken into
a kind of sullen silence; it was now late, and Sidi
Mohammed conducted the whole company into an
apartment that had served, from appearances, as a
stable for mules. They had loudly insisted that we
should lodge in the same place where we had been
before confined, but Rais would not consent, and
declared that his slaves should stay by his side, both
night and day. They had cost him a great deal of
money, (he said) and he was determined not to lose
them. Having thus got into comfortable quarters,
our cloaks were produced from a basket, and we put
them on. Our friend had sent us some hard biscuits,
and boiled meats' tongues—he had also forwarded
tea, coffee, and sugar, and a few bottles of rum, with a
tea-kettle, tea-pot, cups and saucers, all nicely packed
up in a small box. Rais then procured a lighted lamp,
and I gave each of my men a slice of tongue, some biscuit, and a drink of rum:—this revived their spirits
exceedingly, and we all felt as if new life was infused into our hearts, which at the same time swelled

with gratitude to God for his infinite mercy and
goodness. We were next regaled with a very fine
water-melon; and having put on our new shoes to
make our feet warm, and wrapped ourselves up in
large cloaks or *gzlabbias*, we stretched ourselves on
the ground to sleep, whilst Rais, Seid, and his companion, Bo-Mohammed, and Sheick Ali, laid themselves down on a platform made of boards that must
have been brought from the wreck of some vessel,
and was raised two feet from the ground. The food
which I and my companions had eaten, together with
the melon and liquor, caused us such violent griping
pains in our stomachs and intestines, that we could
with great difficulty forbear screaming out with
agony, and we found no relief till morning, after
having passed a sleepless night.

Early in the morning, Rais desired me, in Arabic,
to make some tea—so I took out the kettle, had it
filled with water, made a fire with a few sticks, and
soon had the tea ready for drinking. The men and
boys in and near this village, hearing of Sidi Mohammed's return to his family, came now to congratulate
him and to see the Moor, who directed me to pour
out a cup of tea for each of the men, which he made
thick with sugar. None of the people had ever before
seen such a thing as a tea-cup, nor knew what the
taste of tea was, and it was with difficulty that several
of them could be persuaded to drink it, and they
appeared to be reconciled to it only on account of
the sugar. I waited on them all until they had finished; when Rais, returning to Sheick Ali, said, "I
told you before that Riley was the cook, and now
you see with your own eyes that he is the only one
that can wait upon us." I next made a strong cup
of tea for ourselves, which had a most remarkable
effect in composing and restoring the tone of our
stomachs.

All our things being soon packed up and loaded on
mules we set forward at about eight o'clock. The

Moor had tried to procure mules for us to ride on; but they could not be had in this part of the country at any price. Our company consisted of *Sheick Ali, Sidi Mohammed,* (who had been to Swearah on our account) Seid, our master, *Bo-Mohammed,* (who had assisted in guarding us) and *Rais bel Cossim,* all well armed. Though he could procure no beasts, exclusively for our use, yet Rais managed in such a manner as to let us ride by turns, and Burns all the time, for he was so feeble as not to be able to walk. So soon as we were on the road, Rais bel Cossim begged me to give him an account of my misfortunes and sufferings, and by what miracle my life and the lives of those who were with me had been preserved—I satisfied his curiosity as well as I could by a short narration of the most prominent occurrences. When I had finished, he raised his eyes towards heaven with an air and expression of true devotion, and exclaimed in Spanish, "Praised be God, the most high and holy! for his goodness:" then addressing himself to me, he remarked, "You have indeed been preserved most wonderfully by the peculiar protection and assistance of an overruling Providence, and must be a particular favourite of heaven: there never was an instance (added he) of a Christian's passing the great desart for such a distance before, and you are no doubt destined to do some great good in the world; and may the Almighty continue to preserve you, and restore you to your distressed family. Sidi Hamet (added he) admired your conduct, courage, and intelligence, and says they are more than human —that God is with you in all your transactions, and has blessed him for your sake." I mention this conversation to show the light in which my master had viewed me; and this will account for the interest he took in my restoration to liberty, over and above his motives of gain.

I now inquired who Sheick Ali was, and why he

was going on in company; and said, I much feared him. Rais informed me that all he knew about him, he had learned from Sidi Mohammed, which was, that he is the chief of a very large and powerful tribe of Arabs, who inhabit the hills south of us, and near the borders of the great desert; that Sidi Hamet had married one of his daughters, but had since been at war with him, and that in the contest his father-in-law had destroyed Sidi Hamet's town, and taken back his daughter, but afterwards restored her again on making peace—that this Sheick could bring ten or fifteen thousand men into the field whenever he pleased, and that he was a man of the greatest talents and capacity in war, as well as in peace; but why he was going on in our company in this manner, he could not tell, and agreed with me in suspecting that it could be for no good purpose, yet he observed, "God could turn his evil intentions to our good, and that that power which had protected me thus far, would not forsake me until his will was accomplished."

CHAPTER XXI.

They come near the ruins of a city where two battering machines are standing—description of them—story of its destruction—they cross a river, and a fruitful country—lodge in a city, and are afterwards stopped by Sheick Ali and the Prince of another city

WE travelled on in a south-east direction through a very sandy country, with however here and there a small rising, and a few cultivated spots, for about five hours, at the rate of five miles an hour, when we came opposite the shattered walls of a desolate town or city that stood not far from our path on the right. These walls appeared to inclose a square spot of about three hundred yards in extent on each side, and they seemed to be at least fifteen feet in height. They were built of rough stones, laid in clay or mud, and partly daubed over with the same material. On the north side there was a gateway handsomely arched over with stone, and furnished with a strong heavy-looking wooden gate that was now shut. Over the gate there appeared to be a platform for the purpose of defending the gate, for the wall was not quite so high in that part as elsewhere. Two battering machines were standing against the western angle of the wall, opposite to which a large practicable breach had been made by means of one of those machines. They were both very simple in their structure, but calculated to be very powerful in their effects. I could distinctly see and examine with my eyes the one nearest to us. It was formed, as it appeared to me, in the first place, by laying down two large logs of wood at right angles with the wall, and about fifteen feet apart, the ends of the logs butting against the wall. (See plate, figure 4.) Into the upper side of each of these logs a nitch or mortise was cut to receive the thick ends of two uprights, consisting of two rough trunks of trees, of about twelve inches in diameter at their base, of equal lengths, and rising to the height of about twenty-five or thirty feet. Each upright had a crotch in its upper end, formed by the natural branching of the two principal limbs of the tree, like a common country well-post in America. These crotches being rounded out by art, a stout piece of knotty timber of about from twelve to eighteen inches in thickness was placed horizontally in them. To the centre of the cross-piece a pole of ten or twelve inches in circumference was lashed with a strong rope, and to the lower end of this pole, a huge rough rock was fastened, weighing from appearances several tons. The rock was slung and fastened to the pole by means of thick ropes, formed by braiding many thongs of camels' skins together. After the machine had been fitted together on the ground, it had been raised all in a body by the help of long shores or sticks of timber, not so thick as the uprights, but nearly twice as long; these shores were tied fast to the uprights, near their crotches by ropes, and several to raise and lower the machine at pleasure, and also acted as braces to support it when in action. Two short props or braces were fixed between the uprights and the wall, with one end resting against its base, and the other in a notch cut on the inner side of the uprights to help to keep them steady, and prevent them from falling against the walls. The rock hung within two or three feet of the ground like a huge pendulum; and having a long rope fastened to its slings, stretching off from the wall at least one hundred and fifty feet. The manner of applying it, was by the assailants laying hold of this rope in great numbers, and then hauling off the rock to its greatest extent; all let go at the same instant, and the rock swung back with such impetuosity against those ill-constructed walls, that its repeated strokes soon opened a breach through which the besiegers entered, sword in hand. The other machine was made of four rough sticks of timber, of nearly equal lengths, lashed together at their smallest ends, and raised in form of a common triangle, or rather a quadrangle; from the point of juncture, a large rock was suspended by a rope of camel's skin, braided to the thickness of a man's leg, and slung in such a manner as to be struck against the wall in the same way as the one first described. My companion, *Rais bel Cossim,* gave me all the information I desired relative to these machines. The ground about the breach and near the gate was strewed over with dry human bones; and my curiosity being much excited to know the history of this melancholy scene of carnage and desolation, I requested Rais to communicate to me the particulars; but not being, it seems, acquainted with them himself, he applied to Sidi Mohammed on the subject, who thereupon gave the following relation, while Rais translated into Spanish for me such parts as I did not perfectly understand in Arabic, by which means I was enabled thoroughly to comprehend the whole narrative.

"That city (said Sidi Mohammed, pointing towards it with his staff,) was built by *Omar Raschid*, about forty years ago; he named it *Widnah*. He was a very brave and pious man: and the number of his family and friends, consisting at first of no more than five hundred souls, when the city was built, increased so rapidly, that in a few years they amounted to several thousands: they planted those fig, date, pomegranate, olive, and other trees which you now see near the walls; they cultivated the fields round about, and made gardens; had abundance of bread, beasts, and cattle of every kind, and became exceedingly rich and great for God was with them. In all their transactions, they were respected, loved, and feared by all their neighbours, because they were wise and just. This man was called *Omar el Milliah*, (or Omar the good;) he was my best friend when living (said Sidi) and helped me when I was very low in the world, but the best men have enemies—so it was with *Omar;* he had an inveterate enemy from his youth, who lived among the mountains to the southward of his city whose name was *Sheick Sulmin*. This Sheick, about twenty years ago, came down with a great host and invested the city of Omar, but Omar taking advantage of the darkness of the night, sailed

out of his city at a private passage, with all his forces,
and falling upon his besiegers unawares, killed a
great number, and put the remainder to a shameful
flight—from that time until the time of his death,
(which happened two years ago) he enjoyed a profound peace on every side. After Omar's death, his
eldest son, *Muley Ismael,* (for he caused himself to
be called a prince) took upon him the government
of the city. He was a very effeminate man, entirely
devoted to sensual pleasure, and had a great number
of wives and concubines. The people had long enjoyed a profound peace, and confided in their
strength; when about a year ago one of the brothers
of Ismael, named *Kesh-bah,* who was very ambitious,
and being fired with resentment at the conduct of
Muley Ismael, in taking away from him his be-
trothed wife, left the city and repaired to the mountains, where having found his father's old enemy still
living, he stirred him up to war against the city. The
old Sheick soon collected a powerful army of hungry
and rapacious Arabs on the borders of the desert, and
came down the mountains, bringing on their camels
the battering machines you now see standing there.
When this host approached the city, it was in the
dead of the night and all within were asleep, for
they dwelt carelessly and dreamed of no danger, and
felt so secure, that they did not even keep a watch.
The Sheick and his host drew near the walls in perfect silence, and raised their battering machines un-
discovered: it was now nearly daylight, when both
machines were put in operation at the same instant,
and the gate was also attacked by means of large
stones hung from the upper extremities of long
poles by ropes, which poles stood up on end, and
were managed by the hands of the Arabs. The first
strokes against the walls and gate, shook them to
their very foundations, and awakened the slothful
inhabitants, who flew to the walls in order to make

a defence; but it was too late; the enemy were thundering against them; all was confusion within; those
who attacked the gate were repulsed with great
slaughter by those who mounted the platform over
it, but the walls were already shattered to pieces,
and the assailants entered the breaches over heaps
of their dead and dying enemies.

It was now daylight, and an indiscriminate slaughter of the inhabitants ensued; all was blood and carnage; every male was put to death, except two, who
escaped over the wall to carry tidings of the fate of
the town to their friends and neighbours. All the
women and children shared the same fate, except
two hundred virgins, who were spared for the use of
the conquerors. They next plundered the slain of
their clothing and ornaments; gathered up all the
spoil, and drove off the oxen, sheep, camels, and asses,
and departed, leaving the city before mid-day a heap
of ruins, covered with the mangled carcases of its
once highly favoured inhabitants: they were in such
haste as to leave the battering machines standing,
and made off by way of the plain southward. The
inhabitants of the neighbouring towns soon collected, and pursuing them with great vigour, came up
with them on the side of the mountain the next
morning, while the invaders sending forward their
spoil, took a station in a steep narrow pass, and prepared for battle. It was a very long and bloody fight,
but Sulmin's men rolled down great stones from the
precipices upon their pursuers, who were at last
forced to retreat leaving about half their number
dead and wounded on the ground."

Sidi Mohammed was one of the pursuers, and now
showed me a very large scar from a wound he then
received on his breast by a musket ball. *Sidi Ishem*,
a very powerful prince, had in the mean time heard
the news, and assembled a very large army, and pursued the enemy by another way; but they had fled

to the desert and could not be overtaken. The dead
bodies in and about the city had become so putrid
before the pursuit was over, that none could approach to bury them, and they were devoured by
dogs, and wild beasts, and birds of prey. "They had
offended the Almighty by their pride, (observed
Sidi Mohammed) and none could be found to save
them. Thus perished Widnah and its haughty inhabitants."

I was at that time riding along on a mule next to
Rais bel Cossim and Sidi Mohammed, whilst the latter recounted the transaction in a most solemn tone.
My sensations at beholding the desolate ruins of a
once populous town, whose inhabitants had all been
cut off in a few hours by the unexpected irruption of
a ferocious and unsparing foe, may easily be conceived. I was at first induced to consider the story as
fictitious, but my eyes warranted the belief of it,
and the sight of the battering machines, together
with the breaches in the wall, and the dry human
bones scattered around, afforded conclusive evidence
even to the minds of my fellow-prisoners, who did
not understand the narrative, that here had once
stood a town, which had been sacked and destroyed.

After leaving these ruins, we continued on about
an east course for three hours, when we came to the
bank of a stream or fresh water river, which was
now no larger than a brook, owing to the dryness of
the season. It flowed from the south-east, and bent its
course through a broad valley in a crooked channel,
nearly north, towards the sea-shore. On its left bank,
which was very high land, stood two considerable
walled villages, and a great number of small square-
walled enclosures on the same bank southward, some
in ruins and some apparently in good repair. The
walls were made of rough stones laid in clay, and
the houses had flat roofs. On the margin of the
brook were a great number of gardens fenced in with

dry thorn bushes, placed on the ground, and planted
chiefly with the prickly-pear; but some with
squashes, cabbages, &c. At a distance on both sides
of this stream, we saw a number of square stone sanctuaries, or saint houses, with round domes:—they
did not appear to bε more than ten or fifteen feet
square, and were all nicely whitewashed. This bank
of the river bore strong marks of having been washed
to a very great height from the place where the
stream then flowed; and on inquiring of Sidi Mohammed, I was informed that the whole of the valley
between the two high banks (which from appearances must be five or six miles wide) was entirely
covered with water during some part of the season,
or when great rains fall; at which times travellers
were obliged to go up the banks three days' journey
to a fall before they could cross it: that he himself
had once been that way, but for the last five years
the land had been so cursed with droughts, that it
had not once overflowed its present bed where we
crossed it, and where it was not more than twenty
yards wide, and one foot in depth.

As we passed along close to the prickly-pears, which
hung over the thorn bushes, bearing yellow fruit,
some of my men plucked them and put them in their
mouths, without regarding the sharp prickles with
which these pears were covered, so that their tongues
and the roofs of their mouths were literally filled
with them: on the first touch, they were extremely
painful, and were extracted afterwards with much
difficulty. There were also on both sides of this river
near where we crossed it, numerous herds, and many
inhabitants. We travelled along the right bank of
the river for several miles until it became both wide
and deep, for it met the tide water from the sea;
when coming within sight of a city on the high right
bank, we made towards it. On our approaching within two miles of its walls, we passed large fields of

Indian corn and barley, and gardens filled with most kinds of common vegetables. The borders of these fields and gardens were planted with date, fig, pomegranate, orange, and other fruit trees in great numbers, and many clumps of grape vines: the soil of this spot appeared to be of the richest black mould. As we passed along in a high footway, formed by throwing up the turf from the enclosures, (apparently to make them perfectly level, or all of a gentle descent) we saw hundreds of the inhabitants busily employed in gathering the Indian corn and barley into heaps, for it was now their harvest time, while others (men and boys) were loading it in sacks and baskets on camels, mules and asses, and driving them, thus loaded with the rich products of the soil, into their city. These several enclosures contained, I should judge, one hundred acres of land, divided from each other by mud walls, strewed with dry thorn bushes; the whole were watered by means of a considerable stream brought from the heights near the city, in a large ditch, and carried round each enclosure in small gutters dug for the purpose; so that any one of the owners could either water the whole or any part of his field or garden, at pleasure. Hundreds of oxen and cows, sheep and goats, were feeding in the newly cleared fields, whose thin and famished appearance proved they had been forced to feed on scanty and dried up herbage during the summer months, and that on account of the long and excessive droughts, they had merely been able to exist. Rais also informed me, that the locusts had nipped off and destroyed nearly every verdant thing in the whole country; and that for the last five years they had laid waste whole provinces in the empire of Morocco.

We now arrived at the city, and entered it at a very large gateway, with our camels and mules, and took up our quarters in a smith's shop, near the gate. It was after sunset when we entered this town, and I could observe one broad street, that appeared to run its whole length. The houses were built of rough stones, principally laid in clay, but some in lime; all of one story high, and flat roofed; there were no windows next the street, except a small aperture in each one not a foot square, for the purpose probably of admitting light. They had each a stout plank door strongly made, and furnished with a big clumsy iron lock. The corn continued to pass into the city till dark,—all the camels, oxen, cows, sheep, goats and asses, belonging to the inhabitants, and which were very numerous, were also driven into the city, and the gate shut and barred with four large pieces of timber: this was about eight o'clock and a watch was then stationed on the wall. On entering the city, Rais bel Cossim and Sheick Ali waited on the governor or chief, and obtained permission to remain in his town over night; and a few dates were brought by Rais for our suppers. The shop in which we were permitted to stay was about twenty feet square; a kind of forge was fixed in one corner; two skins were curiously applied, so as to form a bellows to blow this fire with, which was of charcoal; a man stood between them with a hand on each skin, which he raised and depressed alternately, and thus kept up a small and irregular stream of air. They had a large piece of iron for an anvil, which lay so low on the ground, that when they worked on it with the hammer, which was a very clumsy sort of one, they were obliged to squat down. I believe every man and boy in this town came to look at us by turns, and ask questions concerning ourselves, our country, &c. so that we were surrounded with people during the whole night, chatting with each other, and asking our Arab guides an endless string of questions.

These people were of the same nation we had been in the habit of seeing since we came to the river

Nun, yet they appeared to be more civilized. Several of them asked me in Spanish, how I did? and uttered many other words in that language, the meaning of which they did not seem to understand; the most of them being vile oaths and execrations; which proved satisfactorily to me that they had had frequent communications in some way or other with people of that nation. Sheick Ali had all the day after we left Sidi Mohammed's house been lost in a seeming reverie: he would seldom speak, and when he did, it was in a low voice apart with Seid, and I strongly suspected that some plot was in preparation between them. We had travelled the last day about five hours, at the rate of four miles an hour, before we came abreast of the ruins of the city I have described, and we had proceeded five hours afterward at the same rate, making together forty miles.

On the 30th of October, we made ready to start before daylight, and as soon as it dawned, the gate was opened, and we proceeded on our journey. The walls of this city or town, were built of rough stone laid in clay, and were four feet thick at their base in the gateway, and about twenty feet high, but had no outer ditch to defend them, nor any cannon mounted. It appeared to cover a space of about three hundred yards in length along the river's bank, north and south, and one hundred and fifty yards in breadth from east to west. The channel of the river at low stages of the water is about one mile west of the town:—this river is called by the natives, *Woed Sehlem,* or *river Sehlem,* and the town, Rais told me, bore the name; i. e. *Sehlemah:* it is, I should judge from its appearance, fifty yards in width opposite the town at high water, and proportionately deep. I was now informed by Rais bel Cossim and Sidi Mohammed, that there was once a large and flourishing Christian town and settlement near the mouth of this river, and only thirty miles from us: that the town was taken by storm about eight centuries ago, and all the Christians massacred. An Arabian century contains forty lunar years, and is called *Zille,* and they reckon twelve moons to the year. Both Rais bel Cossim and Sidi Mohammed said they had been to the spot, and seen some of the remains of the walls, which were still standing, though nearly all buried up in sand drifted from the sea-shore. They further stated, that there was now a village at a little distance from the ancient ruin, inhabited by fishermen; that the old Christian town was situated on a bay or arm of the sea, and five or six miles broad at its entrance, and that it is an excellent harbour both for large and small vessels: that there was no bar across its mouth, but that the usual bar was formed of sand a few miles below the town we had left. From my own observations on the increasing breadth of the river, I am inclined to think that this bay may contain a fine harbour, particularly as Rais and his companion could have no motive for deceiving me. Rais bel Cossim had been many times in Europe as captain under the Moorish flag, in the grain trade, and insisted that this was a better harbour than Cadiz: if so, it is the only one on that coast, from Cape Spartel, in latitude 34.30. to the latitude of 19. north.

Travelling on at a great rate we entered on a vast plain, over whose surface a few shrubs, and weeds, and clumps of trees were thinly scattered: the boughs of these trees were bending under the weight of a bright yellow fruit, and I learned from Rais that it was the Arga tree, from the nut of which is extracted the Argan oil, very much esteemed by the natives; and it was also highly relished by my companions. This nut, when ripe, much resembles the ripe date in appearance; so much so, indeed, that seeing some of them scattered on the ground, I took one up and bit it, when I found out my mistake, as its bark was extremely bitter. The trees generally

grew in clusters of from three to ten trunks, that
seemed to spring from the same seed: these rise in a
shaft of from ten to fifteen feet in height: and then
branch off in all directions, forming a diameter of at
least one hundred feet; the trunks are from one to
three feet in diameter; the branches are covered with
thorns, which fall and lie so thick on the ground, as
to make it almost impossible to approach them near
enough to shake or knock off the nuts, and they are
consequently left to ripen and drop off spontaneously.

We were now going on at a small trot, mostly all
mounted on the camels, mules, and two asses that
were in company. The Atlas mountains were now
full in view, stretching as far as the eye could reach
from N. E. to S. W. at some distance on our right.
We had seen these mountains for several days past,
in the distant horizon, when we were on the high
ridges, which we were obliged to pass; but we now
beheld them from this wide-spreading plain in all
their awful magnitude: their lofty summits, towering high above the clouds in sharp peaks, appeared
to be covered with never-melting snows. This sight
was calculated to fill the mind of the beholder with
wonder and astonishment. The cold and chilling
blasts of wind which blew directly from the Atlas,
almost congealed our impoverished blood, and made
our feeble frames shake almost to dissolution, notwithstanding the good cloaks and shoes with which
we were provided. Seid and the other Arabs were
also shivering with cold, and ran on foot to make
themselves warm, for the sky was overcast and ob-
scured by thick and heavy clouds, portending tor-
rents of rain. I was now sure we were very near the
emperor of Morocco's dominions, and began to
imagine myself a free man—I felt myself at peace
with all mankind; my mind expanded with gratitude
towards the great Author of my being, and I viewed
this stupendous ridge of mountains, as one of the

strongest proofs of Divine goodness to his creatures; for I considered that all the rivers, and streams, and springs, that water and refresh the northern part of Africa, from the borders of that immense and thirsty desart over which I had travelled, to the streights of Gibraltar, and which empty into the Atlantic ocean, or into the Mediterranean sea, westward of Tripoli, and from the 26th to the 35th degree of North latitude, must either take their rise or have their sources in this vast chain of Atlas. On these burning coasts, seldom refreshed by rains, (and that only in small quantities, and during the winter season), the great bodies of accumulated snow on these mountains, tend in the summer season to cool the atmosphere in their vicinity, as well as to supply water for the use of the animal and vegetable creation.

In the course of this morning, Thomas Burns became so weak (being benumbed with cold) that he could no longer hold on the camel, and tumbled off over the beast's tail with great violence, falling on his head and back, which deprived him for a considerable time, of all sensation:—with much exertion, however, on our part he at length revived, and was again placed on his camel. Proceeding on the plain, we saw a large number of cities, or walled towns, I should reckon at least fifty, some on one side of our path, and some on the other; but mostly on our right, and extending as far as the eye could reach towards the mountains. Those near the path appeared to be three or four hundred yards square: the walls were built of rough stones laid in clay, and with only one gate; they were from twenty to thirty feet in height, and crowned with short turrets about three yards apart all around: at each corner on the top was built a kind of circular sentry box, also of stone, something in the manner of old European castles. Most of the land, at some distance from the vicinity of these towns, was prepared for sowing, and many of the inhabitants were engaged in ploughing. A little nearer, were numerous orchards of fig, date, and other fruit trees; and close to the wells, many gardens of fine vegetables, such as onions, cabbages, turnips, squashes, &c. Round about these gardens, we saw many dung-hill fowls, and at a distance, herds of neat cattle, asses, and flocks of sheep and goats, were feeding upon the scanty and dried up herbage, under the eye of their respective keepers or herds-men. These beasts were very poor, yet the whole seemed to promise abundance of food to the apparently industrious inhabitants, and brought to my mind the ancient Jewish history.

Sheick Ali had been very attentive to me all this morning: he had in imitation of Rais bel Cossim, called me captain, and endeavoured to convince me that I had better go with him to the mountains south-ward, where he had large possessions, and would give me one of his daughters for a wife, and make me a chief in his nation. He had stopped the whole company two or three times to talk over his own affairs, and I now supposed that Seid was leagued with him, and bent on doing me and my men some mischief. We had travelled on thus for ten hours, (say from four in the morning till two in the afternoon) at the rate of five miles an hour, making a distance of fifty miles, when turning aside from our path, as if by choice, we approached the gate of a city. We were both hungry and thirsty, and we seated ourselves down by a very deep well, within one hundred yards of the city gate: Seid and Sheick Ali went immediately into the town, as I supposed, to get some provisions—Sidi Mohammed and Rais bel Cossim were soon invited in also, to partake with them, leaving us on the outside, and under charge of Bo-Moham-med, who stood in Sidi Hamet's stead, and two others. A great many men, and I believe, all the boys belonging to the place, now came out to look at and

make remarks on the slaves; most of them, no doubt
from mere curiosity. The boys, by way of amusement, began to throw stones and dirt at, and to spit
on us, expressing, by that means, their utter contempt and abhorrence of us and of our nation.
Burns and Clark were so far exhausted as to be unable to support themselves sitting, and were obliged
to lie down on the ground; but one man brought a
bucket from the town, and drew water, that we
might allay our thirst; this revived us in some measure. Mr. Savage, Horace, and myself, were in so
weak a state, that I much feared we should not be
able to keep on for the remainder of this day. Burns'
fall had proved him to be too weak to hold on the
camel, and had besides bruised him very much. I
tried my utmost to encourage them and keep up
their spirits, by representing to them that we were
now free, and would soon be in the emperor's dominions, where I presumed we should be out of the
reach of the rapacious Arabs: for I had been informed by Rais bel Cossim, that in the space of one
day's journey we should be within the territories of
the emperor.

Whilst Rais bel Cossim and the rest of his company remained within the walls, the winds from the
mountains, driving before them thick masses of dark
clouds, loaded with vapour, brought on a copious
discharge of rain, and we were directed to enter under the gateway for shelter, which we did, supporting
each other in our weakness, and seated ourselves in
the gate. This was the first rain I had witnessed in this
country; and it continued to fall for about an hour.
I had for a long time looked for Rais bel Cossim and
his companions to come out, and began to apprehend
some disaster or treachery on the part of Sheick Ali,
whose harsh and loud voice I now heard roaring
within. This tremendous clamour between the
Sheick and other persons, continued for about two

hours, when Rais bel Cossim made his appearance, escorted by a number of men: his intelligent countenance bespoke fear, grief, and indignation—he called me aside from my companions, and told me that *Sheick Ali* was the intimate friend of *Muley Ibrahim*, (or prince Abraham,) the king or governor of the city: that *Sheick Ali* had claimed us as his property, alleging that Sidi Hamet was his son-in-law, and owed him a great deal of money, and that he (Sidi Hamet) was now held as a hostage or slave to a *Christian* in Swearah: that he had insisted we should not proceed one step further until fifteen hundred dollars, were produced, together with Sidi Hamet, the husband of his daughter: and that in conjunction with Seid, he had contrived to stop us here by the power of the prince. This news was to me like a clap of thunder; it bereft me of all my fortitude; the fair prospects I had entertained of a speedy liberation from slavery, particularly for the last two days, were now suddenly darkened. *Rais bel Cossim* further informed me that he had argued the matter every way, but all to no purpose—that he had promised the money required, namely, six hundred dollars, as soon as we should get to *Santa Cruz*, in the emperor's dominions, and that he would agree to have the prince and Sheick go along with him and receive it there, and there wait for the return of Sidi Hamet; "but they will not listen to me, (added he) and I must set off immediately and carry this discouraging news to Mr. Willshire, leaving you here until I return, (which will be in six days) and may God preserve you in the meantime from their evil machinations." This was more than I could bear:—tears of anguish, which I had not the power to control, now gushed from my eyes; and my almost bursting heart vented itself in bitter groans of despair. My companions heard my distress, though at a considerable distance from me, and turning fearfully on me their

almost extinguished eyes, begged for an explanation
of the cause.

Rais bel Cossim was just in the act of mounting
his mule to ride off, when Sidi Mohammed, who went
in the first place with my master to Swearah, came
near him and said, "Rais—Muley Ibrahim and Sheick
Ali have determined you shall not go to Swearah;
they fear you will cause a war to break out between
them and the sultan." Observing me in tears and in
great affliction, he took me by the hand, and said,
"Don't be cast down, Riley, I will go to Swearah, and
carry a letter from Rais, and one from you to Willshire; and if he wants a hostage, I will stay with
him. I have two wives and seven children to leave,
and houses, and lands, and herds of cattle; and shall
be a more valuable hostage than Sidi Hamet—he is
your friend, and will come immediately down and
relieve you. God is great and good, (added he, and
will restore you to your family." I kissed his hand in
gratitude, and called him father, and hoped the Almighty would reward him for his benevolence. Rais
now joined Sheick Ali and the prince, who with many
attendants, were seated on the ground, in a circle,
outside of the city gate—here they debated the matter over again. Rais insisted we were his slaves; that
neither the prince nor Sheick had a right to detain
what he had bought with his own money, much less
to stop him like a criminal: that it was contrary to
their religion (which made them all brothers) to
commit such an outrage on hospitality. Sheick Ali,
on the other hand, contended, that Sidi Hamet and
Seid owed him money to a large amount; that we
were their joint property, and that consequently he
had an undoubted right to detain and to carry us off
into his own tribe, or family, and there to keep us,
until Sidi Hamet should return and pay his debt.
Rais insisted he had paid his money for us, and had
nothing to do with Sheick Ali's claim; however, after
extolling the justice and virtue of the prince to the

highest pitch, they both at last agreed to leave it to
Muley Ibrahim to decide what should be done. Muley Ibrahim now asked Sidi Mohammed and Bo-
Mohammed what they knew concerning this business; and they gave testimony in favour of Rais bel
Cossim's previous claim; thus prepared, Muley Ibrahim said—"You, Sheick Ali, my old friend, and Rais
bel Cossim, both of you claim these five Christian
slaves as your own property, and each of you has
some reason on your side—yet, as it is not in my
power to decide whose claim is the best founded, I
am resolved, with a strict regard to justice, and without going into further evidence, to keep the slaves in
my own city, carefully guarded, until messengers can
be sent to Swearah, who shall bring down Sidi Hamet, when you three being confronted, may settle
your claims as shall be found most consistent with
justice." He then proposed that Rais should remain
with him, (like a friend) and without having any
thing to fear. This plan was agreed to by all parties,
and they shook hands upon it like friends.

This done, we were conducted into the city, and
into a house adjoining that where the prince lived.
A mat was spread for the Sheick and Rais, and their
companions to sit on, while we were placed in a narrow corner on the ground among the saddles and
other stuffs—sentinels with muskets and scimitars
were stationed at the door of our apartment and the
other doors, and at the city gate. It was after dark
when the dispute was settled, and soon afterwards a
dish of *Coos-coo-so* was brought in, of which all partook after due ablutions; and they then performed
their evening prayers most devoutly. My companions
were very much cast down; and their bodies and
minds were so much exhausted and debilitated by
their sufferings, that they had become like children,
and wept aloud. I was certain that it would have
been impossible for Clark and Burns to have proceeded further on that day, and I tried to persuade

them all that it was better for us to be detained a little, as it would give us an opportunity of taking some
rest, without which we should be in danger of fainting on our route. Muley Ibrahim, the Sheick, and
Rais, were conversing during the whole night, and
when daylight appeared, (the 2d of November) Rais
furnished me with pen, ink, and paper, and told me
to write to Mr. Willshire, stating our present situation as near as I was able: this I accordingly did,
while a *talb* or scrivener was employed in writing a
letter for him, (as he could not write himself.) At an
early hour Seid, Sidi Mohammed, and Bo-Mohammed, set out for Swearah, taking our letters, and
promising to return as soon as possible. Sheick Ali
also, soon afterwards, left us, promising to return in
four days.

CHAPTER XXII.

Rais bel Cossim gains the friendship of the prince—
good provisions are procured—Sheick Ali's plans
miscarry—they set off for, and arrive at Santa Cruz,
in the Empire of Morocco

BEING now left alone with Rais bel Cossim, I questioned him concerning our detention; he said it
would be but for a few days, and that we needed a
little time to refresh ourselves, in order to enable us
to bear the fatigues of the remainder of our journey:
that he trusted we should make a friend of the prince,
in whose power we all now were, and that he hoped

to be able to effect this by making him a small present. I told him I almost despaired of living to regain my liberty, as I was extremely feeble, and must soon perish. "What! (said he) dare you distrust the power of that God who has preserved you so long by miracles? No, my friend, (added he) the God of Heaven and of earth is your friend, and will not forsake you; but in his own good time restore you to your liberty and to the embraces of your family; we must say, 'his will be done,' and be contented with our lot, for God knows best what is for our good."

To hear such sentiments from the mouth of a Moor, whose nation I had been taught to consider the worst of barbarians, I confess, filled my mind with awe and reverence, and I looked up to him as a kind of superior being, when he added, "We are all children of the same heavenly Father, who watches over all our actions, whether we be Moor, or Christian, or Pagan, or of any other religion; we must perform his will." Rais then called Muley Ibrahim, and had a long conference with him. This prince Ibrahim was a man of a very mild aspect, of a light complexion, about five feet ten inches in height, and rather thin—his countenance was intelligent, and he was very active, though apparently sixty or seventy years of age. By the tenor of the conversation I could understand that Rais was flattering him highly, but in a delicate way: he asked him very affectionately about the prince's wives; and understanding he had but one, he enquired if she had any children; and was answered, she had none: he next wished to know if she had any tea or sugar, and was answered in the negative.

We had not seen the faces of any of the women since we arrived at the town where Sidi Mohammed dwelt. Rais now managed to get a little wood and some water, and we made a fire and boiled some coffee; this was done by the help of a small negro girl who was a slave to Muley Ibrahim; and during the

absence of the prince. Rais, by giving the girl a small
lump of loaf sugar, persuaded her to carry a large
lump to her mistress, and also a cup of coffee thick
with sugar. The Prince had gone out before Rais
attempted to bribe the girl. After carrying in the coffee and the sugar, the girl returned and told Rais
that her mistress was much obliged to him, and
would keep the cup and saucer, for she had never
seen one before, and thought them very pretty, and
begged to know how she might serve him in return.
Rais sent back word that she could serve him most
essentially by striving to make the prince his friend.
About one hour after this, Muley Ibrahim entered
our apartment, and asked Rais what he had been doing with his wife? saying, at the same time, "You
had no need of gaining my friendship through her
influence, for you had it already;" but I could perceive a very great difference in his manner. He
wished to know if Rais did not want to go to the
mosque, which he said was not far distant. Rais accompanied him thither, and I discovered at his return, about two hours after, that all was right between him and the prince, and that he had all the
liberty he required. I had in the meantime, made
some coffee, of which my companions and myself
drank as much as we wanted, and nibbled our biscuits; for our Arab friends had before taken care to
eat up all our boiled tongue. We were, all of us, so
excessively weak, that we were not able to fetch water
for ourselves, and our diarrhœa also continued with
the most distressing hermorrhoides: this day, however, had passed away more smoothly than I had expected. In the evening, the prince came, and prayed,
in company with Rais, and appeared very friendly.
After the prince retired, Rais informed me that he
(Rais) had sent off to a rich man, an old acquaintance of his, who lived about one day's journey south
of us, for money to pay Sheick Ali's demand, and

that he expected his friend would come to him the next day—"but (said Rais) God has made Muley Ibrahim my firm friend; and he has given his princely word that he will protect both me and my slaves, and in case force is necessary, he will provide a sufficient escort for us into the emperor's dominions—he will also provide some fowls and eggs for you in the morning, and you may tell your shipmates they have nothing to fear, for to-morrow *M. Shallah*, (i. e. if it is God's will) they shall have plenty of good food." This news cheered their spirits, and as our apprehensions had in some measure subsided, we rested comfortably.

Early in the morning of November the 3d, Muley Ibrahim brought in some eggs, which we boiled for our breakfast: he gave us salt to season them with, and soon after brought half a dozen fowls, and Rais taking the fowls' wings in his left hand, and turning his face towards the east, after saying aloud, *Besmillah*, (in the name of the most holy God) he cut their throats, and we soon dressed them after our fashion, and put them into an earthen pot with water, and set it a boiling. The prince had furnished us with wood, and brought us water with his own hands; he next went into his garden, and pulled some onions, turnips, and small squashes, with which we enriched our soup; and he also gave us salt and green peppers to season it with. We put in four fowls, and this soup would have been thought good in any country. A more grateful and wholesome dish could not possibly have been prepared for our poor disordered stomachs, that had been so long harassed with the most cruel griping pains, and felt as if they had lost all power of digestion. The prince and Rais had a bowl of the soup, with a part of the fowls, and seemed to relish it exceedingly. The prince insisted on my eating from the same dish with them: inquired concerning my wife and children, wished to know their sex:

and continued from that time during our stay in his city to administer all the relief and comfort in his power, both to me and my desponding and wretched companions, whose last ray of hope had faded away on our being stopped here; although in fact they were not in a condition to continue their journey, particularly Burns and Clark, for they had sunken into a lethargic state, bordering on dissolution. Yet, when I was enabled to explain the causes of our detention, and to inform them that the prince was our friend, and gave them nourishing soups, their spirits came again, and hope raised them from the ground. To the circumstance of this stoppage alone, and the friendship and protection of this good chief, I attribute, under Providence, the salvation of our lives. On the second day of our detention, in the afternoon, the old man, Rais bel Cossim's friend, to whom he had written for assistance, came to see him: he had been riding all night to be with Rais in time. Their meeting was a friendly one: the old man had two mules, on one of which were two baskets, containing a dozen of fowls, and some dry coos-coo-soo; these he presented to Rais, and said he had brought five hundred dollars for his use, as he requested, and that he would bring it in: but Rais had now become the friend of Muley Ibrahim, and therefore did not need the money; yet this old friend insisted on his taking the fowls as a present, with some eggs he had also brought with him; these Rais accepted, for he said they were meant as a present to me. I had some fowls cooked already, and the old man sat down and ate with Rais, and would have me to be one of the company: he told Rais that if he would but say the word, he would go and collect his friends and take the slaves by force of arms, and in spite of Sheick Ali's opposition, would carry us safe to Santa Cruz, and beyond his power: but as Muley Ibrahim had given his word, on which Rais said he could depend, to see us all safe to Santa Cruz, and to use all his force and influence, if that should be necessary, the old man, whose name I am sorry to say I have forgotten, left us and returned to his home. We now lived for three days as well as we could wish.

On the fourth day after Seid's departure, a kind of fair was held at a short distance from our city, and some manœuvre to liberate us, and to get us on towards the sultan's dominions.—A man of great influence lived about five leagues distance from that city. He was called a son of the holy prophet, or *Shariff;* had been to Morocco, and was also called *el ajjh:* (the pilgrim;) he was looked upon by all far and near as possessing supernatural powers, and was obeyed and almost worshipped as a superior being; and his word or dictate was equivalent to a law. Rais went to the fair and from thence to the place of worship, and did not return until the afternoon, when he informed me he had bought a bullock at the fair, the best and fattest he could find, though it was but a small one. He had sent one half of it to the son of the prophet (or Shariff) by the hand of a messenger, on a mule, saying, "when you deliver the flesh to the el ajjh, and he asks you who sent it to him, tell him a pious man, who has lately come from Swearah, and is now a guest with Muley Ibrahim, and wishes to be remembered in your prayers." This, Rais said, was all the message he sent, but he was sure that if the Shariff accepted the present he should see him before the sun went down. Rais had given the other half to Muley Ibrahim, and remarked, that it was not so much the real value of a present that was taken into consideration by the Moors, but the manner of giving it, which laid the receiver under such an obligation as to make him your friend forever. This notion I was at a loss to understand, and therefore supposed it to be some peculiarity in the customs of these singular people. Rais went out to prayers about sunset, and

returned in a short time; when he mentioned that he
had been waited upon by the Shariff, who had asked
him what favour he wanted, that made him send
such a present to a stranger.—Rais told him our
story, and that he had paid his money for myself and
my companions, and begged his assistance to force
Sheick Ali (whose power all dreaded) to consent to
have us removed quietly to Santa Cruz; where Rais
thought his property would be safe: this the Shariff
promised to do, and even to exert all his power and
influence if necessary, to remove and protect Rais
and his property by force of arms, and requested to
be informed without delay when Sheick Ali returned.

On the following day (November 4th) the Sheick
did return; and relying on the friendship of Muley
Ibrahim, had only one attendant: the Shariff was immediately informed of his arrival by express, and
came, to see him as an old friend; then taking him
aside, he advised the Sheick to remove his slaves to
Santa Cruz as soon as possible, asserting at the same
time that he was certain that *Sidi Ishem,* whom the
Sheick well knew and dreaded, would set out from
his city on the morrow with a force, in order to seize
upon the slaves, whom he had before strove hard to
purchase for money without success, and if they were
not in the dominions of the emperor before he came,
another day would place them in his hands, when the
Sheick would not only lose them, but it must also
kindle a war between him and that powerful chief;
which would set the whole country in a blaze, and
after all it would be impossible to deliver them from
his grasp by force. When the Sheick heard the advice
of the Shariff, he returned to our prison, and Rais
contrived to find out what had passed between them,
by again meeting the Shariff at the city gate alone, as
had been before agreed upon. Rais being thus fully
informed and let into the secret, came into the apartment and informed me how matters stood. Sheick

Ali, in the meantime, was unfolding his plan to Muley Ibrahim, and trying to gain his consent to let the slaves be carried off in the night by surprise, but the prince would not consent; they were now within his walls, and he had given his word they should not be removed until the disputed right of property was settled by all parties face to face:—this he should insist on. Finding that plan would not answer any good purpose, and fearing Sidi Ishem's expected arrival, and wishing to make a merit of necessity, this crafty chief addressing Rais bel Cossim, told him, in a flattering way, that he had found him to be a good and an honorable man, and wished to be called his friend; that he did not doubt Rais's word, since he knew his character, and would therefore consent to go on with the slaves on the morrow morning, as far as Santa Cruz, where they would wait for the arrival of Sidi Hamet, and settle the right of property amicably. Rais, on the other hand, as crafty as the Sheick, took care not to evince any desire of going; and being in the whole secret, now told Sheick Ali, that he had stopped him and his Christian slaves at first contrary to the laws of justice and hospitality, and that as he had kept them so long a time, he had no wish to remove them at present, but would wait with patience until Sidi Hamet, should come down, and convince the Sheick that he had done wrong in detaining him.

At last, however, he suffered himself to be persuaded by the united voices of Sheick Ali and Muley Ibrahim, but on the express condition of being escorted to Santa Cruz by the prince, who was a party in the whole secret. He was also to procure camels for us to ride on, and went forth to engage and have them ready for a start at daylight the next morning. Rais bel Cossim now informed me that Muley Ibrahim had previously agreed to accompany us; that we were to ride on camels, and that two hundred horse-

men were to guard us on the road, in order to prevent any treachery on the part of Sheick Ali, who
might already have troops stationed on the way to
seize and carry us off to the mountains: he had also
given private orders to his friends and his vassals, to
hold themselves in readiness in case of an alarm. The
two hundred horsemen were to take stations, so as to
keep us in continual view without exciting suspicion,
and to be ready to carry intelligence. Rais then bade
me kill and boil what fowls and eggs remained,
which I did, with the assistance of my men, who had
very much recovered.

While the fowls and eggs were cooking, I asked
Rais who this Sidi Ishem was? as his name alone had
seemed capable of inspiring such dread. "This *Sidi
Ishem*," said Rais, "is a descendant of the former
kings of Suse, before it was conquered by the Moors;
—he is a man of between fifty and sixty years of age,
possessed of great wealth and power; is very crafty,
and very brave, but rapacious and cruel; he has under his command fifteen thousand horsemen, well
armed: they are of the race of the ancient inhabitants
of the country, from whom the whole country de-
rives the name of *Berberia*, corrupted by the Europeans into *Barbary;*—these Berberians are extremely
fierce and warlike, and are joined by all the renegado
Moors, who escape from the Emperor's dominion, to
evade punishment for crimes they have committed.
These men are always ready to join him in any of his
enterprises, for they always get a share of the spoil.
He lives in the gorge of a mountain, near the town of
Widnoon, on the great route from Morocco across
the great desert, to Soudain, the country beyond the
desart, and the city of Tombuctoo. All the caravans
that travel either to or from the desart are obliged to
go close to Widnoon, and as the Atlas mountains are
on the one side, and the ridge next the sea on the
other, they find it highly necessary to secure his

friendship and protection by presents. Between this Chief and the Emperor of Morocco there exists the most implacable hatred, and a continual jealousy, which a few years ago broke out into an open war. The Emperor sent a powerful army against him, (said to be 30,000 strong) but Sidi Ishem was apprized of its approach in time, and sent off all the women, children, and old men, with all their substance, to the south foot of the Atlas mountains, and on the great desert. The Emperor's army entered his territory, where they found nothing to subsist upon: yet as they met with no resistance, they carried on their work of destruction, by burning all the towns and every thing that was combustible, tearing down the houses and walls of their cities, so that nothing escaped their violence and rapacity. They continued pursuing Sidi Ishem (who hovered about them with most of his men) until they were exhausted by fatigue and hunger; when this chief fell upon them by surprise with his infuriated followers, who had been rendered doubly desperate by the sight of their ruined cities. They slew more than ten thousand on the spot; those who escaped this dreadful carnage, and fled, were hunted down and nearly all destroyed, before they could reach the city of *Tarudant*, (the southern and westernmost town in the emperor of Morocco's dominions) where the few that were left found shelter, and spread such terror and dismay throughout that part of the empire, by the horrid accounts they gave of their disasters, as to render it impracticable to raise another army for the purpose of reducing Sidi Ishem and his men to submission. All the inhabitants were soon recalled by their chief from the mountains and desarts; took possession of their country anew, rebuilt their cities and dwellings, and are at this time more powerful, more feared and respected, than they were previous to that event." This is the account Rais bel Cossim gave me

in Spanish, as nearly as my memory served me, when
I took it down at Mogadore:—he also said that we
had escaped falling into his hands only by groping
our way along a private path on the sea shore. The
substance of this account of Sidi Ishem was confirmed, after my arrival at Mogadore, by Mr. Willshire and others.

Our food being prepared, and every thing packed
up tight for a start, we took a short nap, and at daylight on the morning of the 4th of November, we
were placed on five camels, which were saddled
much better than any we had hitherto rode: they had
on them also bags of barley, and empty sacks, made
of tent cloth, that would hold, I should suppose, ten
or twelve bushels; these altogether made quite a
comfortable seat, though rather a wide one, and we
could hold ourselves on by the ropes that secured the
lading: they placed me on the largest camel I had yet
seen, which was nine or ten feet in height. The camels were now all kneeling or lying down, and mine
among the rest. I thought I had taken a good hold to
steady myself while he was rising—yet, his motion
was so heavy, and my strength so far exhausted, that
I could not possibly hold on, and tumbled off over
his tail, turning entirely over. I came down upon my
feet, which prevented my receiving any material injury, though the shock to my frame was very severe.
—The owner of the camel helped me up, and asked
me if I was injured? I told him no—"God be
praised," said he, "for turning you over; had you
fallen upon your head, these stones must have dashed
out your brains; but the camel," added he, "is a
sacred animal, and heaven protects those who ride on
him! had you fallen from an ass, though he is only
two cubits and a half high, it would have killed you;
for the ass is not so noble a creature as the camel and
the horse."—I afterwards found this to be the pre-
vailing opinion among all classes of the Moors and

the Arabs.—When they put me on again, two of the men steadied me by the legs until the camel was fairly up, and then told me to be careful, and to hold on fast: they also took great care to assist my companions in the same way.

Being now all mounted, we set off to the N. E. leaving *Stuka*, (for that was the name of the place where we had been confined) accompanied by Rais bel Cossim, Muley Ibrahim, and his two servants, and Sheick Ali, with his attendant, all riding on mules and asses: the five owners of the camels went on foot, each driving his own camel, and taking care of its rider.—*Stuka* is built in a quadrangular form; its walls would measure about three hundred yards on each angle; they are built of rough stone, laid in clay, and appeared to be four or five feet thick at their base, and twenty feet in height, tapering off to two feet thick at the top, and were crowned with turrets all around. It has but one gate, which is at its north angle, very strongly made, and swinging on the ends of its back posts which are let into large stone sockets at the bottom and at the top: the gate consisted of two folding leaves, and at night was secured by four heavy wooden bars. The town was divided within, into as many compartments as there were families in it, which I should think might amount to three hundred, probably containing in all five thousand souls. The houses are built of the same materials as the walls; only one story high, and flat roofed: excepting the door, they looked like heaps of mud and stone: even that of the prince bore the same appearance, without any other distinction or ornament than being closer jointed, and more bedaubed with mud.—All the flocks and herds were driven within the walls every night, and each owner makes those that belong to him lie down in his own yard or enclosure.

As we travelled on, we passed between a great

number of cities or towns, similar in appearance to
Stuka, with which this truly vast plain is chequered.
The whole plain seemed very fertile, was planted
with numerous groves and orchards of fig and other
fruit trees, with here and there a clump of the arga
tree, yellow with fruit. The inhabitants were busied
in ploughing up the soil, with a kind of plough
which I shall hereafter describe.—We proceeded on
very rapidly, keeping those on foot running constantly, and had been travelling about six hours,
when we came to the ruins of many towns on our left,
similar in appearance to Stuka; near the shattered
walls of some of which stood several battering machines, but they were at the distance of a mile or
more from us. These places appeared to have been
recently inhabited; for the gardens near the walls
were still green with vegetation. Wishing to know
what had been the cause of such desolation, I was informed by Muley Ibrahim and Sheick Ali, through
Rais bel Cossim, that a family quarrel happened
about one year ago between the chiefs of two of these
towns, which soon broke out into the most dreadful
kind of warfare—each party engaged their friends to
assist them in fighting what each termed their *righteous battles:* the neighbouring towns joined, some
on one side, and some on the other, and the plain
was deluged with blood. This quarrel being only of
a family nature, Sidi Ishem did not interfere, and it
was finally settled by the destruction of seven of
those small cities, and most of their inhabitants.
These ruins were now entirely abandoned, and their
environs laid desolate, though the war continued
only one month. I could scarcely believe it possible
for such devastation to have been committed in so
short a time or on such trivial grounds; but Rais bel
Cossim (who was born near Santa Cruz) assured me
that nothing was more common than such feuds between families in those parts: that he had known

many himself, with every circumstance attending them, and that they were very seldom finished until one family or the other was exterminated, and their names blotted out from the face of the earth.

We continued our journey until about mid-day, still on the plain, when Santa Cruz or Agader was distinctly seen and pointed out to me. It is situated on the summit of a high mountain; its walls are white, and can be descried at a great distance. The plain on which we travelled was nearly level; not a brook or stream of water had we passed since leaving the last mentioned river, but the towns and villages had many deep wells near their walls, from which the inhabitants drew water for themselves and their numerous cattle.—Innumerable clumps of the evergreen arga tree, loaded with the rich oil nut, were scattered over the plain in every direction. Vast numbers of leafless fig trees, and enclosures of grape vines with date, pomegranate, almond, orange, and other fruit trees, promised abundance in their seasons; and delightfully variegated the scene.—Hundreds of the inhabitants were busied in ploughing the soil, which appeared rich, though dry; and sowing their barley; while their herds were browsing on the shrubs round about for the want of grass. Many unarmed men, with droves of camels and asses loaded with salt and other merchandise, were meeting and passing us almost continually. We saw also from time to time, bands of armed men on horseback, of about fifty in each band, most of whom I learned from Rais were the friends of Muley Ibrahim, whom he had requested to ride guard, as I before mentioned, and to be ready to act in our behalf in case of treachery, or of any emergency whatever. Our path led us in a N. E. direction, and the camels were kept most of the time on a great trot, while their drivers were running on foot, and kept up with us, seemingly, with great ease; though I compute we rode at the rate of seven or eight miles an hour.

About two P. M. approaching the coast, we fell in with huge drifts of loose sand on our left, which extended to the sea shore. This sand had been driven from the sea beach by the constant trade winds, and as the sea had retired, (for it was clean coarse beach sand) it had undoubtedly for ages been making its way gradually from the coast, (which was now about twenty miles distant) and had buried, as I was informed, several flourishing villages, towns, and cities, the tops of whose walls were still visible; the circular domes of a considerable number of saint-houses, or sanctuaries, whose bodies were entirely enveloped, were yet to be seen among these barren heaps of overwhelming sands; for the inhabitants take great care to clear away around them, and to give them a whitewashing every year. Muley Ibrahim informed me that a large town called Rabeah, whose ruins we had passed in mounting over the sand hills, was a flourishing place within his remembrance; (probably fifty years ago;) that he himself was born in it—but that large bodies of sand had already encroached upon its northern wall: that as soon as it was overtopped, it fell in, and the whole city was filled with sand in the course of one year after, and its inhabitants forced to seek a new shelter. These drifts extended, as far as we could distinguish sand, on our right.

Having got past the high heaps, which filled a space of eight or ten miles in width, we came to the high banks of an apparently once large river, now called by the natives *el Woa Sta*. This river's ancient bed, and the high banks, which are still perfectly distinct, bear the strongest marks of having been once laved by a stream of four or five miles in breath, and nearly one hundred feet in depth, or by a part of the ocean. The steep, barren, and craggy mountains, rising before us to the eastward and southward, though very high, appeared to serve only as a base to the mighty range of Atlas, whose towering height and grandeur filled my mind with awe and astonishment. Notwithstanding my frame was literally exhausted, yet my imagination transported me back to a time when this region might have been inhabited by men in a higher state of civilization, and when it was probably one of the fairest portions of the African continent. My reasons for imagining this are, first, that it is well known by historians, that the Romans had settlements along this coast as far south as Salee at least, and no doubt much further. Second, that the Portuguese and Spaniards had possessed the settlements of *Mamora, Mazagan, Asbedre, Santa Cruz,* &c. Third, by the traditional information obtained from Rais bel Cossim and Sidi Mohammed, I have no doubt that a large city and settlement of civilized men existed at a former period near the mouth of the river *Schelem,* from sixty to one hundred miles west of Santa Cruz, and I am firmly of opinion that the convenience of these harbours, the luxuriancy of the surrounding soil, and the commercial advantages this part of the country offers, were a sufficient inducement for colonization.

We had now approached to within two miles of Santa Cruz or Agader, (the lower town or port,) when rising an eminence, the ocean opened to our view at a distance, and near-by appeared Santa Cruz bay, which was then quite smooth. Nearly one hundred good looking fishing boats were hauled up on the beach out of the reach of the surf, and numbers of long fishing nets were spread out to dry on the sand and over the boats. This view gave a most favourable idea of the importance of this bay as a fishery.

The sun had not yet set, and Rais informed me he did not wish to enter the lower town till dark, and did not mean to go nearer the fortress than he could help, for fear of insult and detection; so we stopped about a mile short of it, to the southward, where I had an opportunity of examining this bay with a seaman's eye.—It is spacious and perfectly well defended from the common trade winds, say from N. N. W. all round the compass; by the East, and as far as S. W. thence to N. N. W. it is entirely open, and of course is a very dangerous anchorage in the winter months, when westerly winds prevail on these coasts, at which times, as these is no possibility of getting to sea, vessels at anchor in this bay must remain where they are ; not however without the greatest risk of being driven on shore in spite of the best of anchors and cables, and large vessels must ride too far out to make it a good harbour for them at any season of the year. The port of Santa Cruz, or, as it is called by the natives, *Agader,* has been shut by order of the Sultan for many years; yet there are parts of the wrecks of vessels still visible, sticking up through the sand on the beach.

A little while after sunset we entered the lower town, or port, as it is called; this village is situated on the steep declivity of the mountain's base, on which the upper town is built, and near the sea, which washes the south end of the principal street. The steep side of the mountain on which this village is erected has been apparently sloped down by art, so as to make it practicable to build on it; has one principal street and several small alleys: the houses are built of rough stone laid in lime mortar, and are but one story in height, with flat roofs terraced with lime and pebbles. We could see the tops of many houses below us, and the whole made but a miserable appearance. It was not quite dark when we entered the village. The street was soon filled with Moors, (men and boys,) and they saluted us by spitting on us, and pelting us with stones and sticks accompanied with the Spanish words, *"Carajo a la Mierda le Sara, perro y bestias,* and many other chosen phrases equally delicate and polite; but some of the old men now and then uttered a "how de do, Christianos !" in broken English and Spanish. We were conducted through the streets to its further extremity towards the north, where we took up our quarters for the night in the open air alongside a smith's shop ; our camels and asses were then fed with barley. Some of the inhabitants kindled a fire for our company, whilst others were preparing a rich repast for them of boiled and baked fish, and *cous coo-soo,* of which, after they had eaten, they gave us the remains, and we found it excellent food. Numbers of men, driving asses before them, loaded with fish, had passed us going into the country, the day before, and they were of the same kind as those we had tasted soon after our entrance into Suse, and we had also seen the same kind of fish at Stuka: they carry them from Santa Cruz, or Agader, about the country in every direction, where they sell them for a good price, being much in request. This fish very much resembles the salmon both in size, shape, and flavour; weighing (from appearance) from eight to sixteen or twenty pounds; and is extremely fat and delicate. I then recollected to have seen in my several voyages to the Canary Islands, numbers of small vessels arrive from the coast of Africa laden with this species of fish, and to have been told they were caught near that coast: they are highly esteemed in the Canaries, where they call them *Bacalao Africano,* or the African cod-fish, and are sold at from five to ten dollars per quintal, or at least one-third higher than the best of American codfish: they are dried, without salting, on the vessels' decks, and their scent is so strong as to nearly suffocate the crews of merchant vessels that lie near them while discharging. I have been told that no less than one hundred barks, of from fifteen to fifty tons burden, are continually employed in this fishery,

near the African coast from the Canary Islands, and
that scarcely a year passes without more or less of
them being driven on shore by tempests or other accidents, when the crews either perish with the vessel,
or upon their reaching the shore, are massacred by
the natives, or else carried off into the interior as
slaves, where they are never after heard from. After
my arrival in Mogadore, or Swearah, I was informed
that the crew of a bark of this description landed
imprudently on the beach not far from Santa Cruz,
about two years since, where they were surprised by
a sudden attack, but all escaped into the boat except
one man, who was seized and carried off. On the return of the bark to Teneriffe, the wife of the man
who had been left, upon inquiring for her husband,
was informed that he was made a slave: distracted
by this shocking event, she ran, raving as she was, to
the archbishop, and begged of him either to take her
life, or restore to her arms her lost husband, the
father of five helpless children: she was poor, but
her case excited general pity—a subscription was
opened, and the sum of about five hundred dollars
soon raised. The archbishop in the meantime wrote
to Alexander W. Court, then Spanish agent at Mogadore, to ransom this unfortunate man, which he
effected with much difficulty: but as the money did
not come on in time, or from some other cause, this
poor Spaniard, whose name was *Fermin*, remained
in Mogadore for nearly a year without being permitted to go home, when Mr. William Willshire and
Don Plabo Riva, of Mogadore, and Mr. John O'Sulli-
van, of New York, interfered in his favour; furnished him with clothing; procured for him a passage,
and sent him to his disconsolate family. This is said
to be the only Spaniard who has been redeemed in
that part of Barbary, for many years past.

CHAPTER XXIII.

Sheick Ali out-manœuvred again by Rais Bel Cossim —they set off in the night—meet with Sidi Hamet and his brother, accompanied by some Moors with mules sent by Mr. Willshire for the sufferers to ride on—occurrences on the road—meeting with Mr. Willshire near Swearah or Mogadore—they go into that city—are ordered before the bashaw

AFTER supper, Rais bel Cossim told me to keep a good look out; that he would watch the motions of Sheick Ali, who he still feared was plotting against our liberty. After I had informed my enfeebled and desponding companions that we were now out of danger from the Arabs, (having come about fifty miles from Stuka,) and in the emperor of Morocco's dominions, and, consequently, sure of being liberated, and that too in a very few days; and after telling them that we must bear up under our fatigues with fortitude, and exert our remaining strength and spirits, in order to reach Mogadore; we all laid ourselves down to rest; and my companions, though they had the bare ground for their bed, yet as they were wrapped up in cloaks, and had their stomachs well filled with good and nourishing food, soon fell asleep. As for myself, fear, hope, and various other sensations, kept me awake, and I could not close my eyes, but waited with extreme anxiety for the appearance of Rais bel Cossim. Soon after midnight Rais

came, and finding me awake, he roused me and the
owners of the camels, and requested them to get
ready to go on speedily, and then told me that on entering this place, while he was bruised in feeding his
mule, Sheick Ali had stolen off privately to the town,
and visited the governor, who had agreed, on his
representation, to take us into custody in the morning at day-break, and assist in extorting what money
the Sheick demanded; or to connive at our being
stolen and carried back by Sheick Ali's men to Suse.
"I have learned this (said he) from an old friend
of mine, whom I met and commissioned to watch
Sheick Ali's motions when we were coming into his
place: awaken your shipmates: you must depart this
instant: the drivers know the road; it is very rocky:
you must tell your men to hold on as tight as possible: and remember, if you are four leagues from
this town before daylight, your liberty is secured, if
not, you will be again the most miserable of slaves.
Encourage your men to use their utmost exertions,
and I hope, with God's blessing, in three days more
you will be in Swearah with your friend. I will join
you as soon as possible." The camels were by this
time ready: we were placed on them, and proceeded
up the rocky steeps as fast as possible, but with
the most profound silence. Sleep seemed to have literally sealed the eyes of all the Moors in the lower
town, and in the batteries near the path through
which we passed; these batteries rose one above another like an amphitheatre towards the fortress. The
quadrangular walls of the town and fortress of Santa
Cruz, or Agader, crowned the summit of this mountain, on our right, and stand, from appearance, not
less than fifteen hundred feet above the level of the
sea. We went fast forward, in profound silence, which
was not in the least disturbed by the tread of the camels, because their feet are as soft as sponge or leather:
only the hoarse roaring of the surf breaking among
the rocks below us, startled the ear, and exciting in

my mind frightful images of direful shipwrecks, and the consequent miseries of the poor mariner driven on this inhospitable coast.

We had been hurrying on as fast as possible for about two hours, and had gained the distance of probably three leagues from Santa Cruz, when our ears were struck with the clinking sound of iron against the stones, which announced the approach of horses or mules that were shod; and in an instant, though dark, we discovered close by us on our right a considerable number of men riding on mules, and passing the other way. Not a word was uttered on either side, nor could the faces of any be distinguished, though we were not more than three or four yards asunder. A thought darting across my mind, suggested to me that it was my old master: I instantly called out *Sidi Hamet!* and was quickly answered— *escoon Riley?* (who is it, Riley?) the whole company stopped in an instant; and the next moment I had the joy of kissing the hand of my old master and benefactor. Sidi Mohammed, Seid, and Bo-Mohammed, were in his company, together with three or four Moors, whom our kind friend had sent down, charged with the money and mules for our ransom and conveyance. The principal Moor, and who had charge of the money until we were delivered over according to the wish of Sidi Hamet, spoke Spanish fluently: he wanted to inquire of me where Rais bel Cossim was: I told him at Santa Cruz: Sidi Hamet wished to question me himself, and asked me "where is Sheick Ali ?" and when I informed him that I had left him in Santa Cruz, in company with Rais bel Cossim and Muley Ibrahim, he was satisfied; and said Sheick Ali was a bad man, and did not fear God. Seid also pretended to be much rejoiced at our being on the road to Mogadore, and yet I thought I could discover that he was trying to play a deep game of artful duplicity: but old Sidi Mohammed was in truth rejoiced to find us in the emperor's dominions.

Having now been absolutely delivered over to *Bel Mooden*, the Moor who had charge of the money, he paid it over to Sidi Hamet, and three of us were mounted on mules, and proceeded on, while all those whom we met, went towards Santa Cruz, except the three Moors who owned and brought the mules down for us to ride on, and who remained and proceeded northward with us.

All the time we had stopped to make the necessary arrangements above mentioned, the owners of the camels were urging us to go forward, thereby showing a disposition to obey the orders of Rais bel Cossim, and would not for a long time believe that those who stopped us were not our enemies. The backs of the mules were covered with large saddles made of coarse cloth, stuffed with straw, and formed very broad, so as to fit their shape, and reached almost from their heads to their tails: this kind of saddle is too broad for a man to attempt to stride. Over the saddles were placed what the Moors and Arabs call a *shwerry*, which is made like a double basket, and formed of palm leaves woven together like mat work: each of these baskets might contain about two bushels; they art attached together by a mat woven in with and like the rest, of about a foot and a half in width, sufficiently strong to bear a burden, and long enough to let them hang down easily on the sides of the mules: the outer part of this *shwerry* is held up by means of a rope passing through the handle on one side, and tied to that on the other, passing over the mule's back. In this shwerry, they carry their provisions, merchandise, and spare clothing, (if any they have) when on their journeys. The rider sits on the saddle above the shwerry, with both legs on one side, balancing his body exactly, and rides extremely easy, as he can shift his position at pleasure, and the mule's gait is an easy, fast ambling walk, which they are taught when very young; their motion is very slight, and was a seasonable relief to our almost dislocated limbs: the change, with respect to jolting, was so great from the camel to the mule, that we could not keep our eyes open from mere drowsiness, and Burns getting asleep, dropped off his mule, and was so badly hurt as to be from that time incapable of supporting himself; so that a moor was obliged to sit before or behind him, and keep him on, driving the mule at the same time: and this was continued during the remainder of our journey.

We had proceeded in this way until about ten o'clock, when we were joined by Rais bel Cossim, Sidi Hamet, Seid, Sidi Mohammed, and Bel Mooden. I now inquired of Rais what had become of Muley Ibrahim and Sheick Ali, with their attendants, and he told me they had set out for their respective homes. I wanted to know all the particulars of their proceedings, and Rais promised to satisfy me after breakfast, which we now stopped to eat, (viz. biscuit and butter) near a wall that afforded us good water though nearly on a level with the sea. After we were again mounted, he began to relate as follows. " When my friend told me of Sheick Ali's plan, I stole away softly, and came and sent you off without the Sheick's knowledge; but Muley Ibrahim was in the secret and remained with the Sheick to prevent alarm if he should awake during my absence." Rais bel Cossim further told me in substance, that as soon as we were on our journey, he returned and laid himself down to sleep across the door-way, where Sheick Ali slept, and in such a manner as to make it impossible for the Sheick to go out without alarming him; the Sheick awoke at the dawn of day, and finding himself blockaded in the house, awakened Rais, and told him, that they had better wait on the governor this morning, to which Rais consented, but wanted to see the slaves first, so as to have some coffee made: this was agreed on; but when they came where we slept, and found none of us there, nor the camels, nor their drivers, Rais broke out into the most vio-

lent passion apparently; accused the Sheick of having robbed him of his slaves during the night, and
said he would instantly have him seized and delivered up to the governor to be punished according
to the Moorish law. Muley Ibrahim, who knew the
whole affair, joined with Rais, protesting he could
no longer hold friendship with a man who was capable of committing such an act, which he considered
to be one of the worst breaches of faith that ever
disgraced a man of his (the Sheick's) high character.
Sheick Ali was thunderstruck by this unexpected
event—declared, in the solemn manner, that he knew
nothing about our escape; begged he might not be
delivered up to the governor; acknowledged he had
laid a plan the preceding evening for our detention;
wished Rais to leave the governor a small present,
and proceed on the road towards Mogadore in the
hope of finding us, saying, we must have gone that
way, as the gates were shut on the other side, and
there was no possibility of turning back by any other
route. The Sheick added, "I am in your power, and
will go on with you and my friend Muley Ibrahim,
without any attendants, to prove to you that I am
innocent, and that I place the greatest confidence in
your friendship." Thus they agreed to pursue and
endeavour to overtake the supposed runaway slaves;
but soon after they had mounted the hills north of
Santa Cruz, meeting our former masters, with Bel
Mooden and Sidi Mohammed, who had seen us, (as
I before mentioned) they stopped and talked over
their several affairs. Sheick Ali insisted that Sidi Hamet had treated him very ill: that he and Seid owed
him four hundred dollars, which they were to pay
him on their return from the desart, but that they
had passed by his lands three days' journey with their
slaves, without even calling on him to eat bread: he
added, he would have gone with them himself, and
with an armed force through Sidi Ishem's country,
to prevent that chief from taking their property—

"but you wished to cheat me of my money, as you did of my daughter," said he addressing himself to Sidi Hamet. Sidi Hamet, whose voice had been very high before, now lowering his tone, said, it was better to settle their disputes than to quarrel: so he acknowledged he owed his father-in-law three hundred and sixty dollars for goods, but asserted that they were not worth half the money: he would, however, pay the principal but no interest, which would have swelled the amount of debt to more than five hundred dollars; the Sheick agreed to take the principal which was counted out in silver, as he would not take gold doubloons in payment, because he did not know their real value. He then delivered up Sidi Hamet's bond, and said he would return to his tribe. Rais bel Cossim gave Muley Ibrahim a present in cash, and they separated, having first vowed everlasting friendship, and joined in prayer for the success of their several journeys.

Our company now consisted of Rais bel Cossim, Bel Mooden, Sidi Hamet, Seid, Sidi Mohammed, and three muleteers, all armed with muskets, swords, or daggers—the five Bereberies with their camels, who had brought us on from Stuka, and myself and four shipmates. We proceeded along the coast, sometimes on a sand beach, now climbing an almost perpendicular mountain of great height by a winding kind of zigzag road that seemed to have been cut in the rock in many places, by art; then descending into deep valleys by this kind of natural steps; the rocks on our right for a great distance, rising nearly perpendicularly. The path we were now obliged to follow, was not more than two feet wide in one place, and on our left it broke off in a precipice of some hundred feet deep to the sea—the smallest slip of the mule or camel would have plunged it and its rider down the rocks to inevitable and instant death, as there was no bush or other thing to lay hold of by which a man might save his life. Very fortunately for us, there had been no rain for a considerable time previous, so that the road was now dry. Rais told me when it was wet it was never attempted, and that many fatal accidents had happened there within his remembrance; though there was another road which led round over the mountains far within the country.

One of these accidents he said he would mention. "A company of Jews, six in number, from Santa Cruz for Morocco, came to this place with their loaded mules in the twilight, after sunset; being very anxious to get past it before dark, and supposing no other travellers would venture to meet them, or dare to pass it in the night, they did not take the precaution to look out, and call aloud before they entered on it; for there is a place built out on each end of this dangerous piece of road, from whence one may see if there are others on it: not being quite half a mile in length, a person by hallooing out can be heard from one end to the other, and it is the practice of all who go that way, to give this signal. A company of Moors had entered at the other end, and going towards Santa Cruz at the same time, and they also supposing that no others would dare to pass it at that hour, came on without the usual precaution. About half way over, and in the most difficult place, the two parties met—there was no possibility of passing each other, nor of turning about to go back either way— the Moors were mounted as well as the Jews—neither party could retire, nor could any one, except the foremost, get off his mule: the Moors soon became outrageous, and threatened to throw the Jews down headlong—the Jews, though they had always been treated like slaves, and forced to submit to every insult and indignity, yet finding themselves in this perilous situation, without the possibility of retiring, and being unwilling to break their necks merely to accommodate the Moors, the foremost Jew dismounted carefully over the head of his mule, with a

stout stick in his hand: the Moor nearest him did
the same, and came forward to attack him with his
scimitar: both were fighting for their lives, as neither
could retreat—the Jew's mule was first pitched down
the craggy steep, and dashed to atoms by the fall—
the Jew's stick was next hacked to pieces by the scimitar; when finding it was impossible for him to save
his life, he seized the Moor in his arms, and springing
off the precipice, both were instantly hurled to destruction—two more of the Jews and one Moor lost
their lives in the same way, together with eight mules,
and three Jews, who made out to escape, were hunted
down and killed by the relations of the Moors who
had lost their lives on the pass, and the place has ever
since been called 'the Jews leap.'" It is, indeed,
enough to produce dizziness, even in the head of a
sailor, and if I had been told the story before getting
on this frightful ridge, I am not certain but that my
imagination might have disturbed my faculties, and
rendered me incapable of proceeding with safety
along this perilous path. The danger over, however,
and the story finished, we found ourselves mounting
the first bank from the sea on Cape Geer. When we
came on the height, at the pitch of the Cape, I rode
up to the edge of the precipice to look down upon
the tumultuous ocean. The present Cape is about
one hundred feet in height, and appeared to have
been much shattered and rent by the waves and tempests: huge masses of rocks had been undermined,
broken off, and tumbled down one upon another,
forming very wild and disorderly heaps in the water
all around it. I could not help shuddering at the
sight and sound of the surf as it came thundering on,
and burst against the trembling sides of this rocky
Cape, which is about a mile in length, and is already
undermined in such a manner, that the whole road
along which we passed will very probably soon tum-
ble down among the assailing billows. On our right,

the land rose gradually like an inclined plane, and was covered with pebbles and other round smooth stones that bore strong marks of having been tossed about and worn by the surf on a sea beach: it rose thus for about two miles, when it was interrupted by perpendicular and overhanging cliffs of craggy and broken rocks three or four hundred feet in height: these rocks and the whole face of the upper Cape bore as strong marks of having once been washed and beat upon by the ocean, as did the cliff below us, against which it was now dashing with dreadful violence. Along most parts of the inclined plane, and particularly near the upper cliff, were large mounds of lose sand in form of snow drifts. This sand was now flying up from the beach below, being blown out from among the rocks by the strong trade winds at every low tide, and almost as soon as the dashings of the waves among them had prepared it: this sand, and in fact all we had seen since we came to the cultivated country, was the same in appearance as that which we saw and passed through on the desart, and must have been produced and heaped up by the same causes. After passing the Cape, about one hour's ride, we came to the high bank of the river, and descending to its left shore, we found its mouth was filled up with sand that had been washed in by the sea, though the river was about half a mile wide at its end, and appeared quite deep—here we stopped to take some food, namely, biscuit and butter.

Bel Mooden had also brought some dried figs, dates, and nuts. Having finished our repast, we were again placed on our beasts, and proceeded round the mouth of the river on a sandy beach, about one hundred yards wide, and twenty feet above the level of the fresh water within, and thirty feet above the sea water on the beach at high tide. Our guides informed me that this river was called *"el wod Tensha;"* that it had formerly been a very wide and deep one, and

used to empty itself into the sea: that in the rainy
season it was impossible to pass it without going
twenty miles up the country: but for the last few
years there had not been rain enough in this part of
the country to force open its mouth.

Having left the margin of the river, we entered on
a plain, and struck off to our right in a direction
nearly east, and we went forward as fast as possible
towards the high land. We had passed many sanctuaries, but had not observed a single dwelling house,
nor even a tent since we left Santa Cruz. We now
beheld several square walled places, which answered
the double purpose of dwelling house and castle,
crowning the top of the high mountain, which appeared very dry and sterile, mostly composed of
layers of huge rocks and very steep, with a few dry
shrubs scattered thinly about the crevices and small
flat spots or spaces.—Approaching the foot of the
mountain, we came to a very deep hollow, apparently
formed by the washings of a small stream of water,
assisted by rains that have poured through it from
time immemorial. Our way wound up through this
steep hollow, and alongside of the little brook before
mentioned. As we entered it, the eye was delighted
with the beauty of the scene. The bottom of the hollow had been made level by art, and was covered
from its base with gardens, which rose one above another in the form of an amphitheatre: they were
kept up to a level by means of solid stone walls laid
in lime, and had been filled in with rich soil; the
longest was not greater in extent than twenty yards
by ten: the sides of the hollow were so steep, that the
upright walls were not less than ten or fifteen feet in
height between each garden: they were well stocked
with most kinds of vegetables cultivated in kitchen
gardens, and with melons: gutters were curiously
disposed around these gardens to convey water to
every part, at the pleasure of the proprietor: they

had growing on their sides an abundance of fig and date trees, and grape vines running up the sides of the rocks; and a little higher up hundreds of the dwarf Arga tree, whose yellow fruit contributed to enliven the prospect. We were at least two hours in gaining the summit, when it had become dark, and we had to pass down the mountain on its east side through another hollow, though not a fertile one; for here was no running water. The narrow path we travelled in, had been worn into the limestone rock, by the feet of mules and horses that had passed along it, no doubt during the course of many centuries; and assisted by the rain water streaming through it from above, it was in some places channelled out to the depth of ten or fifteen feet, and just wide enough for a camel or mule to pass. In one place it became necessary, for the want of sufficient room to get through, to take the landing from the mules and carry it down by hand. After descending about three hours we came to a plain, and kept on in an eastern direction until about midnight; when we approached the walls of a small city, or dwelling-place, and took up our lodgings near it on the flat top of a long cistern, which afforded plenty of water. The chief men of the city, alarmed by the barking of their dogs, soon came out and welcomed their visitors by the well known Arabic salutation, "Salemo Alikom, Labez," &c.

They furnished our company with a supper of coos-coo-soo, while I and my men ate some dates and dry figs. The night was damp and cold, and this, with my fatigues, rendered it impossible for me to sleep. We stayed here for about three hours, when daylight appearing, (October the sixth) we were again mounted and proceeding on our journey. My companions, as well as myself, were so weak, being really worn out, and completely exhausted, that it was with the greatest difficulty they could be supported on the mules. As daylight increased, we saw a number of towns or dwellings handsomely enclosed with high walls of stone, cemented with lime: the land on the plain was divided off and fenced in with rough stone walls made with great labor: numerous flocks of goats were feeding on the oil nut: some herds of cattle, with a few old horses, asses, and camels, were nibbling off the green leaves and branches of small shrubs, for the want of grass: we also saw many regularly planted orchards of fig trees; and the land was in many places ploughed and ready to receive the seed barley so soon as rain should fall sufficient to ensure its vegetation.

We went forward to the north-eastward, and on rising a hill, we saw two mountains before us to the north, over which I was informed we must pass: the farthest one north appeared to be twenty miles distant. We soon began to climb the nearest, and when we reached its summit, looking to the east, the Atlas was fairly in view, and all its lofty peaks covered with snow. Descending this mountain, we met large droves of camels, mules, and asses, laden with salt and other merchandise, and driven by a considerable number of Moors and Arabs: the Moors were easily distinguished by their dress: they had each, besides his haick, a caftan or close jacket next to his skin, and the most of them had turbans on their heads: they were armed with daggers, or scimitars, suspended from their necks by a cord of red woolen yarn thrown over the left shoulder: the scabbards were such as I have before described—the dagger is worn outside of the haick; its handle is made of wood handsomely wrought: the point of the dagger hooks inward like a pruning knife: when they have occasion to use it, they seize it with their right hand, the lower side of the hand being next to the blade, and strike after raising it above their heads, ripping open their adversary: they never attempt to parry a stroke with their daggers.

The valley between these two mountains had been well cultivated, and would be very productive with seasonable rains, but at this time those dreadful scourges, severe droughts, and myriads of locusts, had destroyed almost every green thing: even the leaves of the trees and shrubs had not escaped their devastations. I was informed by Rais bel Cossim that we were now in the province of *Hah hah*, and that the locusts had utterly laid waste the country for the last six years, so that the land now groaned under a most grievous famine; nor could our company procure any barley or other food for their beasts. This province must be naturally a very strong military country; it is very mountainous, and rendered almost inaccessible by the craggy steeps and narrow roads, or defiles, through which any army would be under the necessity of marching. The cities, or rather castles in which the inhabitants reside, are built strong with stone and lime, and are fifteen or twenty feet in height, generally of a quadrangular form of from fifty to two hundred yards square, and the tops crowned with turrets: within these walls all the flocks and herds are driven every night for safe keeping. All the men in these parts are well armed with long Moorish muskets, and with sabres, or daggers, by their sides: there are no Arabs dwelling in this part of the country, as they always live in tents, and will not be confined within walls; nor had we seen a tent since our arrival at the dwelling of Sidi Mohammed.

The valley now spread out to the right, and might be termed a considerably extensive plain, on which but few castles or dwellings appeared, and we saw no river or stream of water, though there were high mountains on both sides. The little herbage that had sprung up, in consequence of the recent rains, was destroyed by the locusts, which were to be seen

thinly scattered over the ground, and rose in considerable numbers on our approach; skipping like
grasshoppers. Rais bel Cossim informed me that the
flights of locusts, from which these few had strayed,
had gone to some hitherto more favoured part of
the country to continue their ravages.

While we were tranquilly travelling along, I asked
Rais in what manner the oil was extracted from the
nuts that grew in such quantities on the Arga tree,
which entirely covered the sides of the hills. He
told me that in the country these nuts were swallowed
by the goats, (and in fact we saw these animals picking them up under the trees;) that the nut passes
through, after being deprived of its bark, which
though very bitter, was highly relished by the goats,
and when voided the women and children, who tend
them, pick up the nuts and put them into a bag,
slung about them for the purpose, and carry them
home, where they crack them between stones, get out
the kernel, and expressing the oily juice from them,
they boil it down in a jar until it becomes of a proper
consistence, when it is poured off and is fit for use.
The appearance of this fruit growing thickly on the
trees, different in size, and variegated in colour from
green to red, and from that to bright yellow, had a
pleasing effect: the ground beneath the trees was also
covered with them.

Having come to the foot of the high mountain, we
ascended it, winding up its steep side in a zigzag path
very difficult of ascent, and indeed almost impracticable. On our left was a deep gully, with a considerable stream of water running down through it, like
a small mill-stream: it poured over the precipices,
making a loud roaring, that might be heard at a great
distance; though the whole stream seemed to lose
itself entirely in the sand before it reached the bottom of the mountain. The sides of this gully were
shaded by the Arga and the bean tree, and many
other bushes: and near the water I discovered a few

yew or hemlock bushes, that reminded me of scenes I had been familiar with in my own country. As we rode near the top of the mountain, this gully assumed the appearance of a rich valley, filled with gardens one above another, supported by strong stone walls in the same manner as those I have already described, though much larger, and they were apparently well watered by the stream that was carried around them in gutters fitted for that purpose. These gardens looked as if they were well cultivated, and stored with vegetables; and numbers of men and boys were at work tilling and dressing them.

On the highest part of the mountain that we reached, I was much surprised to find a considerable plain spot, nearly covered with stacks of salt, which stood very thick, and must, I think, have amounted to several hundreds. To see marine salt in such quantities on the top of a mountain, which I computed to stand at least fifteen hundred feet above the surface of the ocean, excited my wonder and curiosity; but we stopped short of them, for the camels we had started with from Stuka, were to carry loads of this salt back; so that after Rais had paid the owners of them for their trouble and assistance, they went towards the salt heaps, wishing us a prosperous journey. While we were stopped to settle with them, we were taken from the mules and seated on the ground, when many of the inhabitants came near to have a look at us, *Christian slaves*. They brought with them a few raw turnips, which they distributed among us: they were the sweetest I had ever tasted, and very refreshing. We were soon placed upon the mules again, and I rode a little to the left, in order to find out in what way this great quantity of salt had been procured and deposited in this singular situation; and on a near approach, I saw a great number of salt pans formed of clay, and very shallow, into which water was conducted by means of small gutters cut for the purpose in the clay. The water issues in considerable quantities from the side of the mountain, in the N. W. part of the plain, (which has been levelled down, and regulated with great labour,) and is very strongly impregnated with salt: the pans or basons being very shallow, the water is soon evaporated by the heat of the sun, and a crystallization of excellent salt is the result. It is small grained, and tinged by the reddish colour of the clay of which the pans are formed. The highest peak of the mountain did not appear to rise above the salt spring more than about one hundred feet: a great number of men and boys were employed in raking and heaping up the salt, and numbers more in selling and measuring it out and loading it on camels, mules, and asses. Rais bel Cossim, informed me, that this spring furnished the greatest proportion of the salt that is made use of in the Moorish dominions, and in Suse; and I should estimate the number of camels, mules, and asses that were there at that time waiting for loads, at from four or five hundred. We had met hundreds on the route since we left Stuka, loaded with this article, and I afterwards saw many loads of the same kind of salt enter *Mogadore*, *Saffy*, and *Rabat*.

We proceeded to the northward down the mountain, which is not so steep on its north as on its south side. The country, after descending it, was tolerably smooth, with much of the Agra wood flourishing on every side. Soon after dark we came to a wall that enclosed a space of ground forty or fifty yards square: it was built of stone and lime, six or eight feet in height, with an open space like a gateway on its northern side, through which we entered and took up our lodgings on the ground, which was very smooth. A walled village was near this yard on the west, and on the north, outside of both walls, stood a mosque or house of worship: the inhabitants were chanting their evening or eight o'clock prayers when we entered the yard; yet none of them came out to look at us, their attention being wholly confined to their religious duties. We were taken from the mules and placed near the wall, which kept off the night wind, and after we had nibbled a little biscuit and drank some water, we thanked God for his goodness, and tried to get a little sleep. The wind did not molest us, and we rested until about midnight, when we were awakened by the noise occasioned by a company of men with loaded camels and mules: they had already entered the yard without ceremony, to the number probably of thirty men, with three times as many camels, mules, and asses. I was awakened by the bellowing of the camels, as they were forced to lie down with their heavy loads;—the men did not speak to ours, and as soon as they had tethered their mules by tying ropes around their footlock joints, and fastening them to pegs driven into the ground for that purpose, they laid themselves down to sleep, wrapped up in their haicks.

Our whole company being awake, they saddled their mules, put us thereon, and we proceeded on our journey. It was very dark, and the path lay through a rough stony country. We were so weak, that we could not sit on the mules without one being behind to steady our tottering frames; at daylight we found ourselves near some substantial buildings, and I begged of Rais to buy some milk if it was possible: he rode near the gates and asked some of the inhabitants for milk; but they would not sell any. This to me was a sore disappointment, as I was benumbed with cold, and so much fatigued, that I thought it would be impossible for me to ride much further; which Rais observing, said to me, "keep up your spirits, Captain, only a few hours longer, and you will be in Swearah if God Almighty continues his protection." I was so reduced and debilitated, that I could not support even good news with any degree of firmness, and such was my agitation,

that it was with the utmost difficulty I could keep
on my mule for some moments afterwards. We had
been constantly travelling for three days and most
of three nights, and though I concluded we must be
near Swearah, I did not think we should reach it
before late in the evening. Passing along a narrow
footway between high bushes, we came to a long
string of sand hills on our left, drifted up, like the
sand heaps on the desert, and along the coast: it was
then about eight o'clock in the morning, when
mounting the side of one of those hills, the city of
Swearah broke suddenly upon our view, with the
island of Mogadore forming a harbour, in which was
a brig riding at anchor with English colours flying:—
"take courage, Captain," said the good Rais; "there
is Swearah," pointing towards the town; "and there
is a vessel to carry you to your country and family;—
if God please you will soon see the noble Willshire,
who will relieve you from all your miseries—I thank
my God your sufferings are nearly at an end, and
that I have been found worthy to be an instrument
in the hands of the Omnipotent to redeem you from
slavery." He next returned thanks to the Almighty
in Arabic with all that fervour and devotion, so
peculiar to Mohammedans, and then he ejaculated,
in Spanish, "May it have pleased Almighty God to
have preserved the lives of my wife and children."

We now proceeded down the sand hills towards
the city—but very slowly. Sidi Hamet had been for
some time missing: he had gone privately forward to
be first to carry the news to our deliverer of our
approach; and now Bel Mooden and Sidi Mohammed left us for a similar purpose, and made the
best of their way towards the city. It would be idle
for me to attempt to describe the various emotions of
my mind at this exquisitely interesting moment: I
must leave that to be conceived by the reader. We
soon approached the walls of an imperial palace,
which is situated about two miles southeast of

Swearah, or Mogadore.—The walls are built in a
square of probably one hundred yards at each side,
and about twenty feet in height—they enclose four
small square houses, built at the four corners within,
and which rise one story about the walls: the houses
have square roofs, coming to a point in the centre,
and handsomely covered with green tiles—they, as
well as the other walls, are built with rough stone,
cemented with lime, plastered over and whitewashed.

Near the western angle of the walls we stopped,
and were taken off our mules and seated on the green
grass. A small stream of fresh water, running from
the east, was spreading over the sand near its northern wall, flowing and meandering slowly towards the
bay over the beach, in a number of small rills. The
water in the bay was quite smooth; small boats were
moving gently on its glassy surface, or were anchored
near its entrance, probably for the purpose of fishing: this, together with the sight of great numbers
of men driving camels, cows, asses, and sheep, and
riding on horses, all at a distance and going different
ways, together with the view of the high steeples in
Mogadore, infused into my soul a kind of sublime
delight and a heavenly serenity that is indiscribable,
and to which it had ever before been a stranger.
The next moment I discovered the American flag
floating over a part of the distant city: at this blessed
and transporting sight, the little blood remaining
in my veins, gushed through my glowing heart with
wild impetuosity, and seemed to pour a flood of new
life through every part of my exhausted frame. We
were still seated on the green sward near the western
wall, and the mules that brought us there were feeding carelessly before us at a little distance. Our
deliverer, who had received news of our coming
from Sidi Hamet, having first directed the flag of
our country to be hoisted as a signal, had mounted
his horse, ridden out of the city, and came to the

eastern side of the palace walls, where Rais bel Cossim met him—unknown to me.—I expected him soon, but did not think he was so near: he had dismounted, and was prepared to behold some of the most miserable objects his imagination could paint—he led his horse along the south angle and near the wall: Rais was by his side, when opening past the corner, I heard Rais exclaim, in Spanish, "Allah estan"—"there they are:"—at this sound we looked up and beheld our deliverer, who had at that instant turned his eyes upon us.—He started back one step with surprise. His blood seemed to fly from his visage for a moment, but recovering himself a little, he rushed forward and clasping me to his breast, he ejaculated, "Welcome to my arms, my dear Sir; this is truly a happy moment." He next took each of my companions by the hand, and welcomed them to their liberty, while tears trickled down his manly cheeks, and the sudden rush of all the generous and sympathetic feelings of his heart nearly choked his utterance: then raising his eyes towards heaven, he said, "I thank thee, great Author of my being for thy mercy to these my brothers."—He could add no more; his whole frame was so agitated that his strength failed him and he sunk to the ground. We, on our part, could only look up towards heaven in silent adoration, while our hearts swelled with indiscribable sensations of gratitude and love to the all wise, all powerful, and ever merciful God of the universe, who had conducted us through so many dreadful scenes of danger and suffering; had controlled the passions and disposed the hearts of the barbarous Arabs in our favour, and had finally brought us to the arms of such a friend. Tears of joy streamed from our eyes, and Rais bel Cossim was so much affected at this interview, that in order to conceal his weeping, he hid himself behind the wall; for the Moors as well as the Arabs, hold the shedding of tears to be a womanish and degrading weakness. After a short pause, when Mr. Willshire had in some measure recovered, he said, "Come, my friends, let us go to the city; my house is already prepared for your reception."—The mules were led up, and we were again placed on them and rode off slowly towards Mogadore. Mr. Savage and Clark were on one mule, and Burns and Horace on another, for the purpose of mutually supporting each other; but their debility was such, that they fell off on the beach two or three times before they reached the city;— however, it was on the soft sand, and as they were very light, they seemed to have received no material injury;—they were again placed on the mules, and steadied until our arrival at the gates of Swearah, by Moors walking beside them. The gateway was crowded with Moors, Jews, and negroes—the news of our coming having spread through the city, and a curiosity to see Christian slaves, had brought them together in great numbers; and the men and boys of the rabble were only restrained from committing violence on us, by the gate-keepers and a few soldiers, who voluntarily escorted us to Mr. Willshire's house, and in some measure kept off the crowd: there we were taken from our mules; but some soldiers coming in at that instant, said it was the Bashaw's orders that we should appear before him immediately, and we were constrained to obey: it was but a few steps, and we were enabled to walk there by supporting one another. When we came to the door, we were ushered into a kind of entry-way, which served as an audience chamber, by Mr. Willshire's Jew interpreter, who in token of submission, was obliged to pull off his cap and slippers before he could enter.— We were ordered to sit down on the floor, and we then saw before us a very respectable looking Moor, of about sixty years of age: he was sitting cross-legged on a mat or carpet that lay on the floor, which was terrace-work, drinking tea from a small cup—his dress was the *haick*. After he had finished his cup of tea and looked at us a moment, he asked me, through the interpreter, what countryman I was? where my vessel was wrecked? how many men I had in all, and if the remainder were alive? how long I had been a slave, and if the Arab, my last master, had treated me kindly? He wanted, further, to know how much money from my vessel fell into the hands of the Arabs, and what other cargo she had on board. Having satisfied his inquiries in the best manner I was able, he said we were now free, and he would write to the emperor respecting me and my men, and hoped he would give us leave to go home to our country: he then dismissed us. Mr. Willshire was with us, and answered all the questions that Bashaw chose to put to him, and then assisted us in returning to his house.

CHAPTER XXIV.

The author and his companions are cleansed, clothed and fed—he becomes delirious, but is again restored to reason—the kindness of Mr. Willshire—letter from Horatio Sprague, Esq. of Gibralter—author's reflections on his past sufferings, and on the providential chain of events that had fitted him for enduring them, and miraculously supported and restored him and his four companions to their liberty

UPON our arrival at Mr. Willshire's house, some Jews were ready to shave off our beards, and as the hair of our heads was also in a very unpleasant condition; being literally filled with vermin; that, as well as our beards, underwent the operation of the scissors and razor: the hair was cut off at least as close as the horrible state of our skin and flesh would admit of: this may be imagined, but it is absolutely too shocking for description. Our squalid and emaciated frames were then purified with soap and water, and our humane and generous friend furnished us with some of his own clothing, after our bodies, which were still covered with sores, had been rubbed with sweet oil. Mr. Willshire's cook had by this time prepared a repast, which consisted of beef cut into square pieces, just large enough for a mouthful before it was cooked; these were then rolled in onions, cut up fine, and mixed with salt and pepper; they were in the next place put on iron skewers and laid horizontally across a pot of burning charcoal, and turned over occasionally until perfectly roasted: this dish is called *Cubbub,* and in my opinion far surpasses in flavour the so much admired beef-steak; as it is eaten hot from the skewers, and is indeed an excellent mode of cooking beef.—We ate sparingly of this delicious food, which was accompanied with some good wheaten bread and butter, and followed by a quantity of exquisite pomegranates; for our stomachs were contracted to such a degree by long fastings, that they had lost their tone, and could not receive the usual allowance for a healthy man.—A doctor then appeared and administered to each of us a dose of physic, which he said was to prepare our stomachs for eating. He was a Jew, who had been bred at Moscow in Russia, had studied medicine there, and had since travelled through Germany, Italy, and Spain; he spoke the Spanish language fluently, and I was convinced, before I left Mogadore, that he possessed much medical as well as surgical skill. He had only been in Mogadore two

months, and there was no other physician in that
city, or in that part of the country, except jugglers
or quacks. Good beds had been fitted up for myself
and Mr. Savage in the same room, and after being
welcomed by Mr. John Foxcroft and Don Pablo
Riva, who had heard of our arrival, we retired to
rest.

My mind, which (though my body was worn
down to a skeleton) had been hitherto strong, and
supported me through all my trials, distresses, and
sufferings, and enabled me to encourage and keep
up the spirits of my frequently despairing fellow-
sufferers, could no longer sustain me: my sudden
change of situation seemed to have relaxed the very
springs of my soul, and all my faculties fell into the
wildest confusion. The unbounded kindness, the
goodness, and whole attention of Mr. Willshire, who
made use of all the soothing language of which the
most affectionate brother or friend is capable, tended
but to ferment the tempest that was gathering in
my brain. I became delirious—was bereft of my senses
—and for the space of three days knew not where
I was.—When my reason returned, I found I had
been constantly attended by Mr. Willshire, and generally kept in my room, though he would sometimes
persuade me to walk in the gallery with him, and
used every means in his power to restore and com-
pose my bewildered senses: that I had remained
continually bathed in tears, and shuddering at the
sight of every human being, fearing I should again
be carried into slavery. I had slunk into the darkest
corner of my room; but though insensible I seemed
to know the worth of my friend and deliverer, and
would agree to, and comply with his advice and
directions.

In the mean time, this most estimable and noble
minded young man, had neither spared pains nor
expense in procuring for us every comfort, and in

administering, with his own hands, night and day, such relief and refreshment as our late severe sufferings and present debility required. He had sent off persons on mules to the vicinity of the city of Morocco, more than one hundred miles, and procured some of the most delicious fruits that country can produce, such as dates, figs, grapes, pomegranates, &c.—He gave us for drink the best of wines, and I again began to have an appetite for my food, which was prepared with the greatest care. My men were furnished with shirts, trowsers, and jackets, and being fed with the most nourishing soups and other kinds of food, gained a considerable degree of strength. Captain Wallace, of the English brig Pilot, then being in the port, furnished us with some pork, split peas, and potatoes, and seemed very friendly. Clark and Burns were but the skeletons of men—Mr. Savage and Horace were nearly as much reduced, but not having been diseased in so great a degree, they were consequently stronger. Many of my bones as well as my ribs, had been divested entirely, not only of flesh, but of skin, and had appeared white like dry bones when on the desart; but they were now nearly covered again, though we still might with some reason be termed the dry skeletons of Moorish slaves. At the instance of Mr. Willshire I was weighed, and fell short of ninety pounds, though my usual weight for the last ten years, had been over two hundred and forty pounds: the weight of my companions was less than I dare to mention, for I apprehend it would not be believed that the bodies of men retaining the vital spark, should not weigh forty pounds.

The sight of my face in a glass called to my recollection all the trying scenes I had passed through since my shipwreck;—I could contemplate with pleasure and gratitude the power, and wisdom, and foreknowledge of the Supreme Being, as well as his mercy and unbounded goodness. I could plainly discover that the train of events which, in my former life, I had always considered as great misfortunes, had been directed by unerring wisdom, and had fitted me for running the circle marked out by the Omnipotent. When I studied the French and Spanish languages, I did it from expectations of future gain in a commercial point of view. All the exertions I had hitherto made to become acquainted with foreign languages, and to store my mind with learning and a knowledge of mankind, had produced for me no wealth; without which acquirement a man is generally considered on the stage of the world as a very insignificant creature, that may be kicked off or trampled upon by the pampered worms of his species, who sport around him with all the upstart pride of (in many instances) ill-gotten treasure. I had been cheated and swindled out of property by those whom I considered my friends; yet my mind was formed for friendship;—I do not speak of this in the way of boasting. My hand had never been slack in relieving the distresses of my fellow men whenever I had the power, in the different countries where I had been; but I had almost become a stoic, and had very nearly concluded, that disinterested friendship and benevolence, out of the circle of a man's own family, was not to be found; that the virtuous man, if poor, was not only despised, by his more fortunate fellow creatures, but forsaken almost by Providence itself. I now, however, had positive proof to the contrary of some of those hasty and ill-founded opinions; and I clearly saw that I had only been tutored in the school of adversity, in order that I might be prepared for fulfilling the purpose for which I had been created.

In the midst of those reflections I received, by a

courier from Consul General Simpson, at Tangier, to Mr. Willshire, the following letter:—it speaks the soul of the writer, and needs no comment.

Gibraltar, 13th November, 1815.

MY DEAR RILEY,

I will not waste a moment by unnecessary preamble. I have wrote to Mr. Willshire, that your draft on me for twelve hundred dollars, or more, shall be duly paid for the obtainment of your liberty, and those with you. I have sent him two double barrelled guns to meet his promise to the Moor.— In a short time after the receipt of this, I hope to have the happiness to take you by the hand under my roof again. You will come here by the way of Tangier.

Your assured friend,
HORATIO SPRAGUE.

My sensations on reading this letter, and on seeing that written by Mr. Sprague to Mr. Willshire, I must leave to the reader to imagine, and only observe that my acquaintance with that gentleman was but very slight, (of about ten days,) while I remained at Gibraltar, immediately before my disaster—it was sufficient for him to know his fellow creatures were in distress, and that it was in his power to relieve them. Mr. Sprague is a native of Boston, the capital of the State of Massachusetts, and had established himself as a respectable merchant in Gibraltar a little before the breaking out of the late war.—In the early part of that war a number of American vessels were despatched by individuals with cargoes of provisions, &c. for Spain and Portugal—these vessels were navigated under enemies' licenses, but from some cause or other, many of them were seized on the ocean by British ships of war, and conducted to Gibraltar; where both the vessels and their cargoes were con-

demned, and their crews turned adrift in the streets
without a cent of money in their pockets, and left to
the mercy of the elements. Mr. Gavino, the American consul, would not act in their behalf, because
(as he stated) his functions had ceased by reason of
the war;—when this humane and generous gentleman took them under his protection, hired the hulk
of an old vessel for them to live in, furnished them
with provisions and other necessaries and comforts
for the term of one whole year or upwards, and in
this manner supported for the greater part of that
time as many as one hundred and fifty men—this he
did from his own purse, and out of pure philan-
thropy—of this I was informed by Mr. Charles
Moore, of Philadelphia, and other gentlemen of respectability and veracity. He also furnished and sent
a considerable sum of money to Algiers, which
bought from hard labour our unfortunate countrymen, comprising the officers and crew of the brig
———, Captain Smith of Boston, who were made
slaves by that regency;—in this he was assisted by
Messrs. Charles H. Hall & Co. merchants at Cadiz,
and several other worthy and respectable Americans;
but the loss of the United States' sloop of war the
Epervier, when homeward bound, having on board
all the redeemed slaves after the peace with Algiers,
rendered it impossible for them to communicate their
sense of gratitude for Mr. Sprague's humanity. These
facts were stated to me by several respectable individuals in Gibraltar, and can be fully authenticated.

After my mind had been again tranquillized by a
refreshing night's sleep, my reflections returned to
my providential preservation.

When my vessel was wrecked, I was endued with
presence of mind, judgment, and prudence, whereby
my whole crew was saved in the first instance, and
safely landed. When I was seized on afterwards by
the Arabs, a superior intelligence suddenly suggested

to my mind a stratagem by which my life was saved,
though one of my unfortunate companions was sacrificed to glut the brutal rage of the natives, whilst I
was conducted to the wreck in safety through a tremendous surf that rolled over me every instant. The
ways of Providence were next traced out to my
wondering eyes in the smoothing down of the sea,
so that we were enabled to row our shattered boat
out with safety to the ocean, and in our preservation
in an open boat amidst violent gales of wind, though
her timbers and planks seemed only to hold together
by the pressure of the sea acting upon their outer
side. When destitute of provisions and water, worn
down with privations and fatigues, we were again
landed on the coast, carried on the top of a dreadful
wave over the heads of craggy rocks that must have
dashed us and our boat to atoms without a particular
divine protection. We were next forced to climb over
the most formidable precipices and obstructions, before it was possible to arrive on the dreary desert
above us: these delays were necessary to bring us, at
a proper time, within sight of fires kindled by Arabs,
who had arrived there that day, (and who were the
first, as I was afterwards informed, who had been
there to water their camels within the last thirty
days,) and who were providentially sent to save our
lives, as we could not have existed a day longer without drink. Though my skin was burned off by the
sun's rays, and myself given as a slave to those wandering wretches—the same Almighty power still preserved my life, endowed me with intelligence to comprehend a language I had never before heard spoken,
and enabled me to make myself understood by that
people, and in some degree respected. Sidi Hamet
(though a thievish Arab) had been sent from the
confines of the Moorish Empire before I left Gibraltar: he was conducted by the same unerring wisdom
to my master's tent; his heart was softened at the re-

cital of my distresses, and instead of trading in the
article of ostrich feathers, (which was his whole business there, as he believed) he was persuaded by a
wretched naked skeleton of a slave, merely retaining
the glimmering of the vital spark, against his own
judgment, and whilst directly and strenuously opposed by his brother and partner, who insisted that
if even I told the truth, and had a friend in Morocco
to purchase me on my arrival there, yet my death
must certainly happen long before it was possible
to get me to that place: yet this same brother, one
of the most barbarous of men, was forced, though
against his will, to agree, and to lend the aid of his
property in effecting the purchase, and to exert himself to support and to defend myself and four companions, through the desert, whilst all his schemes
for selling and separating us had constantly proved
abortive. A Spanish barque had been destroyed by
the natives on the coast of Suse, north of Cape Nun,
and nineteen men had been either massacred by the
natives, or were groaning out a miserable existence
in the worst kind of barbarian slavery—this event
alone had furnished a piece of paper on which I
wrote the note, at a venture, to Mogadore: my note
fell into the hands of a perfect stranger, whose name
I had never even heard of, and who was as ignorant
of mine. This excellent young man was touched by
the same power who had hitherto protected me: he
agreed to pay the sum demanded without reflection,
though his utter ruin might have been the consequence, trusting implicitly to the written word of a
wretched naked slave; a person of whom he had no
knowledge, and who was then three hundred miles
distant, and even out of the power of the government
that protected him; and his impatience to relieve my
distresses was so great, that he instantly paid the
money demanded by my master, on his simply agree-
ing to stay in Swearah (Mogadore) until we came up,

but without the power to keep him one instant if he chose to go away; nor would he allow time to the magnanimous Moor, who kindly volunteered to go down after us, at the imminent risk of his life, scarcely to take leave of his family: mounting him on his own mule, and begging him to hurry on, day and night, until he reached us, and to spare neither pains or expense in fetching us to Mogadore.

I cannot here omit mentioning the manner in which Mr. Willshire got my first note. Sidi Hamet (the bearer of it) was one of those Arabs belonging to a tribe, surnamed by the Moors sons of Lions, on account of their unconquerable spirit; when he came to the gate of Swearah or Mogadore, he providentially was met by Rais bel Cossim, who though a perfect stranger, asked him, "From whence come you, son of a lion?" Upon which Sidi Hamet stopped, and made known his business. This Moor was the only one which Mr. Willshire placed confidence in, or treated as a friend: he conducted Sidi Hamet to Mr. Willshire's house, and offered to leave his family, who were then sick, and to do his utmost to restore me and my men to liberty. Providence had also caused us to be stopped at Stuka, where we had time to recover, in part, from our illness, and to gain strength enough to support us through the remainder of our journey; had turned the contrivances of Sheick Ali into nothingness, and finally provided for us such a friend as Mr. Sprague of Gibraltar, one of the most feeling and best of men.

This providential chain of events, thus planned and executed, even against the will of the principal agents employed, filled my mind with unutterable thankfulness and wonder at the wisdom, the goodness, and the mercy of God towards me; and the emotions which these reflections excited kept me almost constantly bathed in tears for the greatest part of a month. When I retired to rest, and sleep had closed my eyes, my mind still retaining the

strong impression of my past sufferings, made them
the subjects of my dreams. I used to rise in my
sleep, and think I was driving camels up and down
the sandy hills near the desart, or along the craggy
steeps of Morocco: obeying my master's orders in
putting on the fetters, or beckets, on the legs and
knees of his camels, and in the midst of my agonizing
toils and heart-sickening anxieties, while groping
about my room, I would hit my head against something, which would startle and awaken me: then I
would throw myself on my bed again to sleep, and
dream, and act over similar scenes. Fearing I should
get out of my chamber and injure myself in my
sleep, I always locked the door, and hid the key
before I went to bed. There was a grating to the
windows of the apartments I slept in, and I often
awoke and found myself trying to get out. My mind
at length became more composed and serene as my
strength increased, and by the first of December I
was able to ride out, and to walk about the city. Mr.
Willshire, whose whole attention had been shown to
me and my companions, tried every means to divert
my mind from the subject of my reflections, and
would ride out with me to a garden two miles out
of the city, accompanied by a Moor, where we passed
away many pleasant hours, which were endeared by
every feeling and sentiment of gratitude and esteem
on the one part, and of generous sympathy and god-
like benevolence on the other.

In this garden stood a venerable fig tree, whose
body and boughs were covered with the names and
initials of the names, of almost all the Europeans and
Americans who had visited Mogadore, carved out
with knives in the thick bark, accompanied with the
dates of their several visits, &c. This was a kind of
monument I delighted to examine; it seemed to say
that Mogadore was once a flourishing city, when its
commerce was fostered by the Moorish government;
but now, that superstition, fanaticism, and tyranny

bear sway, they have swept away, with their perni-
cious breath, the whole wealth of its once industrious
and highly favoured inhabitants;—have driven the
foreigner from their shores, and it seems as if the
curse of Heaven had fallen on the whole land, for
in spite of all the exertions of its cultivators and the
fertility of the soil, severe droughts, and the ravages
of the locusts, have frequently caused a famine in
that country, from whence wheat was exported in
immense quantities but a few years past for Spain
and Portugal, at half a dollar per bushel. Not a single
bushel had been shipped for some years past, and at
this time none was to be had at any price, except
now and then a few bags, brought from the province
of Duquella, which could only be purchased by the
most wealthy: the others were provided with scanty
portions of barley, of which they made their coos-
coo-soo.

CHAPTER XXV.

*The author's motives for requesting of, and writing
down, his former master's narrative of Travels on the
Desart when in Mogadore, together with Sidi Hamet's
narrative of a journey across the great Desart to
Tombuctoo, and back again to Widnoon,
with a caravan*

FROM the time I had a prospect of being redeemed
from slavery, I had determined (if that should ever
happen) to write an account of our sufferings, which
I considered greater than had ever fallen to the lot of

man, and also to embody such observations as I had
been enabled to make while a slave, in travelling the
great desart, &c. &c. for the satisfaction of my family
and the friends of my fellow-sufferers. My late master
was yet in Mogadore, for he remained in the house
of my deliverer about two weeks after our arrival,
and he now mentioned to me that he and his brother
had been three times to Tombuctoo (as he had
before informed Mr. Willshire) with caravans, and
had crossed the desart in almost every direction. I
felt interested in making every inquiry that could
suggest itself to my mind respecting the face and
the extent of the desart and the countries south of it;
and although I was convinced by my own observations, that both he and his brother, probably in
common with the Arabs of the desart, knew the
courses they steered, notwithstanding they had no
compass or any other instrument to direct them in
their journeys, yet wishing to be fully satisfied in
this particular, I took them up upon the roof of
the house (which was flat and terraced with stones
laid in lime cement, and smooth like a floor) one
clear evening, and then told them that I wanted to
know by what means they were enabled to find
their way across the trackless desart. Sidi Hamet
immediately pointed out to me the north or polar
star, and the great bear, and told me the Aragic
names of the principal fixed stars, as well as of the
planets, then visible in the firmament, and his manner of steering and reckoning time by the means of
them. His correct observations on the stars, perfectly
astonished me: he appeared to be much better acquainted with the motions of the heavenly bodies
than I was, who had made it my study for a great
many years, and navigated to many parts of the
globe by their assistance. To convince me that he
knew the cardinal points, he laid two small sticks
across at right angles, one pointing directly towards
the polar star—he next placed two others across,

dividing the circle into eighths, and then in like
manner into sixteenths, so that I was satisfied he knew
the requisite divisions of the compass: and on the
next day I requested him to give me a narrative of
his journeyings on, and across the desart, with which
he very readily complied, and related as follows;—
while I sat in my room with pen, ink; and paper, and
noted it down, having the Moor *bel Mooden* to in-
terpret and explain to me in Spanish such parts of
the narrative as I did not perfectly comprehend in
Arabic. I give it to the reader as nearly as possible
in the words of the narrator, and do not hold myself
responsible for Sidi Hamet's correctness, or his veracity, though for my own part I have no doubt he
meant to, and did tell the truth as near as his recollection served him; and as he had a retentive
memory, and the incidents related were calculated
to impress themselves strongly on his intelligent
mind, I have no doubt that his whole narrative is
substantially true.

SECTION I.

*Sidi Hamet's narrative of a journey from Widnoon
across the great Desart to Tombuctoo, and back again
to Widnoon.*

"THE first time I set out to cross the great desart,
was several years ago, (about nine or ten) being
in the vicinity of Widnoon, where I had the year
before been married to the daughter of Sheick Ali,
(a beautiful woman, who is now my wife, and has
two fine boys and one girl.) I, with my brother Seid,
joined the caravan at Widnoon, by the advice of
Sheick Ali: we had four camels loaded with haicks
and some other goods. The whole caravan consisted
of about three thousand camels and eight hundred
men, with goods of almost every kind that are sold

in Morocco. The men were all armed with good muskets and scimitars, and the whole under the command of *Sheick ben Soleyman* of Waldeleim. (Woled Deleim on the map) with four competent guides. We set out from Widnoon in Suse, which is a great place of trade, late in the fall of the year, and travelled six days to the west, when we came to the last mountain—there we stopped ten days, and let our camels feed on the bushes, while half the men were employed in getting wood from the mountain, and burning it into charcoal, which we put into bags, as it was light, and laid it on the camels over the other goods; then setting off for the desart, we mounted upon its level, which is a great deal higher than the country near it to the north, and travelled four days on the hard level; we then passed amongst the high sand hills, which you saw when we were coming up, in order that we might keep along by the great sea, so as to be sure of finding water; we travelled through and among these great mountains of sand, which were then very bad to pass, because the wind blew so hard, we could scarcely keep together, being almost covered up by the flying sand: it took us six days to get through them; after which the ground was smooth, and almost as hard as the floor of a house, for ten days more, when we came to a watering place, called *Bablah;* there we watered our camels, for they were very thirsty, and eight of them had died and served us for food. We stopped at that great well seven days, and afterwards kept on our journey to the S. W. twenty days, to another well, called *Kibir Jibl,* but there was no water in it, and we were obliged to go six days' journey to the sea-coast, where there was a well close to the sea, the water of which well was very black and salt: here we were forced to unload the camels, and get them down the bank to the water, and after drinking, they yielded us some milk, which had been almost dried

up before:—we found, however, nothing for them
to feed on, and had been obliged to give them of
the coals to eat, once a day for many days: this kept
them alive but it made their milk almost as black
as the coals themselves; yet it was good, and we were
glad to get it. It took up six days to water the whole
of them, when we set out again and travelled near
the sea, where we found wells about every ten days,
like the one we had already visited, but very few
green leaves on the little bushes, in the few small
valleys we saw; for no rain had fallen for a great
while on that part of the desert.

"After a journey of four moons, we came to the
south part of the desert, and went down into the
country of *Soudain,* where we found a little stream
of good running water, and some bushes, and grass,
and a very large tribe of *Bessebes Arabs,* (Libdesse-
bas on the map) who had plenty of barley and maize
or Indian corn, of which we bought some and made
bread, and stopped here one moon. We lost on the
desert more than three hundred camels, which had
died of fatigue, and the want of water and food,
but not one man. All the tribes of Arabs we came
near, took their stuff on their camels, and rode away
as fast as they could, so as not to be robbed, and we
did not find any party strong enough to attack us,
although we saw a great many tribes, but they were
very poor on the *Zaharah,* or great desert." I then
asked him how the face of the desert looked in general, as he passed over it, taking the whole together,
or if there was any material difference in different
parts of it, near the sea-coast? to which he answered:—

"The whole extent of the desert near the sea-coast,
is like that we came over in bringing you up here,
except in one place, where we travelled for nearly
one moon, without meeting with so much as a valley
with green bushes in it for the camels to feed on: the
whole is a trackless waste. Close by the sea we were

obliged to pass mountains of sand that was blown up from the shore before the wind, but the guides always went before us, to show which way the caravan must go, and to find a place to stop in. Our camels had eaten up all the coals we had laid upon them before we got off the desart, and two of them had died, so that my brother and I had only two remaining, but we kept all our goods. After we had rested one moon, and got our camels recruited, we set off to the east on the border of the desert, close by the low country, with mountains in sight to the south, most of the way, and in two moons more we came near Tombuctoo, where we stopped in a deep valley with the caravan, and went every day close to the strong walls of the city with our goods (but without our guns) to trade them off with the negroes, who had gum, and gold rings, and gold powder, and great teeth, such as are sold in Swearah, (i.e. elephant's teeth,) and slaves, and fine turbans: they had plenty of cows, and asses, and a few sheep, and barley, corn, and rice: but the little river that runs close to the wall on the west, was quite dry, and all the people in the city were obliged to fetch water for themselves to drink, with asses, from the great river south of the city, (about one hour's ride on a camel) and we were forced to go there to water our camels, and get our drink.

"After staying near Tombuctoo one moon and a half, the season being far advanced, we set out again for Widnoon. I had not been in the city all the time we stopped here, because I was chosen captain of two hundred men that kept guard all the time about the caravan, to keep off the thievish Arabs and the bands of negroes that were hovering around us to carry off our camels, if any of them strayed away: but we lost only twenty during our whole stay at Tombuctoo, and the Sheick gave me for my trouble a fine young negro girl slave, which I carried home with

me, and she now lives with my wife. We set out for
home from Tombuctoo, in the month of *Rhamadan,*
after the feast, and went back by the same route we
had come—that is to say, we went first to the west,
one moon, along the border of the desert. We durst
not take any thing without paying for it, because we
were afraid of the inhabitants, who were a mixture
of Arabs and negroes, and all of them Mohammedans, but very bad men: they had also many white
men slaves. I saw sixteen or eighteen myself, and a
great many blacks. These true believers have very
fine horses, and they go south to the country of the
rivers, and there they attack and take towns, and
bring away all the negroes for slaves, if they will not
believe in the prophet of God; and carry off all their
cattle, rice, and corn, and burn their houses; but if
they will adopt the true faith, they are then exempt
from slavery, and their houses are spared, upon their
surrendering up one-half of their cattle, and half
of their rice and corn; because, they say, God has
delivered their enemies into their hands. The
negroes live in small towns, fenced in with reeds or
bushes, and sometimes with stones, but the Arabs
live only in tents, and can move off in a minute on
the horses, whilst their wives and children ride on
camels and asses. Before we struck off N. W. on
the desert for the sea-coast, we stopped in the hill
country, and fatted our camels, and burned wood
to make charcoal to carry with us: we were encamped
on the bank of a little river, one day's journey from
a large town of negroes, named *Jathrow.* I did not
go to it, but the Sheick went and bought some corn
and barley, and forty oxen for our provisions.

"After we had prepared our coals, and laid in our
provisions, we went up on to the level desert, and
set off to the N. W., and in three moons and a half
more we reached Widnoon again, having been gone
almost a year and a half. We had lost about five

hundred camels, that either died, or were killed to give us meat; and while we stayed at Tombuctoo, and were coming home, thirty-four of our men had died, and we lost eighty slaves." I asked him what were the goods they carried down at that time? he answered:—

"We had about one hundred camels loaded with iron and knives, and two hundred with salt; all the others carried haicks, and blue and white cloth, and lumber, and tobacco, and silk handkerchiefs, and *chilly weed*, and spices, and a great many other articles. Seid and myself had lost two of our camels, but had got two negro slaves, and some gold dust worth six camels, and ornaments for our wives; but Sheick Ali was not satisfied because I did not give him two slaves; so that he made war against me, and battered down my town which I built, (it was but a small one) and took away all I had, together with my wife, because he said I was a bad man, and he was stronger than me: I myself, however, escaped, and after one year I asked him for my wife again, and he gave her to me with all he had taken, for he loved his daughter: but I had no house, so I removed into the sultan's dominions, near the city of Morocco, close by the Atlas mountains, and lived there with my father and brothers two years, without going forth to trade."

SECTION II.

Sidi Hamet sets out on another journey for Tombuctoo

"About that time one of our party, when we first went to Tombuctoo, named *bel Moese*, came to see me—he was going to join the caravan at Widnoon again, and persuaded Seid and me to go with him; so we bought eight camels between us, and sold off our cattle and sheep, and bought goods and powder,

and went with him to Widnoon, and joined the
caravan. Sheick Ali came to meet me like a friend,
and gave me two camels laden with barley, and
wished me a safe journey. The Sheick who was
chosen by all the people to command the caravan,
was named *Sidi Ishrel;* he was the friend of Sidi
Ishem, who owned almost one-half of the whole
caravan, and we set out from Widnoon, with about
four thousand camels, and more than one thousand
men, all well armed. We laid in an abundant store
of barley, and had a great many milch camels, and
it was determined to go south across the desert,
nearly on a straight course for Tombuctoo, by the
way the great caravans generally travelled: though
there had been several of them destroyed on that
route, that is to say, one within every ten or twelve
years. We went to the south, around the bottom of
the great Atlas mountains, six days' journey; then
we stopped close by it, and cut wood and burned
coals for the camels, for the caravans never attempt
to cross the desert without this article: four hundred
camels out of the number were loaded with provisions and water for the journey, and after having
rested ten days, and given the camels plenty of drink,
we went up on the desert and steered off to the south-
easterly. We travelled along, and met with no sand
for fifteen days; it was all a smooth surface, baked together so hard, that a loaded camel could not make
a track on it to be seen: we saw no tracks to guide
us, and kept our course by the stars, and sun, and
moon. We found only one spot in all that time where
our camels could satisfy their appetites by eating the
shrubs in a shallow valley, but the great well in it
was filled up with stones and sand, so we could procure no water there; at the end of fifteen days, however, we came to a very fine deep valley, with twenty
wells in it; but we found water in only six of them,
because the desart was very dry: here we watered

all our camels, and replenished our bottles or skins, and having rested seven days, we departed for the south-eastward, our camels being well filled with leaves and thorn bushes.

"We travelled along three days on the hard sand, and then arrived among innumerable drifts of fine loose sand; not such coarse sand as you saw near the sea; it was as fine as the dust on a path, or in a house, and the camel's feet sunk in it every step up to their knees: after travelling amongst this sand (which in the day-time was almost as hot as coals of fire) six days, there began to blow a fierce wind from the south-east, called the wind of the desart, bringing death and destruction with it: we could not advance nor retreat, so we took the loading from off our camels, and piled it in one great heap, and made the camels lie down. The dust flew so thick that we could not see each other nor our camels, and were scarcely able to breathe—so we laid down with our faces in the dust, and cried aloud with one voice to God—'great and merciful God, spare our lives!' but the wind blew dreadfully for the space of two days, and we were obliged to move ourselves whenever the sand got so heavy on us that it shut out all the air, and prevented us from breathing; but at length it pleased the most High to hear our supplications: the wind ceased to blow; all was still again, and we crawled out of the sand that had buried us for so long a time, but not all, for when the company was numbered, three hundred were missing—all that were left having joined in thanks to God for his mercy in sparing our lives;—we then proceeded to dig out the camels from the sand that had buried their bodies, which, together with the reloading of them, took us two days. About two hundred of them were dead—there was no green thing to be seen, and we were obliged to give the camels a little water from the skins, to wash their parched throats with, and some charcoal to eat: then we kept on twenty-four days as fast as we could through the dry, deep, and hot sand, without finding any green bushes worth noticing for our camels to eat, when we came to a famous valley and watering place, called *Haherah.* All our camels were almost expiring, and could not carry the whole of their loads; so we threw away a great deal of the salt before we got to *Haherah,* where we intended to stop twenty days to recruit our beasts, but who can conceive our disappointment and distress, when we found there was no water in any of the wells of this great valley: not one drop of rain had fallen there for the last year. The caravan, that amounted to upwards of one thousand men and four thousand camels when we set out, was already reduced to about six hundred men, and thirty-five hundred camels. The authority of *Sheick Ishrel* could scarcely restrain those almost desperate men; every one was eager to save his own life and property, and separately sought the means of relief by running about the valley in a desultory manner, looking for water; this disorder continued for two days, when being convinced that nothing could be done without union, they became obedient, and joined together in great numbers in digging out the different wells. After digging five days without the smallest sign of water, all subordination was entirely at an end. The Sheick, who was a wise and a prudent man, advised and insisted that all the camels should be killed but three hundred, so that the little water found in them, together with their blood might keep the rest alive, as well as all the men, until, by the aid of Providence, they should reach some place where they could find water; but the company would not hearken to this advice, though the best that could possibly be given; no one being willing to have his own property sacrificed. *Sheick Ishrel,* however directed thirty of the oldest and most judicious men to pick out the three hundred camels that were to be spared, who accordingly selected the most vigorous; but when they began to kill the others, a most furious quarrel and horrible battle commenced. The Sheick, though a man of God, was killed in a moment—two or three hundred more were butchered by each other in the course of that dreadful day; and the blood of the slain was drank to allay the thirst of those who shed it. Seid was badly wounded with a dagger in his arm: about five hundred camels were killed this day; and the others drank the water from their bodies and also their blood.

"Fearing there would be no end to this bloody conflict until all had perished, and as I had been a captain in the other caravan, and knew how to steer a course on the desart; and as both Seid and myself were very strong men, we killed four out of six of our own camels that remained, in the first part of the night, and gave their water and blood to the other two: we saved a small package of goods, and some barley, and some meat, and persuaded thirty of our friends privately to do as we had done, and join us, for we meant to set off that night. This was agreed on, for to stay there was certain death, and to go back was no less so. We were ready about midnight, and without making any noise, we moved off with our company of thirty men and thirty-two camels. The night was very cloudy and dark, and it thundered at a distance, as if the Almighty was angry with us for fighting together; but there was no rain. We went towards the south-west, in the hope of reaching *Tishlah*, another watering-place, before our camels died: the desart was dry and hard, and as we went along, we found only now and then a little hollow, with a few prickly shrubs in it: these the camels devoured as we passed among them; but many died, so that on the twelfth day we had only eighteen camels left; when the great God saved our lives by sending a tempest of rain, but he thundered so as to make the whole earth tremble, because of our sins, and we all fell upon our faces and implored his forgiveness: the rain that fell upon the ground gave plenty of water to our camels, and we filled thirty skins with it; when we steered to the south towards the borders of the desert. Nine of our company had died, and many of our camels, before we went down from the desert to the cultivated land, and we then made to the south towards a little river of fresh water, to which some Arabs whom we met with, directed us, after they had first given us some rice and milk, for all our milch camels had died on the desert."

SECTION III.

Tombuctoo—description of that city—its commerce, wealth, and inhabitants.

"Those of us who had escaped with our lives from the desert, only twenty-one in number, with twelve camels, out of a caravan of one thousand men and four thousand camels, stopped near a small town, called *Wabilt*, on the bank of a river about half as broad as from the city of Mogadore to the island, that is to say, fifty yards. We had no provisions, but the negroes seeing us in distress, came out and gave us some meat, and bread made of barleycorn: here we remained ten days to recruit our selves and our camels, which were just alive. The river on whose bank we remained, was called by those who spoke in Arabic, *el Wod Tenij,* and by the negroes, *Gozen-zair.* A very high ridge of mountains, great like Atlas seen from Suse, (but not capped with snow) lie to the south-westward, and at a distance. After resting ourselves and our camels for ten days, we set forward for Tombuctoo. We travelled for four days to the eastward through Soudan, a hilly country, but of a very rich soil, and much of it culti- vated with the hoe." I then asked him what he meant by Soudan? and he said, "The whole country south of the great desart from the great ocean, a great way east, and including the district of Tombuctoo, is called by the Arabs and Moors, Soudan; of which Tombuctoo is the capital. Having watered our camels again, and finding the hill country tedious to get through, by reason of the trees, we bought some barley-corn, and killed two cows, and went north- ward to the border of the desart, and travelled on to the eastward for eight days, when we fell in with the great path used by the caravans, and in two days more came near to the walls of Tombuctoo. We had seen a great many negroes near the river: they live in small towns, fenced in with large reeds, to keep off enemies and the wild beasts in the night: they dwell in small round huts made with cane standing upright, are covered with the same materials, and daubed with mud, to fill up the openings between them. The negroes were afraid of us when we came near their little towns, and those who were outside ran in and blocked up the passage in a minute; but finding we did not come to rob them, as the large companies of Arabs often do, but that we were poor and hungry, they were willing to exchange barley corn and meat for some of our goods. Nearly all the few things we had, were expended to keep us alive until we came near Tombuctoo. The king and the people of that city had been looking out for the caravan from Widnoon for two moons, but not one soul had arrived before us, and we were permitted to go into the city after delivering up our guns, powder, and lead, to the king's officers to keep until we should wish to depart. Tombuctoo is a very large city, five times as great as Swearah: it is built on a level plain, surrounded on all sides by hills, except on the south, where the plain continues to the bank of the same river we had been to before, which is wide and deep, and runs to the east; for we were obliged to go to it to water our camels, and here we saw many boats made of great trees, some with negroes in them paddling across the river. The city is strongly walled in with stone laid in clay, like the towns and houses in Suse, only a great deal thicker: the house of the king is very large and high, like the largest house in Mogadore, but built of the same materials as the walls: there are a great many more houses in that city built of stone, with shops on one side, where they sell salt and knives, and blue cloth, and haicks and an abundance of other things, with many gold ornaments. The inhabitants are blacks, and the chief is a very large and gray-headed old black man, who is called *Shegar*, which means sultan, or king. The principal part of the houses are made with large reeds, as thick as a man's arm, and stand upon their ends, and are covered with small reeds first, and then with the leaves of the date trees: they are round, and the tops come to a point like a heap of stones. Neither the Shegar nor his people are Moslemins, but there is a town divided off from the principal one, in one corner, by a strong partition wall, and one gate to it, which leads from the main town, like the Jews' town, or Millah in Mogadore: all the Moors or Arabs who have liberty to come into Tombuctoo, are obliged to sleep in that part of it every night, or go out of the city entirely, and no stranger is allowed to enter that Millah without leaving his knife with the gate-keeper: but when he comes out in the morning it is restored to him. The people who live in that part are all Moslemin. The negroes, bad Arabs, and Moors, are all mixed together, and marry with each other, as if they were all of one colour: they have no property of consequence, except a few asses: their

gate is shut and fastened every night at dark, and
very strongly guarded both in the night and in the
day-time. The Shegar or king is always guarded by
one hundred men on mules, armed with good guns,
and one hundred men on foot with guns and long
knives. He would not go into the Millah, and we
only saw him four or five times in the two moons we
stayed at Tombuctoo, waiting for the caravan: but
it had perished on the desart—neither did the yearly
caravan from Tunis and Tripoli arrive, for it had
also been destroyed. The city of Tombuctoo is very
rich as well as very large; it has four gates to it; all
of them are opened in the day-time, but very strongly
guarded and shut at night. The negro women are
very fat and handsome, and wear large round gold
rings in their noses, and flat ones in their ears, and
gold chains and amber beads about their necks, with
images and white fish-bones, bent round, and the
ends fastened together, hanging down between their
breasts; they have bracelets on their wrists and on
their ankles, and go barefoot. I had bought a small
snuff-box filled with snuff in Morocco, and showed
it to the women in the principal street of Tombuctoo, which is very wide: there were a great many
about me in a few minutes, and they insisted on buying my snuff and box; one made me one offer, and
another made me another, until one, who wore
richer ornaments than the rest, told me, in broken
Arabic, that she would take off all she had about her
and give them to me for the box and its contents. I
agreed to accept them, and she pulled off her nose-
rings and ear-rings, all her neck chains with their
ornaments, and the bracelets from her wrists and
ankles, and gave them to me in exchange for it: these
ornaments would weigh more than a pound, and
were made of solid gold at Tombuctoo, and I kept
them through my whole journey afterwards, and
carried them to my wife, who now wears a part of

them. Tombuctoo carries on a great trade with all
the caravans that come from Morocco and the shores
of the Mediterranean sea. From Algiers, Tunis,
Tripoli, &c. are brought all kinds of cloths, iron, salt,
muskets, powder, and lead, swords or scimitars, tobacco, opium, spices, and perfumes, amber beads
and other trinkets, with a few other articles; they
carry back in return elephants' teeth, gold dust, and
wrought gold, gum senegal, ostrich feathers, very
curiously worked turbans, and slaves; a great many
of the latter, and many other articles of less importance: the slaves are brought in from the south-
west, all strongly ironed, and are sold very cheap;
so that a good stout man may be bought for a haick,
which costs in the empire of Morocco about two
dollars. The caravans stop and encamp about two
miles from the city in a deep valley, and the negroes
do not molest them: they bring their merchandise
near the walls of the city, where the inhabitants purchase all their goods in exchange for the above mentioned articles; not more than fifty men from any one
caravan being allowed to enter the city at a time,
and they must go out before others are permitted
to enter. This city also carries on a great trade with
Wassanah (a city far to the south-east) in all the
articles that are brought to it by caravans, and get
returns in slaves, elephants' teeth, gold, &c. The
principal male inhabitants are clothed with blue
cloth shirts, that reach from their shoulders down
to their knees, and are very wide, and girt about
their loins with a red and brown cotton sash or
girdle: they also hang about their bodies pieces of
different coloured cloth and silk handkerchiefs: the
king is dressed in a white robe of a similar fashion,
but covered with white and yellow gold and silver
plates, that glitter in the sun;—he also has many other
shining ornaments of shells and stones hanging about
him, and wears a pair of breeches like the Moors
and Barbary Jews, and has a kind of white turban

on his head, pointing up, and strung with different kinds of ornaments; his feet are covered with red Morocco shoes: he has no other weapon about him than a large white staff or sceptre, with a golden lion on the head of it, which he carries in his hand: his whole countenance is mild, and he seems to govern his subjects more like a father than a king. The whole of his officers and guards wear breeches that are generally dyed red, but sometimes they are white or blue; all but the king go bareheaded. The poor people have only a single piece of blue or other cloth about them, and the slaves a breech cloth. The inhabitants in Tombuctoo are very numerous; I think six times as many as in Swearah, besides the Arabs and other Moslemin or Mohammedans, in their Millah, or separate town; which must contain nearly as many people as there are altogether in Swearah."

NOTE BY THE AUTHOR.

SWEARAH or Mogadore contains about thirty-six thousand souls; that is, thirty thousand Moors and six thousand Jews: this may be a high estimation for Tombuctoo: making it two hundred and sixteen thousand inhabitants; yet considering the commercial importance of the place, and the fertility of the country around it, there can be no doubt but it contains a vast number of inhabitants; and I must also observe, that if it was a small town, and contained the riches attributed to it, they would require a very strong force to prevent the Arabs from the desart, together with the caravans, from taking it by surprise or by storm.

The women are clothed in a light shirt or underdress, and over it a green, red, or blue covering, from their breasts to below their knees—the whole girt about their waists with a red girdle; they stain their cheeks and foreheads red or yellow on some occasions, and the married women wear a kind of hood on their heads, made of blue cloth or silk, and cotton handkerchiefs of differ-

ent kinds and colours, and go barefooted. The king and
people of Tombuctoo do not fear and worship God, like
the Moslemins, but like the people of Soudan they only
pray one time in twenty-four hours, when they see the
moon, and when she is not seen they do not pray at all;
they cannot read or write, but are honest, and they cir-
cumcise their children like the Arabs: they have no
mosques, but dance every night, as the Moors and Arabs
pray. The Shegar or king had collected about one thousand slaves, some gums, elephants' teeth, gold dust, &c.
to be ready for the yearly caravans; but as three moons
had passed away since the time they ought to have arrived, he gave them up for lost, and concluded to send a
caravan with part of his goods that came across the desart; viz. some salt, iron, cloths, &c. to a large city at a
great distance from Tombuctoo: and having formed a
body of about three thousand men, well armed with
muskets, long knives, and spears, and three thousand
asses, and about two hundred camels, which were all
loaded with heavy goods, such as iron, salt, tobacco, &c.,
he hired my brother Seid and myself (with ten more
of our companions) to carry loads on our two camels to
Wassanah, for which he was to give us, when we came
back, two haicks each and some gold. As we were completely in his power, we did not dare to refuse to go,
and he put us under the care of his brother, whose name
was *Shelbaa*, who had command of the whole caravan.
It was in month of Shual (——) when we departed from
Tombuctoo for a place we had never before heard of.
We had in the company about two hundred Moslemin,
but the master of the caravan would not permit us,
Moslemin, to keep our guns, for fear we should turn
against him, if he was obliged to fight.

SECTION IV.

*Sidi Hamet Sets Out for Wassanah—Description of
That City, The Country, and Its Inhabitants.*

"ALL being prepared, we went from Tombuctoo,
about two hours' ride, towards the south, to the bank

of the river which is called at that place Zolibib, and was wider than from Mogadore to the island; (i. e. about five hundred yards;) here was a miserable village built with canes, and muddled over: it had about two hundred small houses in it, but no walls: we then set off near the side of the river, and travelled on in a plain even country for six days, every day within sight of the river, which was on our right hand, and running the same way we travelled, and our course was a little to the south of east; when we came to a small town called *Bimbinah,* walled in with canes and thorn-bushes, and stopped two days near it, to get provisions and rest our beasts: here the river turned more to the south-eastward, because there was a very high mountain in sight to the eastward: we then went from the river side, and pursued our journey more southwardly, through a hilly and woody country, for fifteen days, when we came to the same river again. Every night we were obliged to make up large fires all around the caravan to keep off the wild beasts, such as lions, tigers, and other animals, which made a dreadful howling. Here was a small town of black people belonging to another nation, who were the enemies to the king of Tombuctoo, but were friendly to the king of Wassanah; and not being strong, they did not molest us, but furnished us with what corn we wanted, and twenty oxen. We saw a large number of armed black men, nearly naked, on the other side of the river, who seemed to be hostile, but they could not get across to attack us: we also saw two very large towns, but walled in like the others we had passed: we stopped here and rested our camels and asses five days, and then went onward again in about a S. E. direction, winding as the river ran, for three days; and then had to climb over a very high ridge of mountains, which took up six days, and when we were on the top of them, we could see a large chain of high mountains to the westward; those we passed

were thickly covered with very large trees, and it was
extremely difficult to get up and down them; but we
could not go any other way, for the river ran against
the steep side of the mountain; so having gotten over
them we came to the river's bank again, where it was
very narrow and full of rocks, that dashed the water
dreadfully: then finding a good path, we kept on to
the S. E. winding a little every day, sometimes more
to the east, then to the south again: we kept travelling this way for twelve days after leaving the mountains, during which time we had seen the river nearly
every day on our right hand, and had passed a great
many small streams that empty into it: it was now
very wide and looked deep—here we saw many trees
dug out hollow, like the boats at Tombuctoo, and
they were used to carry negroes across the river, and
were pushed along with flat pieces of wood: we also
saw the high mountains on the west side of the great
river, very plainly. Having rested seven days at the
ferrying-place, we then travelled on for fifteen days,
most of the time in sight of the river. When we came
close to the walls of the city of Wassanah, the king
came out with a great army, consisting of all his soldiers, to meet us, but finding we had only come to
trade by the orders of, and with the goods of, his
friend *Shegar* of Tombuctoo, he invited the chief,
and the whole of the caravan, to abide within a
square enclosure near the walls of the city: here we
remained two moons, exchanging our goods for
slaves, gold, elephants' teeth, &c.

"The city of Wassanah is built near the bank of
the river, which runs past it nearly south, between
high mountains on both sides, though not very close
to the river, which is so wide there that we could
hardly see a man across it on the other side: the people of Tombuctoo call it Zolibib, and those of Wassanah call it Zadi. The walls of the city are very large,
and made of great stones, laid up like the stone

fences in the province of Hah Hah, in Morocco, but
without any clay or mud amongst them: they are
very thick and strong, and much higher than the
walls of Tombuctoo. I was permitted to walk round
them in company with six negroes, and it took me
one whole day: the walls are built square, and have
one large gate on each side. The country all around
the city is dug up, and has barley, corn, and other
vegetables planted on it; and close by the side of the
river, all the land is covered with rice, and there are
a great many oxen, and cows, and asses, belonging to
the city, but no camels, nor horses, mules, sheep, nor
goats; but all about and in the city, speckled fowls
abound, and there are plenty of eggs. The people of
the caravan were allowed to enter the city, but only
twenty at a time, and they were all obliged to go out
again before night.

"We had been there more than a moon, when it
came to my turn to go in. I found almost the whole
of the ground inside of the walls was covered with
huts made of stones piled up without clay, and some
reeds, laid across the tops, covered over with the
large leaves of the date or palm tree, or of another
tree which looks very much like a date tree, and
bears a fruit as large as my head, which has a white
juice in it sweeter than milk; the inside is hard, and
very good to eat: the trees that bear this big fruit,
grow in abundance in this country, and their fruit is
very plenty: their huts have narrow passages between
them: the king or chief is called *Oleeboo*, which
means, in the negro talk, good sultan: he is a very
tall, and quite a young man; his house is very large,
square, and high, made of stone, and the chinks filled
up with something white like lime, but not so hard:
they would not let me go into his house, and told me
he had one hundred and fifty wives, or more, and
ten thousand slaves: he dresses in a white shirt, that
looks like the one worn by Mr. Willshire, and long

trowsers made like them you have on, and coloured like an orange." Those I then had on, were common wide sailor trowsers. "He has over his shirt a caftan or robe with sleeves to it, made of red cloth, tied about with a girdle that goes from his breast to his hips, made of silk handkerchiefs of all colours, and has slips of fine coloured silk tied round his arms and legs: his hair is also tied in small bunches, and he wears on his head a very high hat made of canes, coloured very handsomely, and adorned with fine feathers: he has sandals on his feet, bound up with gold chains, and a great gold chain over his shoulder, with a bunch of ornaments made of bright stones and shells, that dazzle the eyes, hanging on his breast, and wears a large dagger by his side in a gold case. He rides on the back of a huge beast, called *Ilfement,* three times as thick as my great camel, and a great deal higher, with a very long nose and great teeth, and almost as black as the negroes: he is so strong, that he can kill a hundred men in a minute when he is mad—this is the animal that the teeth grow in which we bring from Tombuctoo to Widnoon, which you call elephants' teeth, and this was the only one of the animals I ever saw, but they told me these creatures were very plenty down the river from Wassanah." This answers to the description of, and no doubt is, the elephant.

"The king of Wassanah has a guard of two hundred negroes on foot, one hundred of them armed with muskets, fifty with long spears, and fifty with great bows and arrows, with long knives by their sides: they always attend him when he goes out on his beast; he has also a very large army: they fight with guns, spears, and bows and arrows. The city has twice as many inhabitants in it as Tombuctoo, and we saw a great many towns near it on the other side of the river, as well as several small settlements

on the same side below. The king nor the people do
not pray like the Moslemins, but they jump about,
fall down, tear their faces as if they were mad when
any of their friends die, and every time they see the
new moon, they make a great feast, and dance all
night to music made by singing and beating on skins
tied across a hollow stick, and shaking little stones in
a bag or shell; but they do not read nor write, and
are heathens. Though the free people in this place,
do not steal, and are very hospitable, yet I hope the
time is near when the faithful, and they that fear
God and his prophet, will turn them to the true belief, or drive them away from this goodly land.

 "The principal inhabitants of Wassanah are
dressed in shirts of white or blue cloth, with short
trowsers, and some with a long robe over the whole,
tied about with a girdle of different colours: the free
females are generally very fat, and dress in blue or
white coverings tied about their waists with girdles
of all colours: they wear a great many ornaments of
gold, and beads, and shells, hanging to their ears and
noses, necks, arms, ankles, and all over their hair;
but the poorer sort are only covered about their loins
by a cloth which grows on the tree that bears the big
fruit I have told you about before." This fruit, I imagine, must be the cocoa-nut, and I have often in the
West Indies, and elsewhere, observed the outer bark
of this singular palm-tree: it is woven by nature like
cloth, each thread being placed exactly over and under the others. It appears like regular wove coarse
bagging, and is quite strong: it loosens and drops
from the trunk of the tree of its own accord, as the
tree increases in size and age. I had long before
considered that this most singular bark must have
suggested to man the first idea of cloth, and taught
him how to spin, and place threads so as to form it
of other materials that have since been used for that

purpose, and this first hint from nature has been improved into our present methods of spinning and weaving.

"The male slaves go entirely naked, but the women are allowed a piece of this cloth to cover their nakedness with: they are very numerous, and many of them kept chained: they are obliged to work the earth round about the city. The inhabitants catch a great many fish: they have boats made of great trees, cut off and hollowed out, that will hold ten, fifteen, or twenty negroes, and the brother of the king told one of my Moslemin companions who could understand him, (for I could not,) that he was going to set out in a few days with sixty boats, and to carry five hundred slaves down the river, first to the southward, and then to the westward, where they should come to the great water, and sell them to pale people who came there in large boats, and brought muskets, and powder, and tobacco, and blue cloth, and knives, &c.—he said it was a long way, and would take him three moons to get there, and he should be gone twenty moons before he could get back by land, but should be very rich." I then asked him how many boats he supposed there were in the river at Wassanah? he said:—"A great many, three or four hundred, I should think: but some of them are very small: we saw a great many of these people who had been down the river to see the great water, with slaves and teeth, and came back again: they said, the pale people lived in great boats, and had guns as big as their bodies, that made a noise like thunder, and would kill all the people in a hundred negro boats, if they went too near them: we saw in the river and on the bank a great number of fish, with legs and large mouths, and these would run into the water in a minute, if any man went near them, but they told us they would catch children, and sometimes men, when in the boats: ('these are, no doubt, crocodiles or hippopotamus,') the negroes are very kind, and would always give us barley, corn, or rice, milk or meat, if we were hungry, though we could not speak a language they understood. While we stopped at Wassanah, it rained almost every day. Having traded away all the goods we carried there, Shelbar took three hundred slaves and a great many teeth, dazzling stones, and shells, and gold; with these we set off again, and went the same way back to Tombuctoo, which took us three moons, and we were gone from the time we left it, to the time we returned, eight moons. On my arrival at Tombuctoo, we were paid by the chief of the caravan according to promise, and a few days afterwards a caravan arrived there from Tunis, which we joined to return to our own country."

I must here beg the reader's indulgence for a moment, in order to make some remarks, and a few geographical observations that this part of the narrative has suggested. This narrative I, for my own part, consider strictly true and correct, as far as the memory and judgement of *Sidi Hamet* were concerned, whose veracity and intelligence I had before tested: he had not the least inducement held out to him for giving this account, further than my own and Mr. Willshire's curiosity; and his description of Tombuctoo agrees in substance with that given by several Moors, (Fez Merchants) who came to Mr. Willshire's house to buy goods while Sidi Hamet was there, and who said they had known him in Tombuctoo several years ago. From these considerations combined, and after examining the best maps extant, I conclude that I have strong grounds on which to found the following geographical opinions, viz.

1st, That the great Desart is much higher land on its southern side (as I had proved it to be on the north by my own observations) than the surrounding country, and consequently that its whole surface is much higher than the land near it that is susceptible of cultivation. 2dly, that the river which Sidi Hamet and his companions came to within fourteen days ride, and west of Tombuctoo, called by the Arabs *el Wod Tenij,* and by the negroes, *Gozen-Zair,* takes its rise in the mountains south of, and bordering on, the great Desart, being probably the northern branch of that extensive ridge in which the Senegal, Gambia, and Niger rivers, have their sources; and that this river is a branch of the Niger, which runs eastwardly for several hundred miles to Tombuctoo, near which city, many branches, uniting in one great stream, it takes the name of *Zolibib,* and continues to run nearly east, about two hundred and fifty miles from Tombuctoo; when meeting with high land, it is turned more south-eastwardly, and running in that direction in a winding course, about five hundred miles, it has met with some obstructions, through which it has forced its way, and formed a considerable fall: for Sidi Hamet, having spent six days in passing the mountains, came again near the river, which was then filled with broken rocks, and the water was foaming and roaring among them, as he observed, "most dreadfully." This must be a fall or rapid. 3dly, That from these falls, it runs first to the south-eastward, and then more to the south, till it reaches Wassanah, about six hundred miles, where it is by some called *Zolibib,* and by others *Zadi.* 4thly, That as the inhabitants of Wassanah say they go first to the southward, and then to the westward, in boats to the great water; this I conceive must be the Atlantic Ocean, where they have seen pale men and great boats, &c. These I should naturally conclude were Europeans, with vessels; and that it takes three moons to get there, (about eighty-five days) at the rate of thirty miles a day, which is the least we can give them with so strong a current; it makes a distance from thence to the sea of about two thousand five hundred miles: in computing this distance, one-third or more should be allowed for its windings, so that the whole length of the river is about four thousand miles, and is probably the longest and largest on the African continent. 5thly, That the waters of this river in their passage towards the east have been obstructed in their course by high mountains in the central regions of this unexplored continent, and turned southwardly: that they are borne along to the southward, between the ridges of mountains that are known to extend all along the western coast, from Senegal to the gulf of Guinea, and to round with that gulf to the south of the equator: that they are continually narrowed in and straightened by that immense ridge in which the great river Nile is known to have its sources; and which mountains lie in the equatorial region: that this central river receives, in its lengthened course, all the streams that water and fertilize the whole country, between the two before-mentioned ridges of mountains: the waters thus accumulated and pent up, at length broke over their western and most feeble barrier, tore it down to its base, and thence found and forced their way to the Atlantic Ocean, forming what is now known as the river Congo. In corroboration of this opinion, some men of my acquaintance, who have visited the Congo, and traded all along the coast between it and the Senegal, affirm, that the Congo discharges more water into the Atlantic, taking the whole year together, than all the streams to the northward of it, between its mouth and Cape de Verd.

SECTION V.

Journey from Tombuctoo to Morocco.

"THE caravan we joined at Tombuctoo, was a very large one belonging to Algiers, Tunis, Tripoli, and

Fez, four united together. They remained near that city two moons, and bought two thousand slaves, besides a great deal of gold dust, and teeth, and turbans, and gold rings, and chains, and gum; but Seid and I had only our two camels, and they were but partly loaded with gum, for account of *Ben Nassar*, the Sheick of the Tunissian part of the caravan, for there were three Sheicks in it. When every thing was ready, we set off from Tombuctoo, and travelled east-northerly twenty days through the hilly country, crossing a great many little streams of water that ran to the south and west towards the great river, it having rained very hard almost every night whilst we were at Tombuctoo.

When we were going amongst the hills and trees, we saw a great many small towns, or cities, most of them fenced in with good stone walls, but some with cane and thorn bushes. The land of that country is very good, and plenty of corn grows on it, and some rice and dates, and we saw some oxen, sheep and asses, and a few horses. The inhabitants are Moors, and Arabs mixed with the negroes, and almost as black as the latter; all of our own religion: they are very stout fierce men, but they did not attempt to molest us and sold us every thing we wanted at a cheap rate: they wear no clothing but a strip of cloth about their middles, and a ring of bone or ivory round the women's ankles and wrists, and some beads in their hair; they are peaceful people, and never attack the caravan's unless the latter attempt to rob them: they are armed with muskets and with long knives and with bows and arrows. When they are forced to fight, they do it with the greatest fury, and never take prisoners or receive quarter, and only defend their rights. Some of the people in our caravan told us, that a few years ago a caravan, going from Tombuctoo to Tunis, Algiers, &c. in passing through this country, surprised and stole about four

hundred of the inhabitants for slaves, and a great
number of cattle and much corn, and went towards
the desart; but these people assembled a large host,
and came up with them in the night near the edge of
the desart, and cut the whole of them to pieces,
though they were more than two thousand men
strong, and well armed; only about fifty of the people of the caravan escaped and got back to Tunis to
tell the news, and they only by riding on the swiftest
camels without any loads. After having refreshed our
camels for ten days in a beautiful valley, where there
was a good stream of water for them to drink, and
filled the sacks with coals, we mounted up to the
desart, and steered on the flat level away to the north.
As we went along we came to some small valleys,
where the Arabs feed their camels and live on their
milk, and think themselves the most learned, virtuous, and religious people in the world, and the most
happy too, though they have neither bread, nor
meat, nor honey, nor any clothing but a rag tied
round their waist, and live in tents, wandering about.
We steered about north for eighteen days, when we
came to the usual watering-place, called *Weydlah*;
here was a great deal of water in a pond, but it was
black and quite salt, like the water in the wells close
by the great sea: it was very dead and stinking and
tasted of sulphur; it is in a very deep pit and difficult
to get at, there being only one place by which we
could lead the camels down to the water: it is said to
be very deep in the middle, and was never known to
be dry: it was almost covered over by a thick green
scum; we could see the tracks of wild beasts, such as
tigers and lions, near the water. We had seen a great
many of these animals in our travels to Wassanah,
and when we were coming from Tombuctoo to the
eastward. Our caravan consisted of about fifteen
hundred men, most of us well armed with double
barrelled guns and scimitars, and we had about four

thousand camels. It was a long journey to the next well; so we stopped here six days peaceably, having encamped in a valley a little distance west of the pond or lake. We had always made the camels lie down in a circle, placing the goods in the centre, and the men between the camels and the goods: we had two hundred men on guard, and always ready for any emergency. In the night of the sixth day, about two hours after midnight, we were attacked by a very large body of wandering Arabs: they had got to within a few yards of us before they were discovered, and poured in a most destructive fire of musketry, at the same time running in like hungry tigers, with spears and scimitars in their hands, with dreadful yellings: they threw the whole caravan into confusion for a moment; but we were in a tight circle, formed by the camels, which with the guards kept them off for a short time, till the whole of our men seized their arms and rallied. The battle now raged most furiously: it was cloudy and very dark; the blaze of the powder making only a faint light, whilst the cracking of musketry, the clashing of swords, the shouts of the combatants, and the bellowings of the wounded and frightened camels, together with the groans of the wounded and dying men, made the most dreadful and horrid uproar that can be conceived: the fight continued for about two hours, hand to hand and breast to breast, when the assailants gave way and ran off, leaving their dead and wounded on the field of battle. We remained with our arms in our hands all night. I was wounded with a ball in my thigh, and Seid with a dagger on his breast." They then showed me their scars. "In the morning we numbered our men, and found that two hundred and thirty were killed, and about one hundred wounded: three hundred of the camels were either slain or so badly wounded, that they could not walk, and so we killed them. We found seven hundred of our enemies lying on the ground, either dead or wounded; those that were badly wounded, we killed, to put them out of pain, and carried the others that could walk along with us for slaves; of these there were about one hundred. As the enemy fled, they took all their good camels with them, for they had left them at a distance, so that we only found about fifty poor ones, which we killed; but we picked up two hundred and twenty good double-barrelled guns from the ground. The gun which Seid now uses is one of them; we also got about four hundred scimitars or long knives. We were told by the prisoners that the company who attacked us was upwards of four thousand strong, and that they had been preparing for it three moons. We were afraid of another attack, and went off the same day, and travelled all the night, steering to the N. E. (out of the course the caravans commonly take) twenty-three days' journey, when we came to a place called the Eight Wells, where we found plenty of good water. Fifty of our men had died, and twenty-one of the slaves. We remained near these good wells for eleven days: our camels feeding on the bushes in the valleys near them, when we again travelled to the north-westward ten days to *Twati*, a good watering place. For the last three days we waded through deep sands, like those we passed among while going from Widnoon. We rested here two days, and then went down north, into the country of dates, and came to the town of *Gujelah*, a little strong place belonging to Tunis— there we found plenty of fruit and good water, and meat and milk; we stopped there ten days, and then the part of the caravan going to Tripoli left us and went towards the east, by the mountains, and the rest went on to the north-easterly twelve days to *Tuggurtah*, close by a mountain near the river *Tegsah*, that is said to go to the sea near Tunis; here we stopped twenty-five days, and the caravan for Tunis left us.

Tuggurtah is a very large city, with high and thick walls, made tight, and has a great many people in it, all of the true-religion, and a vast number of black slaves, and a few white ones. After stopping here twenty-five days, we set off to the north-westward through a very fine country, full of date and fig trees, and cattle, and goats, camels, sheep, and asses; we then travelled ten days to the high mountains, where the caravan for Algiers parted from us, and we remained with about two hundred camels and eighty men going to *Fez*. We then travelled over the great mountain, which we were told belongs to the same ridge we see close to Morocco and in *Suze;* (the Atlas;) and in two moons more we passed through *Fez*, where what remained of the caravan stopped, and we returned to our father's house, and our families, on the side of the Atlas mountains, near the city of Morocco, having been gone more than two years. We brought back only one camel, and a small load of merchandise, out of the eight camels richly loaded when we set out; yet we thanked God for having preserved our lives; for the whole caravan with which we started had perished on the desart, and out of the twenty-eight men who left it with us, only four reached their homes, and they on foot, and entirely destitute of property. I found my wife and all my children and my father's family in good health. Sheick Ali came to see me as soon as he got the news of my arrival, and after staying with me one moon, he invited me and Seid to go with him to his place, which invitation we accepted, and he furnished us with one camel and some haicks and blue cloth, and advised us to go up on to the desart and trade them away for ostrich-feathers, to sell in Morocco or Swearah: so being poor, we accepted his offer; bought his goods and his camel, and he was to have been paid when we came back. We set off for the desart, and

had passed a great many tribes of Arabs without finding any feathers of consequence, when the great God
directed our steps to your master's tent, and I saw
you. I was once as bad a man as Seid, but I had been
in distress and in a strange land, and had found
friends to keep me and restore me to my family; and
when I saw you naked and a slave, with your skin
and flesh burnt from your bones by the sun and
heard you say you had a wife and children, I thought
of my own former distresses, and God softened my
heart and I became your friend. I did all I could to
lighten the burden of your afflictions: I have endured hunger, thirst, and fatigues, and have fought
for your sake, and have now the high pleasure of
knowing I have done some good in the world; and
may the great and universal Father still protect you:
you have been true and kind to me, and your friend
has fed me with milk and honey; and I will always
in future do what is in my power to redeem Christians from slavery."

Here Sidi Hamet finished his narration: he then
said he wished to go and see his wife and children,
and that as soon as he had rested for a few days, he
would set off again with a large company to seek
after the rest of my men. The next morning I made
him a small present and Mr. Willshire also gave him
some fine powder, and many other small articles.
After he was prepared to go, he swore by his right
hand, he would bring up the remainder of my crew
if they were to be found alive, and God spared his
life: he then took his leave of me by shaking hands,
and all of my companions, wishing us a happy sight
of our friends, and set off for his home. I did not
part with him without feelings of regret and shedding tears; for he had been a kind master to me, and
to him I owed, under God, my life and deliverance
from slavery; nor could I avoid reflecting on the

wonderful means employed by Providence to bring about my redemption, and that of a part of my late unfortunate crew.

CHAPTER XXVI.

An account of the great African Desart—of its inhabitants, their customs, manners, dress, & —a description of the Arabian camel or dromedary

IN giving an account of the great western desart, or Zahahrah, and of its inhabitants, &c. it must be remembered, that in journeying across, or on the desart when a slave, I did not go over but a very small part, comparatively speaking, of that extensive region; I cannot therefore undertake to describe what did not come under my own observation. I can, however, state, without fear of future contradiction the following facts, viz. that the face of this desart, from about the latitude of 22 degrees north, where we were forced ashore in our boat, to near the latitude of 28 degrees north, and from the longitude of *Cape Barbas,* about 19 to 11 degrees west, is a smooth surface, consisting partly of solid rocks, of gravel, sand, and stones mixed, and in some places of what is commonly called soil: this mass is baked down together in most places, by the extreme heat of the sun, nearly as hard as marble, so that no tracks of man or beast are discoverable; for the footstep leaves no impression. The whole surface is as smooth, when viewed on every side, as the plain of the ocean unruffled by winds or tempests, stretching out as far as

the eye can reach; not a break that might serve as
a landmark, or guide to the traveller; not a tree,
shrub, or any other subject, to interrupt the view
within the horizon; the whole is in appearance a
dreary waste; the soil is in colour of a light reddish
brown—not a stream of water (at least for many centuries past) has refreshed this region, which is
doomed to eternal barrenness; but as we went forward on this flat hard surface, we met from distance
to distance with small valleys or dells, scooped out
by the hand of nature, from five to thirty feet below
the plain—those we saw and stopped in, were ten,
fifteen, and twenty miles apart, and contained from
one to four or five acres each—they seem to serve as
receptacles for the little rain water which falls on the
desert; for the inhabitants always expect some in the
winter months, though they are frequently disappointed; and none had fallen on those parts on
which we were thrown for the last two years.

It was already September, and they were offering
up prayers to the Almighty every day, and most fervently imploring him to send them refreshing rains.
These little valleys are mostly scooped out in the
form of a bowl, though in some the sides are steep,
and bottoms nearly level, and the whole irregular.
Here grows a dwarf thornbush, from two to five feet
in height; it is generally scattered thinly over the
valley. The leaves of this shrub, which is almost the
only one that is to be found on that part of the desart, are a fourth of an inch in thickness, one and a
half inches in width, and from two to two and a half
inches in length, tapering to a sharp point, and are
strongly impregnated with salt, so much so, that
neither myself nor my companions could eat them,
though nearly perishing with hunger and thirst, and
a green fresh leaf would have been a great relief to
us, when neither meat nor drink was to be procured.
Such is the face of the desert over which we passed,
until we came within a short distance of Cape Baja-

dor, where we fell in with immense heaps of loose
sand, forming mountains of from one to three hundred feet in height, blown and whirled about by
every wind, and dreadful to the traveller, should a
strong gale arise whilst in the midst of them; for he
and his beasts must then inevitably perish, overwhelmed by flying surges of suffocating sand.

The face of this part of the desart is still the same
as that before described, when laid bare and seen
between the sand hills, by reason of the sand being
blown off. This sand has evidently been driven from
the sea-shore, and in the same degree as the ocean
has retired; by means of the trade-wind blowing constantly on to the desart, and that too very strongly
in the night-time, through a long succession of ages.
The heavy surf dashing perpetually among the rocks
gradually reduces them to grit, which then mixes
with the sand that is washed up upon the shore,
where it is left by the tides that rise on this coast
to the height of twelve or fourteen feet;—his becomes dried by the excessive heat of the sun, and
is whirled about and driven before this constant
gale, upon the surface, and then into the interior of
the desart. Such have unquestionably been the
causes which have produced such astonishing accu-
mulations of sand on that part of the desart; and I
am further confirmed in this belief by the enormous
strings of sand hills to be found all along the coast
of Suse and Morocco, near the sea-shore. These ac-
cumulations are in many parts so great, as to have
raised new bounds to the ocean some miles beyond
its original limits, which have evidently been washed
by the sea at a former period, and the intermediate
spaces are filled up with loose sand hills; which
circumstances all together amount, in my opinion,
to a demonstration of the origin of the sand on this
part of the desart.

Some authors have supposed that there were some fertile spots on the great western desart which were cultivated, &c. &c. but this is, I think, an impossibility: the whole desart being a level plain, it can produce neither spring or stream of water, and no herbage can consequently grow unless by means of rain, and this falls on the desart so seldom, and is so soon evaporated, as to render even a passage across it with a caravan of Arabs and camels, at all times dangerous in the extreme, as is proved by Sidi Hamet's narrative of his journeys, connected with my own observations. That there are more shrubs growing in some parts than in others, is true, from natural causes. The small valleys or dells which now furnish a scanty subsistence for the hardy camel, and that only by feeding on the coarsest shrubs and leaves, serve as basons to catch the little water that sometimes falls there: this is immediately dried away by the intense heat of the sun, which beats down upon the surface in all parts most violently, and scorches like actual fire;—yet that moisture, little as it is, causes the growth of the dwarf thornbush and of two or three other prickly plants, resembling weeds; these grow only among sand, and there are spots on the desart which produce a shrub that grows up in a bunch at the bottom as thick as a man's leg, and then branches off in every direction to the height of two feet, with a diameter of four or five feet. Each branch is two or three inches in circumference, and they are fluted like pillars or columns in architecture, and almost square at their tops: these are armed with small sharp prickles all over, two or three inches long, and yield, when broken off, a whitish liquid that is very nauseous, and bites the tongue like aqua-fortis, so that the camels will nip it off only when they can find nothing else: they are so numerous in some places, that it is difficult for the camels to get along amongst them, and they are obliged to dodge about between these bunches.

In many valleys, the thorn-bushes furnish a few snails. A few ground nuts are also to be found, resembling in shape and size small onions; and there are also to be seen under the shade of the thorn-bushes, an herb known by the name of shepherds' sprouts in America; but like the other things before mentioned, they are very rarely to be met with. These are, as far as came within my knowledge, the whole of the productions of the desart.

It has been imagined by many, that the desart abounded in noxious animals, serpents, and other reptiles; but we saw none, nor is it possible for any animal that requires water, to exist on the desart, unless it is under the care of, and assisted by man in procuring that necessary article. I saw no animal that was wild, except the ostrich, nor can I conceive how that animal exists without fresh water, which it is certain he cannot procure, nor what kind of nourishment he subsists on. There are neither beasts, nor birds, nor reptiles, to be seen on that dreary waste on which we travelled, and it is certain that there are other districts still worse, bearing not the smallest herb nor bush wherewith the camel can fill his stomach: but near the borders of the desart, where more shrubs are produced, sheep and goats are fed in considerable numbers, and we saw many of those light-footed and beautiful animals, called the *Gazelle*, tripping across the sand hills, and near watering-places: some tigers also now and then made their appearance. Such is the great western desert, or Zahahrah, which can only afford a description as dry and as barren as its dreary surface.

Nearly all parts of this vast desert are inhabited by different tribes of Arabs, who live entirely on the milk of their camels, and wander from valley to val-

ley, travelling nearly every day for the sake of finding food for their camels, and consequently food for
themselves: they live in tents formed of cloth made
of camels' hair, which they pull off by hand, and spin
with a hand spindle; this they twist round with the
fore-finger and thumb of the right hand; after they
have pulled out the thread sufficiently long from a
bunch of camels hair, which they hold in their left
hand, whilst the spindle descends to the ground,
when they take it up in their hand again, and wind
off the yarn in a ball, and then spin another length in
like manner: they afterwards double and twist it by
hand, making a thread as thick as a goose quill.
When they have spun a sufficient quantity, and have
agreed to stop for two or three days in one place,
(which they always do when they can find sufficient
food for their camels) they drive into the ground
two rows of pegs, in parallel lines, sufficiently wide
for a tent cloth, that is, about two and a half feet
apart: they then warp the yarn round the pegs, and
commence weaving it by running a kind of wooden
sword through the yarn under one thread, and over
another, in the manner of darning this sword they
carry with them, and it appears to have been used for
ages: they can then tuck through the filling by hand,
after turning up the sword edgeways; haul it tight,
and beat it up with the sword. They weave it the
whole length which they intend the tent to be, and
then roll up the pieces or length, until they have
made enough to finish a tent. This, in my opinion,
must have been the very first method of weaving
practised in the world, and the idea, I imagine, was
taken from a view of the outer bark of the cocoa-nut
tree, as I have before observed. The tent is then
sewed together with the same kind of twine, through
holes made with an iron bodkin. After it is sewed
together to a proper width, from six to ten breadths,
they make four loops on its ends, by fastening short

crooked sticks to the cloth, and two on each side. When they are about to pitch the tent, they spread it out, stretching the cords by which it is fastened, and driving a stout peg into the ground for each cord: this is done with a hard smooth stone, which they always carry with them, in place of a hammer; then getting under the tent and raising it, they place a block; whose top is rounded like a wooden bowl, under its centre, and set the tent pole into a hole made for that purpose, and set the pole upright, which keeps the tent steady in its place. After the tent is raised, all the ropes that hold and steady it, (ten in number) are tautened: these ropes are made of skins partly dressed, or of camels' hair, so that the tent is suspended in form of an oblong umbrella, and about two feet from the ground. In the day-time they raise up the south part of their tents (as those on the desart are always pitched facing the south) with two small stanchions fixed under the cords that hold it in front, so that they can go under the tent by stooping: this tent serves all the family for a shelter. Each family has a mat, which serves as a bed for the whole: they lie down on it promiscuously, only wrapped up in their haick or blanket, if they have one; if not, in the skin that covers their loins only, and lie closer together, to keep off the cold winds which blow under the tents in the night: the children lie between the grown persons; their heads are as low, and frequently lower than their feet, and their long bushey hair, which is never combed, and resembles a woollen thrumb mop, serves them instead of a pillow. The families consist of the father, and one or more wives, and the children that are unmarried, (generally about four to a family, but sometimes six or eight) and their slaves, who are blacks.

The rich Arabs have one, two, or three slaves, male and female; these are allowed to sleep on the same mat with their masters and mistresses, and are treated in all respects like the children of the family in regard to apparel, &c.—they are not, however, permitted to marry or cohabit with the Arab women, under pain of death, and are obliged to take care of the camels and follow them, and to do other drudgery, such as getting fuel, &c. but they will not obey the women, and raise their voices higher than their master or any of his children in a dispute, and consequently are considered smart fellows. They marry among their own colour while they are slaves, with the consent of their masters, but the children remain slaves. After a slave has served his master faithfully for a long time, or has done him some essential service, he is made free: he then enters into all the privileges that the free Arabs enjoy, and can marry into any of their families, which he or she never fails to do, and thus become identified with the families of the tribe in which they were slaves, and may rise to the very head of it. The negroes are generally active and brave, are seldom punished with stripes, and those who drive the camels do not scruple to milk them when they are thirsty, but take care not to be discovered: they are extremely cunning, and will steal any thing they can get at to eat or drink, from their masters, or indeed anyone else. If they are caught in the act of stealing, they are only threatened, and promised a flogging the next time. The father of the family is its absolute chief in all respects, though he seldom inflicts punishment: his wives and daughters are considered as mere slaves, subject to his will or caprice; yet they take every opportunity to deceive or steal from him: he deals out the milk to each with his own hand, nor dare anyone touch it until it is thus divided: he always assists in milking the camels, then puts the milk into a large wooden bowl, which has probably been in the family for ages: some of the largest bowls will contain five gallons: they are frequently split in every direction, and the split parts are fastened together with small iron plates, with a rivet at each end, made of the same metal. All the milk is thrown into the great bowl; then, if in the old man's opinion, there is a sufficient quantity for a good drink round, he takes a small bowl, (of which sort they generally have two or three,) and after washing or rubbing it out with sand, he begins to distribute the milk, by giving to each grown person an equal share, and to the children in proportion to their size, measuring it very exactly, and taking a proportionate quantity to himself. If there is any left, (which was very seldom the case with those I lived among) he has it put into a skin, to serve for a drink at noon the next day: if there is not a sufficient quantity of milk for a good drink all round, the old man fills it up with water (if they have any) to a certain mark in the bowl, and then proceeds to divide it as before related.

The camels are driven out early in the morning, and home about dark, when they are made to lie down before the tent of their owner, very near, with their tails towards it: a doubled rope with a large knot in one end is then put round the knee joint when the leg is doubled in, and the knot being then thrust through the double part at the other end, effectually fastens the knee bent as it is, so that the camel cannot get up to walk off, having but the use of three of his legs. This kind of becket is also fixed on the knees of the old camels that lead the drove; and the others remain quiet when their leaders are fast: in this manner they are suffered to lie until about midnight, when they have had time to cool and the milk to collect in their bags—the becket is then taken off, and as soon as they get up, the net which covers the bag to prevent the young ones from consuming the milk, is loosened: this is fas-

tened on by two cords, that go over the back of the
camel, and are knotted together. As each camel is
milked, the net is carefully replaced, and she is made
to lie down in the same place again: here they lie
until daylight, when all the camels are made to get
up; a little milk is then drawn from each, and the
young ones are suffered to suck out the remainder,
when the net is put in its place again, not to be removed until the following midnight. While the
head of the family is busied milking the camels and
suckling the young ones, assisted by all the males,
the wife and females are striking and folding up the
tent, selecting the camels to carry the stuff, and
bringing them near, where they make them lie down
and pack on them the tent and all their other materials. This being done, they fasten a leather or skin
basket, about four feet wide, fitted with a kind of
tree, like a saddle on the back of one of the tamest
camels, in which the women place the old men and
women that cannot walk, and young children, and
frequently themselves, and proceed forward according to their daily custom. The women take care of
the stuff and the camels that carry it, and of the
children: the other camels are driven off by slaves,
if they have any, if not, by some of the boys, and
kept where there are some shrubs to be found, until
night. The old man, or head of the family, generally precedes the women and stuff, after having described to them the course they are to steer. He
sets off his camel, with his gun in his hand, at a full
trot, and goes on until he finds a fit place in which
to pitch the tent, when he gives the information
to his wife, who then proceeds with all possible
despatch to the spot, unloads her camels, and lets
them go; then she spreads her tent, puts all the
stuff under it, clears away the small stones, and
spreads her mat, arranges her bowls, hangs up the
skins containing water, (if they have any,) on a kind

of horse or frame that folds together, &c. &c. They
start long before sun rising in the morning, and calculate to pitch their tents at about four o'clock in
the afternoon, if they can find a convenient spot;
otherwise a little sooner or later. When one family
sets off, the whole of that part of the tribe dwelling
near, travel on with them; and I have frequently
seen from five hundred to one thousand camels in
one drove, all going the same way, and I was greatly
surprised to see with what facility they could distinguish and separate them; each knowing his own
camels, even to the smallest: they would sometimes
march together for half a day; then in a few minutes
they would separate, and each take his own course,
and would generally pitch within a few miles of each
other. As soon as the place is agreed on, the men
go out on their camels, with their guns, different
ways to reconnoitre and see if they have enemies
near.

When they rise in the morning, after having first
milked their camels, and suckled the young ones,
they next attend to prayers, which is done in the
following manner: they first find a sandy spot, then
unwrap themselves, and take up sand in both their
hands; with this they rub their faces, necks, arms,
legs, and every part of their bodies, except their
backs, which they cannot reach: this done, as if they
washed with water, they stand erect, facing towards
the east; wrap themselves up as neatly as they can
in their blankets or skins; they look up towards
heaven, and then bow their heads, bending their
bodies half way to the ground, twice crying aloud
at each time, *Allah Hooakibar.* They next kneel
down, and supporting themselves with their hands,
they worship, bowing their faces in the dust, twice
successively; then being still on their knees, they
bend themselves forward, nearly to the ground, repeating, *Hi el Allah-Sheda Mohammed—Rasool Al-*

lah; then rising, they again repeat, *Allah Hooaki-bar,* two or three times; and this is the common mode of worshipping four times a day. In addition to this, at sun-setting, they implore the Almighty to send rain to moisten the parched earth; to cause the food to grow for their camels; to keep them under his special care, with their families and tribes; to enrich them with the spoils of their enemies, and to confound and destroy them that seek their hurt; they thank the Almighty for his past mercies, for food, raiment, and his protection, &c. &c.—they then repeat part of a chapter from the Koran, in which God's pretended promises to the faithful are made known by the Prophet; and repeating at all times the *Hi el Allah,* or, "great is the Almighty God, and Mohammed is his holy prophet." Their times of prayer, are, before sun-rising in the morning, about noon, the middle of the afternoon, about sun-setting, and again two or three hours after the sun has set: this makes five times a day, washing themselves (at least their faces, and hands, when they have water) before praying; when they cannot get water, (which is always the case with those on the desart,) they perform their ablutions by substituting sand. Mohammed, their prophet, when he arrived with an army on the desarts of Arabia, found that there was no water either for himself or his followers to wash in; yet by laws he had already promulgated, ablutions could not be dispensed with; a new chapter, however, of revelation, soon relieved him from this dilemma, and he directed his followers to use sand, when no water was to be had. In the ninth chapter of the Book of Numbers, it appears that Moses, in a similar dilemma, found it necessary to apply for a new command from the Lord on a particular subject.

The Arabs always wash when it is in their power, before they eat, nor does any business divert them from the strict observance of their religious ceremonies: and with respect to particular stated times, while pursuing their journies, and going on in the greatest haste, when the time for prayers arrives, all stop, make the camels lie down, and perform what they conceive to be their indispensable duty; praying, in addition to the usual forms, to be directed in the right course, and that God will lead them to wells of water, and to hospitable brethren, who will feed them, and not suffer them to perish far from the face of man: that he will enrich them with spoils, and deliver them from all who lie in wait to do them mischief; this done, they mount again cheerfully, and proceed, encouraging their camels by a song, a very lively one, if they wish them to go on a trot; if only to walk, something more slow and solemn.

The Arabs who inhabit the great western desart, are in their persons about five feet seven or eight inches in height; and tolerably well set in their frames, though lean: their complexion is of a dark olive: they have high cheek bones, and aquiline noses, rather prominent; lank cheeks, thin lips, and rounded chins: their eyes are black, sparkling, and intelligent: they have long black hair, coarse, and very thick; and the men cut their's off with their knives, to the length of about six or eight inches, and leave it sticking out in every direction from their head. They all wear long beards—their limbs are straight, and they can endure hunger, thirst, hardships, and fatigues, probably better than any other people under heaven: their clothing in general is nothing more than a piece of coarse cloth, made of camel's hair, tied round their waists, hanging nearly down to their knees; or a goatskin so fastened on, as to cover their nakedness; but some of the rich ones wear a covering of linen or cotton cloth over their shoulders, to their knees, hanging some-

thing like a shift or shirt, without sleeves, and some
have, besides, a haick or a woollen blanket, about
four feet wide, and four yards long, which they wrap
about them; but this is the case only with the rich,
and their number is very small. These haicks, and
blue shirts they get from the empire of Morocco, in
exchange for camels' hair and ostrich-feathers; the
only commodities in which they can trade. The Arab
women are short and meager; and their features
much harder and more ugly than those of the men;
but they have long black hair, which they braid and
tuck up in a bunch on their heads, and fasten it
there by means of thorns. They generally wear strings
of black beads round their necks, and a white circular bone, of three inches in diameter, in their hair
with bands of beads or other ornaments around their
wrists and ankles. Their cheek bones are high and
prominent; their visages and lips are thin, and the
upper lip is kept up by means of the two eye-teeth.
They take great pains to make these teeth project
forward, and turn up quite in front of the line of
their other fore-teeth, which are as white and sound
as ivory. Their eyes are round, black, and very expressive, and extremely beautiful, particularly in the
young women, who are generally plump and lasciv-
ious. The women wear a dress of coarse camels' hair
cloth, wihch they manufacture in the same way they
make their tent cloth: it covers their shoulders, leaving their arms and breasts naked; it is sewed up on
each side, and falls down nearly to their knees; they
have a fold in this, like a sack, next their skin on
their shoulders, in which they carry their little children; and the breasts of the middle aged women become so extremely long, lank, and pendulous, that
they have no other trouble in nursing the child
which is on their backs, when walking about than
to throw up their breasts over the top of their shoulders, so that the child may apply its lips.

All the Arabs go barefoot; the children, both male and female, before they come to the age of puberty, run about entirely naked, and this exposure to the sun is one great cause of their black colour. The males are all circumcised at the age of eight years, not as a religious rite, but because it is found necessary as a preventive of a disease incident to the climate. The men are very quick, active, and intelligent—more so, taken collectively, than any other set of men I had ever come across in the different parts of the world I had before visited. They are the lords and masters in their families, and are very severe and cruel to their wives, whom they treat as mere necessary slaves, and they do not allow them even as much liberty as they grant to their negroes, either in speech or action: they are considered by the men as beings without souls, and consequently, they are not permitted to join in their devotions, but are kept constantly drudging at something or other, and are seldom allowed to speak when men are conversing together. They are very filthy in their persons, not even cleansing themselves with sand, and are covered with vermin. The continual harsh treatment, and hard drudgery to which they are subject, have worn off that line edge of delicacy, sensibility, and compassion, so natural to their sex, and transformed into unfeeling and unpitying beings; so much so, that their conduct towards me and my companions in distress, was brutal in the extreme, and betrayed the extinction of every humane and generous feeling.

The Arab is high-spirited, brave, avaricious, rapacious, revengeful; and, strange as it may appear, is at the same time hospitable and compassionate: he is proud of being able to maintain his independence, though on a dreary desart, and despises those who are so mean and degraded as to submit to any government but that of the Most High. He struts about

sole master of what wealth he possesses, always ready
to defend it, and believes himself the happiest of men,
and the most learned also; handing down the tradi-
tion of his ancestors, as he is persuaded, for thousands
of years. He looks upon all other men to be vile, and
beneath his notice, except as merchandise: he is
content to live on the milk of his camels, which he
takes great care to rear, and thanks his God daily for
his continual mercies. They considered themselves
as much above me and my companions, both in intel-
lect and acquired knowledge, as the proud and pampered West India planter (long accustomed to rule
over slaves) fancies himself above the meanest new
negro, just brought in chains from the coast of Africa.
They never correct their male children, but the females are beat without mercy. The men were not
cruel to us farther than they thought we were obstinate, and always gave us a small share of what they
themselves had to subsist on.

I never witnessed a marriage among them, but
was told that when a young man sees a girl that
pleases him, he asks her of her father, and she becomes his wife without ceremony. Polygamy is
allowed, but the Arabs of the desert have but very
seldom more than one wife, unless amongst some of
the rich ones, who have need of servants, when they
take another wife, and sometimes a third.

They all learn to read and write: in every family
or division of a tribe, they have one man who acts as
teacher to the children: they have boards of from
one foot square to two feet long, and about an inch
thick by eighteen inches wide: on these boards the
children learn to write with a piece of pointed reed:
they have the secret of making ink, and that of a very
black dye: when a family of wandering Arabs pitch
their tents, they set a part a place for a school: this
they surround with broken shrubs in the desert to
keep off the wind—here all the boys who have been

310 SUFFERINGS IN AFRICA

circumcised of from eight to eighteen or twenty
years old, attend, and are taught to read and to write
verses from the Koran, which is kept in manuscript
by every family on skins: they write their characters
from right to left—are very particular in the forma-
tion of them, and make their lines very straight: all
the children attend from choice or for amusement.—
The teacher, I was told, never punishes a child, but
explains the meanings of things, and amuses him by
telling tales that are both entertaining and instructive; he reads or rehearses chapters from the Koran
or some other book, for they have a great many
poems, &c. written also on skins: when the board is
full of writing, they rub it off with sand, and begin
again: they enumerate with the nine figures now in
use among all European nations, and in America,
and were extremely astonished to find that I could
make them, and understand their meanings, saying
one to another, " This man must have been a slave
before to some Arabian merchant, who has taught
him the manner of using the Arabic figures, and contrary to his law, unless indeed he is a good man and
a believer." The boards on which they wrote seemed
to have lasted for ages—they had been split in many
places, and were kept together by small iron plates
on each side, fixed by iron rivets: these plates, as
well as their rude axes, of which each family has one,
are made of tempered iron by the smiths which belongs to and journey with the tribe. I saw several of
them at work. They burn small wood into charcoal,
and carry it with them on camels: their anvil is made
of a piece of iron a foot long, and pointed at the end
—this they drive into the ground to work on—the
head of the anvil is about six inches over: they make
their fire in a small hole dug in the ground for that
purpose, and blow it up by means of two skins
curiously fixed; so that while one is filling with air,
they blow with the other, standing between them—

with a hand placed on each, they raise and depress them at pleasure. By means of a clumsy hammer, an anvil, and hot irons to bore with, they manage to fix the saddles for themselves to ride on, and to make knives and a kind of needles, and small rough bladed axes. This forge is carried about without the smallest inconvenience, so that the Arabs even of the desert are better provided in this respect than the Israelites were in the days of Saul their King, Samuel, chap. XIII. verses 19 to 23—"Now there was no smith in all the land of Israel; for the Philistines said, Lest the Hebrews make them swords or spears."

There appeared to be no kind of sickness or disease among the Arabs of the desert during the time I was with them: I did not hear of, nor see the smallest symptoms of complaint, and they appear to live to a vast age: there were three people I saw belonging to the tribe in which I was a slave, namely, two old men and one woman, who from appearance were much older than any I had ever seen: these men and the woman had lost all the hair from their heads, beards, and every part of their bodies—the flesh on them had entirely wasted away, and their skins appeared to be dried and drawn tight over the sinews and the bones, like Egyptian mummies: their eyes were extinct, having totally wasted away in their sockets, the bones of which were only covered by their eyelids: they had lost the use of all their limbs, and appeared to be deprived of every sense, so that when their breath should be spent and their entrails extracted, they would in my opinion be perfect mummies without further preparation; for from their appearance there was not sufficient moisture in their frames to promote corruption, and I felt convinced that a sight of such beings (probably on the desart of Arabia) might have given the Egyptians their first idea of drying and preserving the dead bodies of their relations and friends. An undutiful child of civilized parents might here learn a lesson of filial piety and benevolence from these barbarians: the old people always received the first drink of milk, and a larger share than even the acting head of the family when they were scanted in quantity: whenever the family moved forward, a camel was first prepared for the old man, by fixing a kind of basket on the animal's back; they then put skins or other soft things into it, to make it easy, and next lifting up the old man, they place him carefully in the basket, with a child or two on each side, to take care of and steady him during the march, while he seems to sit and hold on, more from long habit than from choice.—As soon as they stopped to pitch the tents, the old man was taken from his camel, and a drink of water or milk given him, for they take care to save some for that particular purpose. When the tent was pitched, he was carefully taken up and placed under it on their mat, where he could go to sleep:—this man's voice was very feeble, squeaking, and hollow. The remarkably old man I am speaking of belonged to a family that always pitched their tent near ours, so that I had an opportunity of witnessing the manner of his treatment for several days together, which was uniformly the same.

After I was redeemed in Mogadore I asked my master Sidi Hamet of what age he supposed this old man to have been, and he said about eight *Zille* or Arabic centuries. Now an Arabic century, or *Zille*, forty lunar years of twelve moons in each year, so that by his computation he must have been nearly three hundred years old: he also told me that it was very common to find Arabs on different parts of the great desart, five Zille old, retaining all their faculties, and that he had seen a great many of the ages of from seven to eight Zille. He further said, that my old master from whom he bought me had lived nearly five Zille or centuries, though he was very

strong and active; and from the appearance of a
great many others in the same tribe I could have no
doubt but they were much older. I then asked him
how they knew their own ages, and he answered—
"Every family keeps a record of the ages and many
of its children, which they always perserve and pack
up in the same bag in which they carry the Koran."
I told him that few people in other parts of the world
lived to the age of two Zille and a half, and the
people of those countries would not believe such a
story.

"The Arabs who live on the desert (said he) subsist entirely on milk of their camels; it is the milk of
an animal that we call sacred, and it causes long life:
those who live on nothing else, have no sickness nor
disorders, and are particularly favoured by heaven;
but only carry the same people off from the desert,
and let them live on meat, and bread, and fruits, they
then become subject to every kind of pain and sickness when they are young, and only live to the age
of about two Zille and a half at the most, while a
great many die very young, and not one tenth part
of the men or women live to the age of one Zille. I
myself (added he) always feel well when I live on
the milk of the camel alone, even though I do not
get half as much as I want, for then I am strong and
can bear heat, and cold, and fatigue, much better
than when I live on flesh, and bread, and fruit, and
have plenty of good fresh water to drink, and if I
could always have as much camel's milk as I could
drink, I would never taste of meat again: but I love
bread and honey very much."— This account from
an Arab who was my friend and the preserver of my
life, and one who had traversed the desert in many
directions, and who was also a good scholar for an
Arab, and on whose veracity I could rely, together
with what fell under my own observation, has removed all doubt from my mind on that subject, and I

am fully of opinion, that a great many Arabs on this vast expanse of desart, actually live to the age of two hundred years of our calendar. My reasons for this belief, in addition to those already given, are,

1st. That their lives are regular, from the day of their birth, to the day of their death.

2d. That there is no variation in their food, which is of the most pure and nutritive kind, and cannot cause in them disorders originating from indigestion, &c. &c.

3d. That the climate they inhabit, though hot, is perfectly dry, and consequently must be healthy for those born there; and,

4th. That in their wandering life they are never subjected to hard bodily labour, and their daily movements afford them sufficient excercise to promote a due circulation of the fluids; nor do they ever taste wine or any ardent spirits, being entirely out of the way of those articles, and are besides strictly forbidden by their religion. I am no physician, and cannot therefore enter into any learned disquisition on this subject, but merely give my own impressions respecting it, without pretending to be less liable to err in judgement than others. It cannot be doubted but that the Arabs existed as a wandering race long before the time of the Greeks, and it is possible that they possessed in those early ages the art of writing, and reckoned time by the same method they do at this day; say forty lunar years for a Zille or century, and that in translating or quoting from their writings, a Zille may have been taken for a hundred of our years.

The tribe of Arabs to which I belonged, owned four horses, or rather mares: they were the general property, and were fed on milk, and watered every two days: with these animals they hunt the ostrich, and with this view, having agreed on the time and place, the whole of the men assemble before daylight

on their camels, and surround a certain spot of
ground where they calculate on finding ostriches,
with the horses to windward, and their riders with
loaded muskets in their hands: they then approach
each other until they start the ostriches, who seeing
themselves surrounded on all sides but one, run to
the southward before the wind, followed by the
horses, which it is said run extremely swift, and pressing on the ostrich very hard, the bird runs himself out of breath in about three hours, when the
men on horseback come up and shoot him: but let
these birds run against the wind, and no horse can
overtake them, for then they do not lose their breath.

After my arrival at Mogadore, I heard of the
Heirie, or small swift camel of the desert, but I never
saw any camel that differed from the common one
either in size or shape, and can only suppose that it
may be a camel of the same race trained for running
swift, and fed on milk like the horses. The common
camels can easily travel one hundred miles in a day.
A good new milch camel gives at one milking when
on the desart about one quart, which is very rich
and good: this is besides what suffices to sustain the
young camel, and is drawn at midnight—they only
draw about a gill in the morning.

Most of the Arabs are well armed with good
double-barrelled French fowling pieces, (which have
excellent locks) and with good scimitars and knives:
each has a kind of bag to carry his slugs, &c. in, slung
by his neck and hanging down to his waist on the
left side: their big powder-horn is suspended in like
manner: this contains coarse powder, and is used
for loading the muskets, but they all have a little
horn in which to carry their fine powder for priming.
Many of the gun barrels that I saw were worn
through, and the holes were stopped up by brazing:
—they have procured many of their guns no doubt by
shipwrecks on the coast of the desart; many more

from caravans that they have overpowered, and
others in the way of trade from the French settlements of Senegal, and from Tunis, Tripoli, and
other ports on the Mediterranean Sea. I did not see
a single Moorish musket or lock during the time I
was among the Arabs of the desert: they were all
made in Europe, and generally in Paris, with the
maker's name on the locks. They have tolerably good
powder, which they say they know how to manufacture, but do not make it fine, so that the first rate
English or French musket powder is much in request,
and looked upon as invaluable for priming. Their
swords or scimitars they most probably obtain by the
same means as their muskets: they are ever ready to
attack an inferior, or even an equal force, and fight
for the sake of plunder.

Their language is the ancient Arabic; is spoken
with great fluency, and is distinguished for its powerful emphasis, and elegant cadence. When they con-
verse peaceably, (and they are much given to talking
with each other) it thrills on the ear like the breath-
ings of soft wind-music, and excites in the soul the
most soothing sensations; but when they speak in
anger, it sounds as hoarse as the roarings of irritated
lions, or the most furious beasts of prey. They attack
the small towns in the vicinity of the desert, on all
sides; which are walled in to ward off their incur-
sions: if they are successful, they put all to the sword,
burn the towns, and retire again to the desert with
their spoil. Such is the wandering Arab of the great
African Desart: his hand is against every man, and
consequently every man's hand is against him.

Lightning Source UK Ltd.
Milton Keynes UK
UKHW021815110822
407174UK00008B/1907